Culture, development, and democracy

Note to the reader from the UNU

Soedjatmoko was an internationally reputed intellectual, diplomat, and social thinker from Indonesia and served as Rector of the United Nations University from 1980 to 1987. The present volume has been compiled from the papers presented at the UNU symposium on Culture, Development, and Democracy: The Role of Intellectuals that was held in Jogyakarta, Indonesia, in December 1991 as a tribute to his memory. Soedjatmoko was very concerned with, and wrote a number of articles dealing with, the complex interactions among culture, development, democracy, freedom, and human rights, particularly in the developing regions. In the changing world of today, a renewed search is under way for cultural and historical roots of societies and communities. The reader of this book will find various perspectives on these issues that will serve as guiding marks for reflection.

Culture, development, and democracy: The role of the intellectual

A tribute to Soedjatmoko

Edited by Selo Soemardjan and Kenneth W. Thompson

TOKYO • NEW YORK • PARIS

The views expressed in this publication are those of the authors and do not necessarily reflect the views of the United Nations University.

United Nations University Press
The United Nations University, 53-70, Jingumae 5-chome, Shibuya-ku, Tokyo 150, Japan
Tel: (03) 3499-2811 Fax: (03) 3406-7345
Telex: J25442 Cable: UNATUNIV TOKYO

Typeset by Asco Trade Typesetting Limited, Hong Kong
Printed by Permanent Typesetting and Printing Co., Ltd., Hong Kong
Cover design by Apex Production, Hong Kong

UNUP-854
ISBN 92-808-0854-0
03500 P

Contents

II. Reflections on the role of intellectuals

An outline of Soedjatmoko's life

Date of birth:	10 January 1922
Place of birth:	Sawahlunto, Sumatra, Indonesia
Date of death:	21 December 1989
Nationality:	Indonesian
Spouse:	R.A. Ratmini Subranti Gandasubrata
Children:	Kamala Chandrakirana
	Isna Marifa
	Galuh Wandita
Education:	Medical College, Jakarta, Indonesia, 1940–1942; Littauer Graduate School of Public Administration, Harvard University, USA, 1950–1951
Profession:	Social scientist, public servant

Positions

1945	Deputy Head of Foreign Press Dept., Ministry of Information, Government of Indonesia;
1946	Chief Editor, *Het Inzicht*, Ministry of Information, Government of Indonesia;
1947	Deputy Editor, *Siasat* magazine;
1947–1952	Member, and later Alternate Permanent Represen-

	tative, Indonesian Delegation to the United Nations, New York;
1950–1951	Chargé d'Affaires, Embassy of Indonesia, London;
1950–1952	Counsellor, Embassy of Indonesia, Washington, DC;
1952–1960	Associate Editor, *Pedoman* daily newspaper;
1952–1960	Editor, *Siasat* magazine;
1953–1961	Director, PT Pembangunan Publishing Company;
1956–1959	Member, Indonesian Constituent Assembly;
1956	Adviser, Indonesian Delegation to the First Asia-Africa Conference, Bandung;
1961–1962	Guest Lecturer in South-East Asian History and Politics, South-East Asia Program, Cornell University, Ithaca, NY;
1966	Vice-Chairman, Indonesian Delegation to the twenty-first session of the UN General Assembly;
1967–1977	Personal Adviser to the Minister of Foreign Affairs, Government of Indonesia;
1968–1971	Ambassador of Indonesia to the United States of America, Washington, DC;
1970–1980	Member, Jakarta Academy;
1971–1980	Special Adviser on Social and Cultural Affairs to the Chairman of the National Development Planning Agency, Government of Indonesia;
1972–1973	Adviser, National Defence College (LEMHANAS);
1972–1973	Adviser, National Security Council (WANHANKAMNAS);
1975–1980	Member Governing Board, Social Science Foundation (Yayasan Ilmu-ilmu Sosial);
1976–1980	Adviser, Association for the Advancement of the Social Sciences (HIPIS);
1976–1980	Adviser, Foundation for the Traditional Arts (Yayasan Seni Tradisionil);
1980–1987	Rector, United Nations University, Tokyo, Japan.

Major international memberships

- Co-convener, with John D. Rockefeller III and Saburo Okita, of the annual Williamsburg meetings on problems of Asia and the Pacific, 1971–1981;
- International Fellow, American Academy of Arts and Sciences, 1971–1989;

- Board of Governors, Asian Institute of Management, Manila, Philippines, 1972–1975;
- Club of Rome, 1972–1989, the Executive Committee, 1984–1989;
- Board of Trustees, the Ford Foundation, New York 1972–1984;
- International Institute for Strategic Studies, London, England, 1967–1989;
- Council of International Foundation for Development Alternatives, Switzerland, 1978–1982;
- Board of Governors, International Development Research Center (IDRC), Canada, 1973–1977;
- Board of Management, Association of Development Research and Training Institutes of Asia and the Pacific (ADIPA), Kuala Lumpur, 1985–1989;
- International Council of the Asia Society, 1982–1989;
- The Palme Commission on Disarmament and Security Issues, Stockholm, Sweden, 1981–1989;
- Board of Trustees, Aspen-Berlin Institute for Humanistic Studies, 1968–1984;
- Board of Directors, International Institute for Environment and Development, London, 1978–1982; Advisory Council, 1983–1989;
- Board of Governors, Foundation for International Training, Canada, 1983–1986;
- Scientific Advisory Board, Conference on Long Term Worldwide Biological Consequences of Nuclear War, Washington, DC, 1983;
- North South Roundtable, Member, 1978–1984: Steering Committee, 1984–1989;
- Advisory Committee, Third World Foundation, 1982–1989;
- Steering Committee, Third World Forum, Rome, 1983–1989;
- Board of Directors, World Resources Institute, Washington, DC, 1983–1986;
- Independent Commission on International Humanitarian Issues, Geneva, Switzerland, 1982–1989;
- Executive Council, World Futures Studies Federation, Rome, 1986–1989;
- Board of Trustees, International Institute for Humanistic Studies, Aspen, Colorado, 1968–1989.

Major distinctions

- Honorary Doctorate of Laws, Cedar Crest College, Pennsylvania, USA, 1969;

- Honorary Doctorate of Humane Letters, Yale University, USA, 1970;
- Award for Education, Service and Science, Ministry of Education, Government of Indonesia, Jakarta, 1971;
- Magsaysay Award for International Understanding, the Philippines, 1978;
- Honorary Doctorate of Law, Williams College, Williamstown, Pennsylvania, USA, 1980;
- Honorary Doctorate in Technology, Asian Institute of Technology, Bangkok, Thailand, 1981;
- Award for Distinguished Service, National Defence Institute, Jakarta, Indonesia, 1981;
- Honorary Doctorate in Letters, Universiti Sains Malaysia, Penang, Malaysia, 1982;
- Medal of the President of the Italian Republic, Rimini, Italy, 1986;
- Honorary Doctorate, University of Hawaii;
- Award from Indonesian Association for Development of Social Sciences and National Congress of Social Sciences, 1990.

Introduction

Kenneth W. Thompson

In the early 1970s, Soedjatmoko and I collaborated on a Hazen Foundation report. When it came time to write the subject sentence it was he who proposed: "It's time to listen." We addressed those words especially to the people of the Northern countries. Viewed against the background of the 1970s the application seemed to be beyond criticism. The message was not merely that the more favoured countries should help the less fortunate ones. The Marshall Plan and Point Four had established that principle, we thought for all time. Self-interest no less than humane instincts buttressed international cooperation. We all believed in foreign aid, even questioning whether "foreign" was the right word. The lesson of the Second World War and its aftermath was that no man and no nation could remain an island separate and apart.

Soedjatmoko intended to point up another truth. With the exception of the Marshall Plan, programmes of post-war international assistance were *designed by the strong* for the benefit of the weak. By contrast, General Marshall had insisted that Europe must define its own needs and priorities and formulate a programme before the United States would respond. The leader of the Grand Alliance was saying, in effect, "It's time to listen." Under the spell of his words and example, the American people awakened from their long sleep of isolationism. Winston Churchill may have exaggerated when he spoke of the Marshall Plan as "the most magnanimous act in the history of statecraft." However, it was clear that a light had been kindled and a sense of responsibility for others been made part of the American foreign policy agenda.

Soedjatmoko's vision went farther than General Marshall's. His boundaries were global, not merely regional. Moreover, his sense of urgency found its centre primarily along a North-South axis, not East-West. While he recognized that international initiatives are always a blending of self-interest and moral purpose, he understood that cooperative programmes that involve the powerful and less powerful depend on a larger component of moral responsibility. Because the vision of nations in particular is limited and moral consensus fragile and ever-changing, Soedjatmoko understood how vital it was that there be communication. For this reason he reiterated that it was time that those who sought to help should understand those to whom they sought to give assistance, and at an ever deeper level.

In part the task was one of discovering a new moral consensus. The less developed countries were in part the recipients of values that had been imported and were not indigenous. Having come of age as nations in the post-war era, they found themselves in the throes of a search for new moral and political values. Without listening to one another, North and South had little chance of building a new moral consensus.

Soedjatmoko understood that values were not singular but plural and as such in competition with one another. The most to be hoped for was that a balance might be struck, say, between order and social justice. The goal, as Dr. Okita reminds us in his introduction to Soedjatmoko's thought, is "a dynamic balance among order, change, and social justice. . . ." Elsewhere Soedjatmoko writes of the balance between development and freedom. He would undoubtedly have agreed with Oliver Wendell Holmes, who observed: "Some praise the man of principle. My admiration is for the man who can find his way through a maze of conflicting principles." If anyone doubts that Soedjatmoko was engaged in a never-ending quest for a better understanding of moral principles that spanned divisions between North and South, the reading of the chapters that follow should remove most doubts. A careful reading of his collected works will repay the reader in much the same way. Each paper serves to illuminate key aspects and basic tenets of his philosophy.

Soedjatmoko often spoke of the essential disjunction between power and morality, a disjunction never wholly resolved in any country, which leads to the religious concept of the tragic dimension of life. Abraham Lincoln understood that the essential irreconcilability of power and morality forces any leader to bow in humility and to throw himself on the mercy of Providence. In looking abroad, a nation's people ought to be able to recognize the limits of virtue and the capacity for evil in every people and find ways not of eliminating it but channelling and containing it.

Soedjatmoko kept returning to the need to build new constructs of theory and practice for the achievement of development with freedom. Most development theories lead away from freedom. In the period before the Second World War, Japan and Germany gained development by abandoning freedom. In the process, they became totalitarian monsters. Only military defeat made it possible for liberal forces to re-emerge. Outsiders who would help must face up to the fateful clash between freedom and growth in the developing world. Soedjatmoko believed that the United States, while preaching freedom, was training thousands of economists, scientists, and military leaders who returned to their own countries with a narrow and élitist technocratic view of development. Against such trends, there are in third world countries countless people who yearn for development but remain respectful of freedom. When they look at most of the universities in the West, however, they find among both liberal and socialist thinkers an acceptance of the notion that development requires the subordination of freedom.

Soedjatmoko asked who is doing anything to help with the search for alternative development models? It is not persons concerned with freedom such as civil rights leaders, theologians, or philosophers but Western social scientists who are training the economists of the world. In politics, Soedjatmoko believed those who seized on the simple and legitimate issues of human rights were taking an easy way out when the essential and the hard question was, Can we shape a viable democratic development theory? That area, he asserted, remained an intellectual desert. He maintained that Western intellectuals did little; hard-pressed national leaders were too embattled to think straight. Latin American *dependencia* theories help explain certain weaknesses and give vent to nationalist anger but failed to provide guidelines for development. At the same time, as Dr. Okita points out, "there is no inherent reason why the organized pursuit of material improvements should automatically result in freedom, respect for humanity, and social justice."

Soedjatmoko pursued all these issues and more in *The Primacy of Freedom in Development*. He asked, "Is freedom possible?" He analysed the impact of political systems on development and the management of structural transformation. "Perceptions of Social Justice" led on to "Religion and the Development Process." Finally he threw the spotlight on the intellectual in a developing nation. We shall return to this theme in conclusion.

If freedom and development and the role of the intellectual in that regard were important to Soedjatmoko, he gave equal if not greater attention to the issue of universalism and particularism. All around him he saw evidence of emergent universalism and many of his initiatives within the United Nations University bespoke his conviction that forces in the world were driving the world toward increased interdependence. He was preoccupied with global problems such as the deterioration of the environment, the worldwide population explosion, especially in the less developed countries, and the threat of nuclear conflict. What set Soedjatmoko apart from most advocates of universalism was his recognition that universalism was not the single all-controlling force in the world. Particularism was competitive with universalism and will continue so in the foreseeable future.

In my discussions with Soedjatmoko I found him to be especially concerned with the claims nation states often make for the universality of their moral systems. What stood out for Soedjatmoko as he surveyed the world was the absence of a single moral framework. He found that American debates about morality and foreign policy were often narrow and ethnocentric. What was missing from such discussions was concern for a philosophy of history or interest in where humanity was going. These concerns had marked earlier periods of world history. Today not only have the millennial views of Christianity come under question but the communist Utopia has, for now at least, been replaced by democratic regimes in some former republics and authoritarianism in others.

Soedjatmoko had no doubts that we live in a pluralist world order but he spoke often about the difference in attitudes around the world concerning the role and the future of the nation state. For many scientists, including social scientists, the nation state has outlived its usefulness. In the developed world, the logic of the situation requires that states transcend their national loyalties. In the third world, the problem is the direct opposite. There the nation state is the appropriate negotiating unit for the promotion of a better world. It is also the necessary instrument for achieving social justice, political freedom, and national unity. It is the arena in which interests and ethnic and tribal groups advance their claims. Nations provide a legitimate framework in which competing ethnic interests can be arbitrated and resolved.

Nations, and particularly the United States, must recognize that they do not speak with one voice to the peoples of other nations. He frequently observed that Americans speak to the world with many voices, not all of which represent the nation's best side. All nations have their darker, subterranean side and he mentioned the problems of violence in the cities, loneliness, and alienation. Americans and other peoples should seek to be more honest; intellectuals and scholars in particular should not flinch from portraying the darker side of our society and then trying to put it in perspective. Honesty of this kind will not derogate from the world's appreciation of a nation's moral standing. If a nation is honest in Lincoln's sense of himself and his nation, it will invite others to join in a common quest for the strengthening of moral and political systems.

Soedjatmoko saw the United States and other developed nations falling short of a national morality that might become universal in character. Whereas most great powers can be indicted for moralism or cynicism at some time in their history, the particular weakness of the United States today was that its innocence was frequently linked up with national self-righteousness. No one could have been more conscious than Soedjatmoko of the far-reaching importance of morality for a people but for individual nations morality is seldom universal. They need to recognize the proper and inevitable tension between their approximation of righteousness and the limits and relativity of their moral base.

Reflecting on the United States, the Indonesian philosopher and diplomat raised questions about the efforts of the Carter administration to universalize its human rights policy. He credited President Carter with having restored a self-doubting and uncertain people to a sense of awareness of its national purpose. He agreed with the need to institutionalize its mission and forge administrative mechanisms to achieve it. However, Soedjatmoko asked himself whether the nation in rediscovering anew its historic moral beliefs could succeed in relating them to a rapidly changing world. The danger was that America's particularism would use human rights as an instrument of foreign policy. Rather human rights should be the avenue along which Americans sought a new morality that was relevant to the needs of the world's people. Against the background of striving to understand the needs and values of others, a more universal human rights policy might emerge.

Further, Soedjatmoko warned of the risks for nations in general, and for democratic states in particular, in the involvement of the great mass of the people in foreign policy with all their innocence and naïvety. The people in their innocence can be led down the garden path by jingoists, populists, or demagogues. In their participation, the people introduce an additional element of uncertainty into foreign policy. Viewed in more positive terms, people-to-people relations are important as are the relations across national boundaries of the representatives of parliaments and political parties. Indeed, Soedjatmoko warned that leaving all public declarations addressed to other countries to the chief executives of nations could be dangerous. He warned of exhausting prematurely the court of last resort and asked why, especially in Western countries, legislatures, parties, and civic and religious organizations could not share the responsibility of speaking out. Only ties between the world's people can foster a modest form of universalism.

Thus Soedjatmoko appeared to be calling for a pluralist and democratic international order. The pathway to such an order is more than the acceptance of cultural differences. It requires trust in those who are members of different cultures and political systems. Within every system we can find those who share common values. Soedjatmoko worried about the present outlook in some Western countries which he described as an almost desperate crusade to get other political systems to accept a common code. Instead he favoured a conscious effort to identify and help recognizable people in different systems to embrace common values. In this connection, he asked, "Who are such people?" They are dissidents in authoritarian and totalitarian states but dissidents are no more than the tip of the iceberg. In the long and protracted history of humanity going back to biological origins, innate belligerency has always required that there be an enemy. Now we are approaching a juncture in history where man has to learn to develop moral positions without directing them at a single identifiable enemy. The root question is whether we are capable of trusting the essential humaneness of other peoples even when the man at the top of the regime may be a gangster. Once we are capable of doing this, we will find those who share our ideals. It would be sad if we were incapable of transcending our nature in earlier, more primitive, societies.

Soedjatmoko was in no way oblivious to the problem of growing violence in the world. Terrorism is changing the whole complexion of the moral problem. It has given power to the powerless and in many countries minorities no longer need to remain without a voice. The availability of plastic bombs may force governments to come to terms with a determined minority. Most American discussions of a pluralist world order lack full awareness of the ethical issues raised by violence. The present world order is seen by a large part of the world as unjust. Calls for a new international economic order are manifestations of the unacceptability of a system where the rich become richer and the poorer ever poorer. More violence may be around the corner, and when it erupts it will be perceived by those who use it as moral. As we are repelled by violence, we should reflect on this aspect of the problem.

Another question follows. In what kind of a world order will the struggle against violence take place? Soedjatmoko saw such an order as pluralist in character in which no single nation will be able to define the moral centre. The search for values will go on through negotiations, blind groping, and partly articulated adjustments. What is most needed is a new morality in which fledgling nation states seek viability without overturning the international order. The further question is, "How, given the inevitability of political and social change, can societies reduce the cost in human suffering?" Soedjatmoko responded not by offering a single stratagem but through an overall approach to universalism and particularism, many of his points having been noted above. He was clear that no one nation in the world can impose its authority on the international order. Speaking to Americans in particular, he noted that the American era of absolute power had been relatively brief, adding "not by any fault of the United States." Its decline had been signalled by Viet Nam and to some this had come as a great shock. Its power and hegemony during the Carter administration was still very great, but he predicted that its capacity to shape events in the future would depend on its adjustment to new realities.

Another important question is whether the projected international order will be autocratic or democratic. Henry Kissinger often said that peace was the highest moral value in international affairs. Soedjatmoko added "yes," but peace must be seen in context. A peace which is unjust or is seen as unjust will never be lasting. A moral international order or universal international system must reflect the goals and values of all the world's peoples. It will require developed nations to join with others to resolve their political and ethical dilemmas. We need to understand that the foreign policies of nations are determined by what their publics openly or tacitly accept. An unsolved problem for most nations is how to connect up a vision of a future world order with the people's sense of participation, perhaps the most poignant example of the relationship between the universal and the particular. According to Soedjatmoko, no one was facing up to this problem in the 1960s and 1970s. Some futurologists assume an authoritarian order and in their scenarios push aside the political nature of foreign policy. Nor has freedom for people to participate been a hallmark of the United Nations. However, world conferences on the environment, food, women, and population can provide opportunities for people as well as governments.

In the end Soedjatmoko came back to his appeal for a philosophy of history and religion. Without such a philosophy, the problems of violence and social change can never be resolved. He observed that the head of the Lutheran World Federation was a black militant. Did this make him moral? Soedjatmoko began as a pacifist believing that Indonesia would gain its independence because its cause was just. However, he dropped pacifism during the struggle for independence. In any conflict, it is tempting to become a moral relativist and justify the unlimited use of force. If humanity could develop a shared sense of the direction in which it is going it might be possible to keep violence within bounds.

Soedjatmoko made plain that in speaking of a philosophy of history he was not speaking of Hegelian or Marxian concepts under which only certain social groups are designated as history's chosen instruments. A closed system always perpetuates injustice. He found no seductiveness in a rigidly coherent political philosophy or a system of ends which seeks by its claim of inevitability to justify the use of dubious means. Put in the simplest terms, Soedjatmoko was thinking of a general evolving scheme of values. At any given moment, societies may give different degrees of emphasis to, say, freedom and justice. In the long view or history, however, it may not matter where societies start. It is true that countries which begin with an exclusive concern for justice end up with the loss of freedom. As early as the 1970s, if not earlier, Soedjatmoko suggested that out of Soviet terror, a new system might emerge. It is moral arrogance to imagine that all mankind would limit its political choices to a single system.

The present world order and any foreseeable new world order is a pluralistic and multiple-value universe. During the Cold War, Soviet leaders took pride that the Soviets had chosen justice over freedom, but other nations choose freedom over justice. The argument over sequences and priorities is endless; in the final analysis nations must find their own acceptable modes. History and circumstances limit every nation. If mankind is to find a way out of particularism and relativism it would more likely be found in religion, not politics. The search for meaning in the international order must not be dissociated from humanity's search for meaning. Americans who are pragmatic and positivist are sometimes embarrassed by talk of the need for universals and a new religious faith. We may ask what can anyone do about man's quest for an ultimate faith.

Soedjatmoko's answer was "probably nothing" except to recognize the need to associate the search for religion with the secular problems of the world. Secular problems may be impossible to solve apart from a religious dimension. No discipline exists within the range of man's scientific and intellectual arsenal that can give answers to meaning. In these terms, someone should be making the case for religion but theologians shy away from doing so. New religious groups tend to be authoritarian and fail to match faith with tolerance. For the first time in history survival depends on combining the two. Soedjatmoko believed that a legend from a Japanese mystical religion might help:

> God is at the top of the mountain. One man lives east, another west, another north, and another south of the mountain. No other path is open than for each man to reach the top by his own road. Each seeks the top but each must find his own way.

This legend, Soedjatmoko believed, casts light on how to match faith with tolerance.

Part I of the United Nations University volume honouring Soedjatmoko comprises four theoretical papers beginning with the paper by Dr. Okita to which attention has already been called. Professor Farhang Rajaee of Tehran University in Iran asks: Are intellectuals guardians of tradition or vanguards of development? Karl Mannheim saw their special task for society as providing "an interpretation for the world." Some question existing authority regardless of its legitimacy. At one and the same time, intellectuals must explain and interpret the existing order, thus preserving tradition when necessary while also comprehending the need for change and development. Rajaee provides a framework for approaching the role of intellectuals in the context of culture and development. Soedjatmoko spoke often of the need for intellectuals to define the fundamental issues.

Professor Mine Eder of the University of the Bosphorus in Turkey, the University of Virginia, Washington and Lee University and Lewis and Clark University, goes back to the Greeks, the Chinese, medieval

Europe, the Muslim world, the Renaissance, nineteenth-century Russia and France, and the modern era to explore changing definitions of intellectuals. Detached from ideology or as political dissenters, they are the creators of political ideas. Having considered and compared their differing roles, she examines the issues of economic democracy and what intellectuals can do. She finds that they have a responsibility for education that can turn the entire society into a "society of intellectuals." They can act as a synthesizing force to generate collective action and can continue to give society a "guilty conscience," thus helping it to improve itself. Regarding intellectuals, Soedjatmoko believed that if they were to prove influential, a "critical mass" was essential. They needed a mutual protection society.

Sulak Sivaraksa of Thailand sees intellectuals as independent thinkers and social critics. They should believe in the common man, speak out for the less fortunate, defend the "robbed" against the "robbers," sustain cultural freedom, and help ordinary people to choose leaders who are "unworldly without being saintly, unambitious without being inactive, warm-hearted without being sentimental." Whoever may be in power, there must always be freedom of speech and a system to counterbalance power and that, as Sulak sees it, is the responsibility of the intellectual. This may involve a more exclusively activist role than Soedjatmoko envisaged for intellectuals. Is this role defined as dissent too one-dimensional?

Dr. Alexander King is co-founder and honorary president of the Club of Rome. In his chapter, "Technology and Dr. Faustus," he follows closely the themes of culture, technology, and democracy, concepts integrally identified with Soedjatmoko's thinking and writing. He treats them as interwoven subjects and approaches their interaction using a term coined by the Club of Rome, "the world problematic." This term for him describes that intertwining difficulties and problems that constitute the human predicament. To understand the context of the predicament, Dr. King discusses the three environments in which man lives: the external environment of the planet of earth, water, and atmosphere; the social environment or the arena in which individuals interact along a vast spectrum of alliances from the family to the United Nations; and the internal world within each individual which undergirds the social environment.

Dr. King begins his discussion focusing on the internal environment which is often swallowed up in the claims by some philosophers that ultimately man is rational. Dr. King finds such thinking spurious, overlooking as it does the irrationality of political and international relationships. Those who have listened to Soedjatmoko can imagine his using the same words as Dr. King who writes: "The problems of individuals and society reside deep within human nature" and later that "egoism is the driving force of innovation and progress" but also of selfishness, brutality, and dominance over others. It is the struggle between the two aspects of egoism, its positive and negative sides, that constitutes the eternal Faustian drama. If the egoistic urge is unchecked by countervailing forces, it may give rise to a dynamic society but one marked by exploitation and social injustice. However, too much controlled egoism brings apathy and stagnation. What is true of individuals is also true of nations and great collectivities. Nationalism may reflect love of country or ethnic continuity or it can become chauvinism and xenophobia leading to war. I often told Soedjatmoko that his views on human nature were reminiscent of Reinhold Niebuhr's and the same could be said of Dr. King.

Throughout his essay, Dr. King discusses concepts that invite us to reflect on the contributions of Soedjatmoko. This is true of his discussion of development no less than of human nature. Following the Second World War, development was cast in a Euro-American mould and equated with the idea of progress expressed as economic development and less often as socio-economic development. Cultural and traditional aspects were glossed over or ignored. In time, the assumptions that undergirded development in the early decades of the United Nations were increasingly challenged. Such questioning led to new development strategies that emphasized rural problems and the third world's rural poor. The developed countries' model of development proved lacking and Dr. King therefore turns to a consideration of culture and development with technology being considered a part of culture.

The first of the country papers has as its subject Indonesia. Before I ever visited Indonesia, I had heard about Professor Selo Soemardjan. He is a world-class sociologist who had close personal ties with Soedjatmoko. They found they were in agreement on several fundamental issues, including the role of the intellectual in society. Thus Soedjatmoko would have agreed with Professor Soemardjan's view that what sets the intellectual apart is his or her "independent thinking as distinct from placating the opinion of others. . . ." Koko would also have agreed with Soemardjan's longer definition which emphasizes careful observation, searching for underlying causes, and formulating conclusions that can be communicated to others. Another telling distinction is the one that asserts that rural development does not require university graduates as much as it does intellectuals. Soedjatmoko's complaint was that some of the American-trained economists became technicians, not independent thinkers, on their return from study abroad. As he used to say, they were "too brittle" to deal with Indonesia's most basic problems.

Another topic which preoccupied Soedjatmoko was identifying the social and religious groups that produced leaders in Indonesia. He spoke and wrote often of the aristocrats, the religious leaders, and the intellectuals. With regard to the first, he recognized the historical factors that had enabled colonial leaders and their aristocrat allies to maintain power through policies of indirect rule. But he also described Indonesian aristocrats as father figures who brought a certain amount of stability to the region. The aristocracy had survived all the messy political and social change that Indonesia experienced. Religion as well had become an "integral part of the culture." I recall Soedjatmoko saying that the religious parties had reached a peak in Sukarno's time but had either declined or been dissolved in the Suharto era. It was a third group, the intellectuals, who interested Soedjatmoko most and he would have found especially rewarding Soemardjan's wide-ranging discussion of education; early attitudes toward university graduates, especially graduates of Dutch universities; the link between the aristocracy and the Dutch and between non-government intellectuals and religious leaders. The latter were closer to the people. The intellectuals were feared by the Dutch and many were exiled. Soemardjan brings this discussion to a close by describing the period of Japanese occupation and Indonesia's post-war independence from the Dutch.

In discussing the post-war era, Soemardjan is in effect revisiting a period in the 1950s and early 1960s in which he and Soedjatmoko played an important role. The intellectuals divided themselves into nationalists and communists, and the religion-oriented group was the third leg of the tripod. Sukarno in 1959 seized all power, dissolving the Constituent Assembly and Parliament. He ridiculed intellectuals and passed over many of them as politically unacceptable. Soemardjan notes the excesses of Sukarno's regime and praises Suharto's action in creating "a rational and realistic" development planning agency called Bappenas. Its staff was composed exclusively of professors, university graduates, and consultants. Fifteen of the 22 members of the first Suharto cabinet were technocrats or professors still active in their universities. Soemardjan finds that intellectuals both in the public and private sectors have been influential in development planning, although not in political decision-making. Soedjatmoko was wary of university persons being drawn too closely into governmental affairs. I suspect he might put a somewhat different emphasis on the strength and weaknesses of the technocrats. Soemardjan ends his discussion by analysing the role of intellectuals during various stages of development.

The second of the country papers written from the perspective of an Asian country, with overlays of Spanish and American culture, is an essay by F. Sionil José of the Philippines. Mr. José asks why the Philippines, which was comparatively better off than all other South-East Asian countries in the 1950s and 1960s and even ahead of Korea and Taiwan, had fallen so dramatically behind in the 1990s. He identifies one cause as the tendency of Filipinos to live in a "blame culture." Whenever the Philippines falls into decline, they affix the blame on some other group or country.

José places the blame for the Philippines' condition on a Filipino oligarchy of 400 top families. In this connection, he quotes Salvador de Madariaga that "a country need not be a colony or a foreign power; it can easily be the colony of its own leaders." The Philippines have been colonized by the rich at the expense of the poor.

José takes the reader inside the culture of Philippine society and writes about life in his family's village. Its poverty and its intermixing of different ethnic groups, each of whom periodically placed a few leaders in high offices, remain lasting features of village life. In describing his village, José maintains he is describing "the lives of millions of Filipinos to this day." Life revolves around the rice crop and planting and harvesting. The medical doctor is summoned only after the herb doctor has been consulted. Power relations stem from ethnicity not ideology, and poverty is unchanging. José observes that Filipinos would have liked to import American technology without American culture. That culture, he maintains, has been degrading.

American initiatives in the Philippines, José argues, came in waves and too often were imposed from above. Community development centres, reading centres, the Green Revolution, and commercial and business ventures were all introduced from the outside and in a matter of years fell into decline. The reason for this is that after a time they are left unattended by the Filipinos and fall victim to corruption. José maintains that outsiders seek stability for the Filipinos but "the instability I want for my country is the harbinger of change and, therefore, of justice." I believe Soedjatmoko would have sympathy for the emphasis on justice and respect for the defence of indigenous culture. He would also applaud the challenge to Filipino artists and writers to recast the national character. He would, however, question whether a people's habits and history can so easily be written out of existence. Whereas José urges that development be equated with justice, Soedjatmoko would rather have said that development and justice are in creative tension. I cannot imagine Soedjatmoko, the universalist, writing that

> Filipino development hinges primarily on the capacity of Filipinos to "kill" their Western father and do it alone, never to eschew violence as an alternative, for it is the intellectual revolutionary after all who is the real modernizer. I do not propose a hermetically sealed culture, although, on second thought, it may not be such a bad idea after all.

In other words, Soedjatmoko would see the pathos of the Philippine situation but would place it in a broader context. Village life has deeper roots than José acknowledges and more to lose by adopting a nihilistic view of the more positive aspects of modernization. He would reinforce what José mentions in passing, however, that the nation's leaders are sometimes the product of villages such as his and of the ethnic groups that populate the villages. Rather than reporting, as José does, that educational and scientific projects, such as reading centres or the Green Revolution, ultimately failed, Soedjatmoko would have discussed how they could succeed. He would also have brought to the surface more explicitly what he might identify as Philippine culture and democracy. As for the intellectuals, whereas José sees them as the spokesmen for revolution and change, Soedjatmoko might look to them also for political wisdom and practical morality.

Dr. Alexander Kwapong presents the first of the regional perspectives in the volume, a perspective on culture, development, and democracy, and the role of the intellectual from the vantage point of Africa. It is evident from his essay that he and Soedjatmoko were not always in agreement in their seven years together at the United Nations University. It would be surprising if they had thought alike, one being an African trained in the classics at Cambridge and the other an Asian who began in medicine but gravitated to philosophy and diplomacy.

Kwapong sketches in the broad outlines of a portrait of contemporary Africa. He considers the views of the pessimists who write of "this giant troublesome continent" but also those who witness "the new crusade for African democracy." Clearly, Kwapong views himself as a member of the second group. As for the region's development, Kwapong is closer to Soedjatmoko than José when he prescribes "a comprehensive, sustained, and systematic response, with a long-term focus on all fronts – economic, social, and political." Development in Africa must be an African inspired effort "designed, implemented, and owned" by the African countries. For this Africa requires "technical, analytical, management, and institutional capacities." To achieve this goal, Africans must advance as their highest priority "the building of African human and institutional capacity." Africa suffers from the decline of education at all levels. Side by side, a shortage of skilled manpower coexists with the unemployment and underemployment of graduates of African universities. "The brain drain has become a haemorrhage" but donor agencies are beginning to respond to this problem. More needs to be done in building centres for research and training and a critical mass of researchers.

As one reads Kwapong's comprehensive analysis of African development and culture, the enormity of the challenge comes through. It must "overhaul its educational system; attract capital; stem the brain drain; conquer desertification, drought, and famine"; and get through the next 10 years. But it must also master high science and technology for the long term. Does this not call for a clear sense of priorities? Soedjatmoko would have said so and I look back on my career in development and wonder if sending electron microscopes to the third world countries in the 1960s and 1970s was out of phase with their capacity and needs. One of Soedjatmoko's foremost contributions was to recognize that culture was related to development and democracy in a most fundamental way. For that reason he called for indigenous entrepreneurs and skills and tools that served their needs.

The author of the second regional perspective is Rodolfo Stavenhagen, research professor at El Colegio de Mexico and visiting professor at Stanford. The founder of El Colegio, Don Daniel Cosio Villegas, was Mexico's foremost economic historian. In establishing El Colegio, he brought together some of Mexico's most respected intellectuals: the economist Victor Urquide, diplomats such as Francisco Cuevas Cancino, legal scholars such as Caesar Sepulveda and others who joined as the institution gained international recognition. My impression then was that a major task of this group was to train their successors. From this effort an impressive group of younger scholars emerged in international relations, political economy, anthropology, sociology, and history.

Professor Stavenhagen, after having begun as an applied anthropologist in south-eastern Mexico, has continued the pioneering work of El Colegio. Although his paper is entitled "The Culture of Resistance in Latin America," his work calls to mind the problem of minorities around the world. As one learns about the plight of indigenous people on the American subcontinent, parallels come to mind in other countries. For example, the distinguished American historian Arthur M. Schlesinger, Jr., in his recently published *The Disuniting of America* asks whether *e pluribus unum* can survive the cult of ethnicity. Elsewhere the war in Yugoslavia symbolizes the challenge of ethnicity to national unity throughout Eastern Europe and the former Soviet Union. In Germany, France, and Britain, the influx of Eastern Europeans, North Africans, West Indians, Turks, and South Asians offers new challenges within the European continent. What sets Latin American culture apart is the fact that its minority population is indigenous and not the result of a flood of immigrants coming to its shores in the last 50–200 years. Whatever the differences, the phenomenon of the separated minority is near universal.

Professor Stavenhagen provides a brilliant analysis of indigenous peoples on the Latin American subcontinent. He demonstrates how deep the rift is among Latin American intellectuals confronted with a problem that goes back 500 years. Liberators such as Simón Bolívar asked whether viable nations could be built from such mixed populations. The search for national identity by a divided population is still a principal concern of Latin American intellectuals. A subordinate Indian peasantry stands apart from the small ruling groups and the landowners. Whereas the ruling élites identified with liberal democracies in the West, copied the US Constitution and considered themselves a part of Western civilization, the native Indian peoples lived in isolated villages or tribal communities, practising their ancestral customs and speaking one of many hundred Indian languages. By the twentieth century, the mestizos were to become the majority ethnic element in most Latin American countries. Indians remained at the bottom of the pyramid and some argued that change would come about only by improving the "biological stock" through large-scale European immigration. A racist viewpoint led to the exclusion of Indians at least through the nineteenth century. For the rapidly increasing mestizo population, their status changed in the twentieth century as their population increased and the number of "pure" whites and "pure" Indians declined. They became the driving force for nationalism and the growing urban middle class. Whereas in the nineteenth century, mestizos were thought to combine the worst traits of the other two groups, by the turn of the century they were seen as combining the best.

One could wish that Professor Stavenhagen had felt freer to generalize more often, as Soedjatmoko would surely have done, about the comparability of similar yet different situations in the world. It is evident that he profoundly understands the larger issues as when he writes:

> While the European was regressing to the myth of racial purity and superiority, the white supremacy was still legally enshrined in the United States, the idealization of the mixed-blood mestizo in the Latin America of the nineteen twenties and thirties could be considered as something of a heterodox if not a revolutionary position.

He traces how the culture of whites and mestizos came to be considered superior while the backwardness of Indian culture led to government policies called *indigenismo*, or "national integration." Indian culture, including language, education, legal systems, and self-government, was intended to yield to assimilation. The discussion of Indian culture by Stavenhagen is a worthy tribute to Soedjatmoko's study of culture.

Elise Boulding's paper "The dynamics of reshaping the social order: Old actors, new actors" is an imaginative quest for a new or transformed social order. Its contents reflect both points of convergence and divergence with Soedjatmoko's thought. Boulding finds the basis for a new social order in the ideas and undertakings of 18,000 international non-governmental organizations and the 10,000 societies of indigenous and ethnic peoples. By contrast, Soedjatmoko and the United Nations University are more often seen as anchored to existing universities, which Boulding argues are too disciplinary in their approaches. Boulding admits that what she describes is a utopia (a "not-place") but then defends its usefulness as one would defend the age-old image of the Good Society in Plato or Mount Zion. Soedjatmoko more often found realities in the practical wisdom of Aristotle and his successors.

Looking back, Boulding asks why Spencer's dream of the industrial age as an age of peaceableness gave way to fear of extinction of the human race. She finds the cause not in human nature but in developments in science and technology. It manifests itself in nuclear war and environmental destruction. Soedjatmoko would more often have thrown the spotlight on man struggling with other men and with intractable social realities. Boulding evidently is optimistic about man's transformation, while Soedjatmoko holds to a view of man that puts some but not exclusive stress on continuity.

Dr. Boulding argues that we should think about the Now (the present) in the context of what she calls the "200-year present." The processes of change move "more rapidly and more slowly" than we can comprehend; we need an expanded time frame but one we can understand through our own life experience. Her "200-year present" begins 100 years ago today, on the birth of centenarians in our society. The other boundary is the hundredth birthday of babies born today. This image gives boundaries $3\frac{1}{2}$ generations each way in time. It gives a span of history understandable to contemporary man.

In this "200-year present," the major contribution of the intellectual community is the formation of vast numbers of transnational networks. As I read Boulding's euphoric praise of the peripatetic intellectuals of the global community who go back and forth as members of these networks, I could not but remember Soedjatmoko's enthusiasm when he visited Universidad del Valle in Cali, Colombia, which he called the most impressive developmental university he had seen. Koko, with all his global instincts, also preferred some fixed place with its ongoing activities as contrasted with the sometimes short-run exhilaration of networkers on the move.

None the less, Boulding sees participants in the early INGOs as pioneers whose concepts of social and economic development precede by half a century their use by organized states. She calls for peace education necessary to train future generations, yet she acknowledges the short-lived existence of some of these efforts. It remains to be seen how much and how well peace education prepares us to live in a harsh and conflict-ridden world. On the other hand, Dr. Boulding would be quick to point out that the world has suffered from forms of education that failed to emphasize peace. On one issue and with one exception, Boulding and Soedjatmoko agree. Both put great emphasis on culture. However, Soedjatmoko would be sceptical of calling the period from 1988 to 1997 the World Decade for Cultural Development. Henry Kissinger had a penchant for naming a decade the decade for development. So apparently does Dr. Boulding. More importantly, both agree that culture is basic to the development of a community.

The final chapter in our volume is a brilliant essay by Professor Wang Gungwu. He has kindly consented to its use even though it will be published in another form as part of a larger work. It is addressed to "spaces people occupy" in an increasingly global society.

Historians characteristically study the relations of people over time. His essay examines what happens to "the space people leave and the space they move into" when they leave their own country. Wang Gungwu identifies three forms of migration: first, large group migrations of tribes or nations leading either to conflict or defeat; second, enforced migrations of smaller groups driven out of their homes by famine or other disasters; and those he calls sojourners who are economic refugees, go abroad in response to opportunity, and who eventually settle as migrants.

Wang Gungwu finds sojourning a way of overcoming opposition to migration, especially in East Asia and South-East Asia. It is one of three core subjects in his discussion. The other two are the growth in modern nation states of formal structures to control and assist migration and new varieties of migration leading to informal linkages of people across boundaries. The author points up differences between this form of migration and movement such as the Jewish Diaspora and the settling of the Americas. Indeed, his great contribution is to go beyond the traditional studies of migration and to link his findings with global development around the world.

Wang Gungwu acknowledges that some of his views of migration as a contributing factor to a global society might lead to a new Whig interpretation of history and a new theory of progress. However, he is quick to say that the need persists for national and local history where much of political and social action continues. Migration studies of the kind he describes are essential because of the trends in global development brought about by migration and reinforced by new forms of communication. Of all that has been written about global development it would be difficult to think of a work comparable to Wang Gungwu's in breadth or profundity, unless it was Soedjatmoko's writings.

It is a sign of the profundity of Soedjatmoko's thought that he addresses virtually all the issues raised in our little volume. As if by some kind of miracle, he responds to our writers in his earlier essay on "The Intellectual in a Developing Nation" with the wise and trenchant analysis we have long associated with him.

With an emphasis that characterizes almost all his essays, Soedjatmoko analyses the role of the intellectual in terms of culture and democracy. He insists upon the need to recognize that the intellectual is "continually and crucially concerned" with the cultural and moral problems of "identity and expression, purpose and direction, structure and meaning...." The overall challenge continues to be relating universally held values to each successive concrete situation. For the intellectual in uniform, a conflict exists between the military and civilian cultures in which he lives. For the intellectual who has been a leader for national independence, he confronts the unfamiliar experience of leadership in governance in the post-independence world. Often for the first time he confronts the dilemmas involved in exercising responsibility.

The first dilemma which interestingly enough only a few of the contributors to the volume acknowledge or discuss is the dilemma of power. The main source of strength for the intellectual is clarity of vision, whereas the exercise of power calls for "inevitable compromises," gradual change and concessions to popular prejudices to reinforce one's power base. Moreover, responsibility in government requires concessions to the achievement of a minimum of order and orderly change which threaten the intellectual's insistence on freedom. Soedjatmoko suggests that intellectuals faced with this dilemma become either mandarins known for their disinterested public service, faceless bureaucrats, or cynical *apparatchiks*. Confronted with such choices, other intellectuals choose "unstructured influence to power," a choice with which Soedjatmoko was familiar at certain stages in his career.

One change that almost all post-independent intellectuals experienced in coming to office was a heightened awareness of the reality of power including its character, its function, and its limitation. They came to experience the need for a strong central government that was capable of nation building. Alongside the reality of power was an awareness of the need for balancing and countervailing power to check abuses of power. In such a balancing process, Soedjatmoko concluded that a sufficient number of intellectuals must stay outside of government to secure a balance between state and society. In such a role, the intellectual becomes a prophet, seer, sage, or defender of fundamental values in part because of his disinterest in power. Yet because he is detached, he may be more convincing to society. He may help others identify the actions which require the exercise of power as well as those for which the use of power is precluded.

If a society fails to achieve economic development, this fact may cause the people to fall back on traditional patterns of social organization. They may trade insecurity in the pursuit of new goals for the "comfort of tradition." Thus a society becomes "locked in a vicious circle of underdevelopment." In this circumstance, the crisis may call forth intellectuals to prepare the people for the new challenges of modern existence both within communal groups and in developing a national vision and the attendant national loyalties.

Raising consciousness and heightening positive actions on behalf of national unity and security, freedom and growth are tasks for the intellectual. Rather than maintaining the posture of critic and dissenter, the intellectual helps legitimate such values. He must articulate the differing perceptions of central values as they relate to the structuring of interconnected balances. Progress and civility depend on such balances. In a phrase that prefigures the dangers created by political and religious fanaticism, Soedjatmoko observes that "the exclusive pursuit of one particular goal, beyond a certain point ... will call forth a backlash of passion and violence ... resulting in general retrogression."

At the same time, the intellectual must show how the pitfalls to national unity may be avoided and the society's cohesion enhanced. He must listen to the unarticulated yearnings of those in society unable to express their aspirations and help them enter into a spirit of national self-consciousness. In all they do, intellectuals must heed the importance of safeguarding their own intellectual roots while entering into dialogue with peers in other groups. In other words, intellectuals must preserve their "strong and separate identity while pointing to strong national and cross-communal intellectual institutions."

The question of the validity or non-validity of dissent is a perennial problem in the third world because of the fragility of the new nation states. The intellectual must continue to spell out alternative courses of action, while recognizing the threats to national unity and solidarity. A people's attitude toward dissent is inextricably linked up with social responsibility and its competing interpretations. He asks, What if a people have achieved their national independence through solidarity and self-discipline but have little or no idea of what is meant by a loyal opposition? What are the consequences for democracy? Intellectuals who have participated in the struggle for national independence have learned to measure the social and political consequences of their individual actions. Their experience of civil war and bloodletting adds to the sense of social responsibility. They must understand the nature of politics in the third world and what Soedjatmoko called "the politics of instability." They are likely to face intolerance from part of the citizenry, yet they must persist.

Soedjatmoko knew full well that whatever role the intellectual chooses to play, he must pay a price. His aim should be to help his society choose *meaningful* courses of action. In so doing not only can he be subjected to criticism and ridicule but in pursuing hard-fought goals he may risk "losing his soul." In pursuing the ends of modernization, he may discover that his own rational approach may touch only the tip of a volcano of powerful and deep-seated irrational forces and feelings that may trigger violence. The intellectual who initially sought to eradicate traditional values and cultures may learn he must first rearrange and build on them to achieve modernization.

Soedjatmoko had doubts that any of the world's great ideologies, whether communism, socialism, or democratic capitalism, were sufficient to meet the third world's need for development. The unique problems of the third world arising from the context in which industrialization and technology are applied tends to make the answers of three ideologies irrelevant. Their applicability as strategies of development for a society at the subsistence level is problematical. Almost in passing, Soedjatmoko takes note of the fact that communist ideologies have had some success in countries that are culturally and ethnically homogeneous but have been rejected in heterogeneous societies. He concludes that none of the great ideologies provide adequate models but "home grown ideologies compounded of elements adapted from the major ideologies are more likely to shape these societies."

All this has led the third world intellectual to decide that he must stand on his own. The older intellectuals were more inclined than younger ones to look for approval from their Western mentors. While the former suffered anguish when they moved beyond the approval of their teachers, the latter have a tendency toward becoming a consumerist, Western-oriented élite. The younger intellectuals have found answers in the social sciences but in so doing have overlooked the importance of cultural and moral evaluations. Soedjatmoko's conclusion regarding the social science approach is unmistakable:

> As long as development theories avoid dealing with basic normative issues ... as long as these theories ignore the central questions of power, the political preconditions for development, and the relationship of social change to the power structure; and as long as development strategies are not linked to political dynamics, there is not much hope that through these models we will be able to come to grips with the basic problems of our stagnant societies (*The Primacy of Freedom in Development*, p. 70).

Soedjatmoko saw a danger for the young social scientists in losing themselves in the kind of social science research that was a mere extension of the academic approach of the more stable developed Western countries. By comparison, the most important intellectual challenges in the new societies include defining the national purpose, relating unfolding value patterns to changing social realities, illuminating the routes to the future, discovering alternative pathways, pointing out the pitfalls, and explaining the significance of each new development in terms of common goals.

Two requirements are essential in confronting these challenges. First, new societies require a theory of society to understand the social and cultural forces that can sustain modernization. Soedjatmoko explains that in the quest for such a theory moral indignation or idealism can be destructive. He speaks of the heavy concentration of combustible materials in the society such as high population growth, a low median age level in the population, rising expectations, slow growth rate, limited resources, and a high potential for regional and communal conflict. Those who advocate simple unilinear solutions such as an agrarian revolution are courting disaster. The task of the intellectual is to help steer the nation through transition and development. Nothing short of the capacity for moral reasoning will do. Throughout the intellectual must give highest priority to the goals of freedom and social justice. The complexities of the intellectual's relationship to power, reason, tradition, national and communal groups constitute the ultimate dilemma.

Intellectuals face another dilemma that cannot be overestimated. One aspect of the commitment must be to find the courage for political engagement, not blindly but with a deep understanding of the needs of society. The intellectual's dilemma arises because however great the fascination with power, he must also step back from the political battles of the day to rethink the perceptions of the problems the nation faces. Paradoxically, his political responsibility is to strengthen the political process so that development can be depoliticized. He must do this by operating at three levels, the national, the communal, and the transcommunal levels.

Finally, the intellectual is society's link with the outside world which is itself in a state of continuous change. Faced with such changes the intellectual must continually review his assumptions concerning modernization. No one may have ready answers but this makes the leaders' independence of thought that much more important. Because most major problems are intractable, the contribution of the modernizing intellectual becomes part of the stream of history's unfolding drama.

We deem it appropriate to pay tribute to one of the century's foremost intellectuals both in these introductory reflections and in the papers that follow.

I. Tribute to Soedjatmoko

1

Culture, economic development, democracy: A tribute to the late Soedjatmoko

Saburo Okita

There are three threads running through the legacy left by the late Soedjatmoko. The first of these is that the central issue in any society is that of ensuring a dynamic balance among order, change, and social justice in the development process, and that the social costs of failing to achieve such a balance are enormous. Second is that there is no inherent reason why the organized pursuit of material improvements should automatically result in freedom, respect for humanity, and social justice. And third is that it is ultimately impossible to expect to resolve the many issues we face with material values alone.

Ideology is no guarantee of a dynamic balance in the development process, and it is better to consider the possibilities for simultaneously following the pursuit of economic growth, equity, human rights, and political freedom through the balanced workings of a system in which government seeks to achieve popular goals, the market economy provides the necessary coordination, and culture and other factors preserve society's identity. The formation of a new international order for the resolution of environmental and North-South problems is a crucial issue for mankind, and intellectuals have a major role to play here.

Soedjatmoko was very much aware of the need for a dynamic so-

The author would like to acknowledge the assistance of Shinji Mizukami, on the staff of the Institute for Domestic and International Policy Studies, in the preparation of this paper.

cial balance encompassing the political, cultural, and more. One of the hypotheses that he drew from the lessons of history is that the central issue for society is that of achieving a dynamic balance among order, change, and social justice, and that ignoring this balance ultimately leads to social disintegration and a transitional period imposing very high-risk changes in the social order. He thus focused on the question of whether or not it would be possible to manage change in the development process in an orderly manner and without slipping into social turmoil and chaos. Recognizing that the State is the main force for development in the developing countries, which means that it is a political system within the State that must manage the changes commensurate upon development, Soedjatmoko recognized that social order and stability rest upon the freely given consent of the governed and the coercive power of the State, with the balance between the two determined by the degree to which society as a whole deems the prevailing order to be just.[1] In effect, he said, society rests on the balance between the State's right to protect itself and the basic human rights of society and its members to live democratic lives.[2]

The State exists to achieve certain ends – ends which must be such that they contribute to the purposes of the society as a whole. While the existence of a social consensus facilitates the pursuit of such legitimate government authority as taxation and the allocation of public works disbursements, and this in turn promotes development, it is important to consider whether or not such a social consensus does in fact exist. For Soedjatmoko, this is a question of whether or not social justice is being served. While society encompasses a wide variety of concepts as to what is just, society's cohesiveness and vitality depend upon a tacit agreement as to the acceptable limits of injustice and unfairness, and this concept of social justice is subject to changes with the changing conditions of development.[3]

It is considering the questions of what concepts of social justice are appropriate within the development process and what conditions must exist for the attainment of this social justice that Soedjatmoko introduces and defines the question of individual freedom. This is the issue of the relationship between development and freedom.

As Soedjatmoko stated, the relationship between development and freedom is one of the most troublesome and most important unresolved issues of our time. Whether or not mankind will be able to achieve a future of freedom and justice will depend to a considerable extent on whether or not the third world is able to eradicate poverty and develop relatively free and open societies.[4] As such, he postulated the question of whether there is something inherent within the development process that is at conflict with freedom and what the future outlook is for the great masses of the third world peoples who seek to achieve not only more materially comfortable lifestyles but also freedom. This he did because he fervently hoped it would be possible to discover developmental paths that supported rather than negated freedom and respect. In effect, he was looking for democratic theories of development.

It is instructive here to start by looking at development itself. As defined by Soedjatmoko, the ultimate purpose of development is "to make the population of a country (especially the weak and the poor) not only more productive but also more socially effective and self-aware."[5] Development is not simply for the attainment of growth and the accumulation of resources and wealth but is to help all of society's constituent people and groups acquire the social, economic, and political skills they need for growth and learning through this acquisition process.[6] At the same time, he emphasized that we must learn both from the past and the future. I believe this is a universal approach to neither North nor South, for his definition of development makes it clear that we must learn from the past and study the future's potential. Just as the developing countries can and should learn from the industrial countries – their partners in development – so can and should the industrial countries learn from each other and the developing countries, and so can and should the developing countries learn from each other in exchanges of experiences and information as part of South-South cooperation. There are many issues where North and South must cooperate and learn together for the future, including global environmental issues and the tremors generated by scientific and technological advances and the information revolution.

Soedjatmoko warned that we must not see development as a straight-line progression. Rather, the very process of development engenders numerous issues of changing values and value judgements. To borrow Soedjatmoko's own terms, "the heart of the problem of development and of freedom is located in the difficulty of conciliating the needs of the centre for the most rational and efficient allocation of scarce developmental resources with the requirement of development from below, with its ingredients of autonomy and self-reliance."[7] While concentrating authority at the centre during the development process countervails the ethnic, religious, values and other diversities that tend to weaken social cohesion, it also happens that, just as the rise of new interests is disruptive to the political linkages developed under the older social order, development mandates changes in the systems for reconciling the various interests that arise with changes in political and social circumstances. There is a very good likelihood of friction and conflict within this shift of power and power-sharing. It is thus necessary, Soedjatmoko wrote, for society to have the flexibility and adaptability to ride out this social crisis, which in turn demands that the social climate be one of respect for diversity. Such a society's existence can only be guaranteed by institutionalized legal rules and equal access to the legal means of redress, and it takes time to create a diverse society and foster social pluralism.

It is also important to recognize that there are limits to the extent and speed of development and modernization that the people can and will accept, and there is a very real danger that the society could fragment if its development and modernization are incompatible and unreconcilable with the culture and traditional values. "At all times this (developmental effort) must be capable of relating the development effort to the moral core of the nation, to the 'deep structure' of a particular culture and its basic values."[8] Culture functions to maintain and preserve the patterns of society, and such aspects as popular values, beliefs, practices, and behavioural patterns help significantly to preserve social cohesiveness. There are, thus, considerable doubts today about the assumption that development will automatically socialize people to the existing political system. It was most likely based upon awareness of this fact that the South Commission's *The Challenge to the South* emphasizes the importance of people-centred development strategies. Postulating the creation of a democratic climate guaranteeing basic human rights as both an essential goal of development and as an important means of accelerating development, *The Challenge to the South* says that democratic institutions should be strengthened and the formation of spontaneous grassroots organizations encouraged.[9]

I suspect Soedjatmoko went through such a philosophical journey in considering democracy's potential as a stabilizing mode able to effect both order and balanced social change in promoting development. Transitional democratic governments are weak because they have yet to consolidate their political foundations, and they are arguably not as effective as authoritarian governments in promoting reform in societies where there are clear forces of political opposition.

Yet the World Bank has stated flatly in its 1991 *World Development Report* that democratic systems are positively linked with the overall aspects of development and welfare.[10] The development effectiveness implications of democratic government and authoritarian government are crucial in considering Soedjatmoko's second hypothesis.

The second hypothesis that Soedjatmoko derived from the lessons of history is that there is no guarantee that the organized pursuit of material betterment will automatically translate into freedom, respect for human rights, and social justice. Thus, the next step, as already noted, is to recognize the need for a strategy for democratic structural change. Soedjatmoko characterized the trickle-down theory as naïve and emphasized that economic growth alone is not an adequate condition for ensuring subsequent equity and justice.

Unfortunately, many of the people who formulate policy in the developing countries may be unduly enamoured of a sequential progression going from economic growth first to the attainment of social equity second and then to the attainment of human rights and political freedom only third.

It is also worth noting here that Soedjatmoko discoursed on the limits to what ideology can do in the quest for social equity. While ideology can be useful in considering what kind of a society is wanted, "freedom is not the product of any particular ideological construct," and "no ideology can sustain itself as a motive force for more than one or two generations" in the face of global complexities and uncertainties, the speed of change, and the enormity of the transformations taking place today.[11] This is almost prophetic in light of the recent changes in the Soviet Union and Eastern Europe.

In terms of social functionality, there are generally very close interrelations among the government, which serves to introduce purposeful change in society, the market economy, which provides the necessary coordination, and the traditional cultural mores, which seek to preserve the underlying social order, and it is in light of these interrelationships that order and balance are kept and that it is possible to consider any policy structures making it possible to pursue simultaneously economic growth, social equity, and political freedoms. And this is also a pragmatic approach that avoids the pitfalls of any particular dogma, be it the primacy of planning or *laissez-faire*'s myth of market omnipotence.

It is interesting to look at this issue in terms of the government and the market. Unlike the industrial countries, the developing countries can be said to need government intervention not only to offset market failures but also because their private-sector economies are less mature and their markets underdeveloped compared to those in the industrial countries. On the one hand are countries in which it is government policy that fosters the private sector and creates the climate and coordination necessary to enable market mechanisms to function to the best effect, and on the other hand are countries which have well-developed market economies and in which fully developed private sectors can adequately anticipate government policy directions. And as a country develops, it should move from the first to the second group. Even in the first group, government intervention – although perhaps prerequisite to getting the full benefits of early development – is not by itself enough. Whether or not government intervention is effective depends not on the extent but on the quality of the intervention. The danger of inadequacy and error is ever present, and different countries are able to pursue their policy objectives differently and achieve different results even though they may intervene in the markets to the same extent and employ the same policy tools. What then is entailed in the concept of policy quality? Basically, policy quality is determined by the mix of three aspects: (i) the enhancement of administrative capabilities and policy guidance for market function complementarity; (ii) long-term policy consistency and compatibility, and (iii) consideration for cultural factors.

Looking at the first of these three aspects, just as Soedjatmoko pointed out that development must take place in a situation of continuously changing parameters beyond government control,[12] it is necessary to appreciate the market's coordinative functions, to take fullest possible advantage of market mechanisms' ability to work through the interaction among individual economic entities to create a general equilibrium with conditions conducive to the attainment of social balance. By so doing, it should be possible to avoid excessive administrative bloating, the emergence of vested interests and corruption that make it difficult to effect policy changes with government intervention, massive fiscal deficits, and other failures of government. Instead both should be able to enhance administrative capabilities and approach a situation in which all of the entities concerned are able to conduct free and market-based economic behaviour – to reach what might be called economic democracy.

Looking specifically at the Japanese example by way of explanation, the government of Japan announced an income-doubling plan in 1960. At the time, I was one of the people responsible for drawing up this plan, which was drawn up with the full awareness of the Japanese economy's growth trends in an effort to eliminate the barriers to growth, rectify the various disparities that existed and otherwise focus on lessening social and economic inequalities. There were five main policy goals postulated under this plan: (i) the enhancement of social capital; (ii) the achievement of an advanced industrial economic structure; (iii) trade and economic cooperation promotion; (iv) the development of human resources and the promotion of science and technology; and (v) the drive to secure social stability by mitigating the structural dualism. These five policy goals are similar to the market-function-complementary development strategy approach set forth in the *World Development Report* with its emphasis on the importance of the linked interworkings of the four factors of investing in people, global linkages, a stable macroeconomy, and a competitive microeconomy.[13] It is especially important that development planners and strategists realize how very vital the government's role is in the development of human resources. Although elementary education, health and hygiene, nutrition, and the other basic human needs generally yield low short-term financial returns, it should be noted that they can yield a very high economic return if they are effectively planned and implemented.

The second aspect, long-term policy consistency and compatibility, highlights the importance of planning based on the assumptions of liberal economic structures. The significance of long-term planning is that most governmental and corporate policy planning tends to be too caught up in short-term issues and objectives, and planning – part forecast and part persuasion – should stimulate governmental and corporate policy makers to take the longer-term perspective. Economic plans must thus serve three roles, being educational tools when they centre on forecasting, stating long-term commitments when they focus on governmental policy implementation, and being tools for the conciliation of interests and the formation of social consensus when they elucidate current and emerging realities.

The important thing about government plans in connection with the relationship between development and freedom is that their role in the formation of national consensus can, through promoting broader dissemination of information and encouraging public hearings and debate, clarify the directions in which the government and private sector are heading, heighten awareness of the importance of a cooperative relationship, and hence, contribute to enhanced cohesiveness for development. At the same time, because so many problems arise and are highlighted in the process of forging a social consensus, the public development of plans is also thought to contribute to minimizing the social risk of policy implementation. I believe that this is one of the key factors in ensuring that economic democracy is accepted and takes root.

In the third aspect of the government's role in the cultural field, the South Commission has written that culture must be a central component of development strategies in a dual sense: on the one hand, the strategies must be sensitive to the cultural roots of society, and on the other hand, they must include the development of culture itself as a goal.[14] Because traditional culture functions to preserve the existing social order, it is essential that development be compatible with the basic social and cultural characteristics. At the same time, it is also imperative that consideration be paid to rural and urban development, and other development modalities to the impact that living conditions have on culture. Conversely, it is also true that there may be a number of factors within the traditional culture that are undesirable in light of the crucial importance of human rights and respect for humanity. As Soedjatmoko pointed out, "many of the traditional cultures in Asia have not felt the need to make human freedom an explicit value in their own perception of their cultures."[15] Awakening development awareness and heightening social cohesiveness, introducing such universal cultural elements as democracy, social justice, and the scientific mind by simultaneously buttressing self-organization abilities and the capacity to make independent decisions, enhancing managerial skills, and forming and strengthening new kinds of cultural identity can therefore be a motivating force for development. Taking the labour market as an example, if it is possible to promote the ethical homogenization of society and social fusion by popularizing universal values and working to integrate the labour market by eradicating the gender, religious, occupational, and other divisions that keep it splintered, this should then lead to a reduction of wage disparities and, hence, enhance the drive for a more equitable society. Likewise, a gender-sensitive approach should be adopted that builds on the emerging awareness of the role of women in development, recognizes the interrelations among poverty, population growth, inequality, and other problems, and assumes that women will naturally play a key role in production, family planning, and family budgeting. Similarly, the provision of education is, as the South Commission has noted, a crucial component of the right to culture,[16] and we should be fully aware of the important role that the diffusion of education has to play in enhancing productivity, reducing income disparities, and engendering social unity by making people more literate and, hence, making it more possible for them to acquire knowledge and skills, to access information, engage in wider communication, and hone their planning, organizational, and management skills. In this regard, we must not forget the crucial impact that science and technology, especially the technological revolution in information and communications, has on the sociocultural aspects.

The third hypothesis that Soedjatmoko gleaned from lessons of history is that it is impossible either to define our problems or to seek their solution in purely material terms. Stating that one of the most important lessons of the twentieth century is that of the earth's inherent limits,[17] Soedjatmoko pointed out that the development issues of one country work and reverberate throughout the international system so that they are at the same time issues for the whole of the global community. Among the issues illustrative of this are the environmental and resource limitations, the international structural dualism that reinforces income and technology differentials between North and South, the rigidity of the international order in the face of change, and the issue of international morality.

Mankind is today limited by environmental considerations and resource finiteness, and it is essential that we mobilize our full technological and financial resources in a global response to these constraints. The environment is the very basis of mankind's continued survival, and it is impossible to believe that the human race will prosper unless we use the environment wisely so that future generations can also enjoy its blessings. At the same time, given that development is imperative if the developing countries are to eradicate poverty and enable all peoples everywhere to live in a more civilized fashion, it is essential that we approach this with a view to reconciling the dual imperatives of environmental conservation and economic development. This in turn demands the concept of sustainable development. As Soedjatmoko emphasized, some degree of material affluence is essential to the attainment of market economies and democratic government, and the pursuit of material affluence necessarily entails energy consumption. Thus, the attainment and maintenance of market economies and democratic government demands that development and growth, as well as expanded energy consumption, be tolerated to some extent. Yet measures must also be taken at the same time to alleviate and even reverse the environmental impact. Once it is realized that poverty itself is closely interrelated to environmental degradation, it is clear that official development assistance must be provided in modes that are conducive to international compatibility between development projects and projects to improve and sustain the environment. Likewise, environmental technology cooperation and international cooperation in environmental impact assessments for development projects are also essential.

Yet as Soedjatmoko pointed out, this is not only an issue for the developing countries' development strategies, for the industrial countries' assistance systems, and the international agencies' development strategies, but also and even more an issue of morality and lifestyles. This concept of environmental ethics was also discussed at the 1989 Tokyo Conference on the Global Environment and Human Response Toward Sustainable Development that I chaired,[18] the International Chamber of Commerce has issued a *Business Charter for Sustainable Development; Principles for Environmental Management*,[19] and Japan's Keidanren (Federation of Economic Organisations) has published a *Global Environment Charter*.[20] In the same vein, the South Commission report stated flatly that, "A development strategy designed to imitate the lifestyles and consumption patterns of the affluent industrial societies is clearly inconsistent with our vision of development for the South."[21] It seems clear to me that there is an emerging awareness of the global environment and the fact that it affects us all equally. It is here that we transcend the need to solve economic and social issues and come face to face with the question of our humanity and what it means to be human. Based upon his long observations, Soedjatmoko said that this all ultimately comes back to the question of human resources. Development demands human growth, and human growth demands expansion of the personal self – specifically a greater sense of empathy, solidarity, and responsibility.

Economic issues are typically discussed in terms of the concept of scarcity, which is basically defined by the disparity between the level of human wants and the level of actual attainment. Growth strategies are thus strategies to raise the level of attainment relative to the level of desire. Yet with the global constraints on the level of possible attainment, it seems imperative that we also work to lower the level of our wants and take another look not at the quantity of our possessions but at the quality of our lives. This is why Soedjatmoko was so adamant in stressing the importance of the humanities.

In looking at the role of intellectuals, I suspect that – given his profound insights and vast energy – Soedjatmoko himself is a worthy subject of such humanistic studies. It is imperative that intellectuals divine the proper directions for society based upon foresight, the ability to discern the ebb and flow of history, and the wisdom to see what lies ahead for mankind, and intellectuals are especially important as beacons of illumination in the developing countries. At the same time, what we need are not the intellectuals of the great struggles for national independence but intellectuals who can provide constructive leadership appropriate to the end of the Cold War and today's greater awareness of the limitations to ideology. Even more than participating in national and international decision-making, we need intellectuals who can bridge North and South and who can work tirelessly to promote understanding and educate international opinion. Soedjatmoko hoped that today's younger people would create a new consensus on international morality and contribute to the management of the international community in line with this new morality. I cannot but agree, and I hope that such people will spring forth in both North and South. In closing, I would like to quote the following passage of encouragement by Soedjatmoko:

> Clearly,... freedom should not be seen as the automatic result of successful development.
>
> It is important for those of us who cherish freedom to realize that love of freedom alone is not enough. Freedom may well depend on our capacity to actualize a multiplicity of conflicting values simultaneously, necessarily in a socio-economic and political setting that makes this possible. In this context, the determined pursuit of a single value or a single goal is the greatest enemy of freedom.
>
> Vitally involved in the struggle for freedom are those single individuals who are willing to stand up not only for their own rights but also for the rights of their neighbour. A great deal of courage and tenacity is required; but above all, the intelligence to discern how to wage the struggle for freedom without destroying it in the process is crucial. History often has demonstrated, in the more distant past as well as in more recent times, that struggles for freedom did not always bear the fruit of freedom.
>
> But by the same token, history has revealed to us many splendid examples of the indestructibility of the human spirit in its search for freedom.[22]

Notes

1. Soedjatmoko, *Development and Freedom* (Tokyo: The Simul Press, Inc., 1980), p. 19.
2. Ibid., p. 33.
3. Ibid., p. 19.
4. Ibid., p. 9.
5. Ibid., p. 90.

6. Soedjatmoko, "Development as Learning" (Tenth Vikram Sarabhai Memorial Lectures), Ahmedabad, India, 19–20 January 1985.
7. Soedjatmoko, *Development and Freedom*, op. cit., p. 28.
8. Ibid., p. 38.
9. *The Challenge to the South: The Report of the South Commission* (London: Oxford University Press, 1990), p. 80.
10. The World Bank, *World Development Report 1991: The Challenge of Development* (London: Oxford University Press, 1991), p. 134.
11. Soedjatmoko, "The Search for Freedom: Lessons for the 21st Century" (Tokyo: Asahi Shimbun International Symposium: A Message to the 21st Century), 24 October 1984, p. 1.
12. Soedjatmoko, *Development and Freedom*, op. cit., p. 15.
13. The World Bank, op. cit., p. 6.
14. *The Challenge to the South: The Report of the South Commission*, op. cit., p. 132.
15. Soedjatmoko, *Development and Freedom*, op. cit., p. 34.
16. *The Challenge to the South: The Report of the South Commission*, op. cit., p. 133.
17. Soedjatmoko, "The Search for Freedom: Lessons for the 21st Century," op. cit., p. 5.
18. Chairman's Summary, Tokyo Conference on the Global Environment and Human Response Toward Sustainable Development, Tokyo, 11–13 September 1989, p. 3.
19. *The Business Charter for Sustainable Development: Principles for Environmental Management*, International Chamber of Commerce, April 1991.
20. Keidanren, *Global Environment Charter* (Tokyo: Japan Federation of Economic Organisations), 23 April 1991.
21. *The Challenge to the South: The Report of the South Commission*, op. cit., p. 80.
22. Soedjatmoko, *Development and Freedom*, op. cit., p. 39.

2

Intellectuals and culture: Guardians of traditions or vanguards of development

Farhang Rajaee

Today, many societies, particularly the ones within the third world, face the challenges of political change, modernization, economic development, social planning, population increase, urbanization, and now the globalization of democratic institutions.[1] Due to their education, awareness, and universal outlook, the intellectuals can play a crucial role. A couple of factors make this role a difficult and sophisticated task. The first relates to the fact that the intellectuals of the third world have to operate within the unequal encounter of their societies with the pressure of technical and industrial civilization. The second relates to the nature of the extent and the speed by which modernity imposes itself on the third world. The all-encompassing characteristic of the modern technical world makes the relation ambiguous, confusing, and chaotic, which in turn causes greater demand on the intellectuals, particularly, as has been noted, "in circumstances of confusion and chaos intellectuals tend to have great salience."[2]

The present chapter aims at presenting a theoretical analysis of the dilemma of intellectuals within the "third world" societies, as well as suggesting a pattern of behaviour which might help their societies find solutions or ways of balancing the competing demands for development. To that end, I consider a workable definition of intellectuals which would include their specific functions in a civilization but within the differing situations of either its normal course or the time that the civilization experiences encounter with one another. Sometimes the encounter occurs between two perceived or actually equal civilizations, and in some others it happens when there is a perceived or actual inequality between the two encountering civilizations. It seems that the greatest challenge presents itself in the latter situation, and intellectuals of the third world, indeed, operate in such a condition.

The following questions support the argument: What is the function of men of thought, better known today as the intellectuals? Do their functions differ according to society and culture? How about the effect of time and place? Should one see them as the propagators of prevailing ideology or are they a living conscience in their environment? How far should they be allowed to raise questions about their polity and society? Are they subversive regardless of the place where they live and function? If their mandate forces them to consider issues which the powers that be might feel threatened by, what should their relation be with the political establishment? In short, are they the guardians of the existing value system or the vanguards of changing the status quo?

Intellectuals, definitions and characteristics

In general, intellectuals are a group who basically work with their intellect. This is the least contested definition for this group within any given society. It is not time, place, culture, or civilization bound. But, it merely presents a general demarcation. A more comprehensive definition is that of Edward Shils, who writes:

> In religion, in art, in all spheres of culture and politics, the mass of mankind in all hitherto known societies have not, except for transitory interludes, been preoccupied with the attainment of an immediate contact with the ultimate principles implicit in their beliefs and standards.... In every society, however, there are some persons with an unusual sensitivity to the sacred, an uncommon reflectiveness about the nature of their universe and rules which govern their society.[3]

Based on this passage regardless of time and place and culture, there exists a minority of people who will act as the conscious mind of the society and help in providing meaning to its life. This rather insightful account sheds light on the position of the intellectuals in the life of the society. However, it provides very little understanding on the character or the nature of their functions. For that we turn to Karl Mannheim, who devoted a good deal of his academic career to the question of intellectuals. He writes: "In every society there are social groups whose special task it is to provide an interpretation of the world for society. We call this the 'intelligentsia'."[4] They make sense out of the life of society and guarantee that its members feel their existence is a worthwhile experience. Through these two accounts, the position and function of the intellectuals are relatively stated.

But, what about their *modus operandi* in terms of the way in which they present their "interpretation of the world"? Here, it is much harder to find an accepted definition. Any account of their characteristics and their mode of operation depends on the way in which one sees their attitude towards existing political order. Some consider intellectuals as a group who question the existing authority regardless of the degree of its legitimacy. For others, intellectuals are skilled and trained individuals who work with their mind for the attainment of societal goals. Still others see intellectuals as detached observers of the affairs of society who offer insights into the workings of their environment. But, should they be evaluated in terms of the existing order or, rather, should they be considered within the context of the society? Unfortunately, today the state has grown so large that it has surpassed the society and sees itself as the *mater* of the political society (or the *polis*, in the language of Greek thought). This is all the more true of many societies within the third world in which the state sees itself not as the representative of the society, but as its master. Regardless of such development, intellectuals are not evaluated according to their proximity to positions of power. Instead, they are the conscious mind of the society, who also pave the way for new ideas and practices regardless of the impact of either action on the existing order. An interesting account of either action in a Persian classic presents a definition which answers many of these concerns and settles the issue of definition and main characteristics as well.

Reporting on how the Iranian mythical figure, *Jamshid*, divided the people into groupings appointing each to a specific task, Ibn Balkhi writes that the first group were those who possessed the qualities of

> perspicacity, wisdom, intelligence, and perception, some of them he appointed to contemplate on religious sciences so as to guard the boundaries of the nation, and some others he appointed to study practical wisdom so as to refer to them on the issues of worldly interest. Based on their counsels, the order of the land will be preserved.[5]

Considering that, unlike modern times when science presents competing claims to religious world views, religious sciences at the time meant the only theoretical framework by which one would define one's existence. It would be correct to summarize the above passage as follows.[6] People of wisdom and prudence were appointed to guard the theoretical as well as the practical boundaries of social life. Thus, Balkhi presents a definition which not only combines those of Shils and Mannheim, but also provides us with the general characteristics of this class in the society. It is due to their "wisdom and prudence" that they are better able to understand the world and thus better equipped to present an interpretation of the world. By so doing, they guard the theoretical and practical boundaries of social life.

The key concept is that of guardianship. Some complementary points to Balkhi's definition merits attention. First, to achieve this end an intellectual's basic feature must be that of the mastery of the complexity of his culture and place. He must be the man of his age in that he must have knowledge of his own environment, his surroundings, and the world of his time. Thus, in terms of performing his social function, he is place and culture bound. One consequence of such perception means that he is the person who knows the value system of his society. Since no value system of a culture stays unchanged, it is the intellectuals who contribute to its updating. At the same time, he knows that modification must occur within the framework of the prevailing *Weltanschauung* of his society, otherwise it will not take any roots. If the intellectuals merely explain and maintain the existing order and contribute to the preservation of the status quo, they become tools in the hands of the powers that be and a part of the existing ruling machinery. Such attitude demands the impossible task of freezing social life in a particular social setting and in a specific time. If they dream of utopias and idealize a distant future, however, they become anachronistic and out of touch with their immediate time and place. They must live both in the past and the future at the same time. They are on the threshold with those who uphold the past and herald the future. The constant closing of the gap between the persistent endurance of what Max Weber calls the "eternal yesterday," and the constant demands of what I term *à la* Weber, the "eternal tomorrow," with its pressing need for change marks the function of an intellectual. Without the "eternal yesterday," he has no foundation, i.e., he works in a cultural vacuum, and out of touch with realities, while without a solid comprehension of the demands of the "eternal tomorrow" he will not be able to communicate with the new generation or to present a new horizon for a prosperous and thriving society.

Considering the above-mentioned arguments, one could say that the intellectuals are a group of self-conscious men of wisdom, intelligence, and perception who present an unanachronistic interpretation of the world for their society and thus close the gap between the pressure of the "eternal tomorrow" and the demands of the "eternal yesterday" in the mind of the average citizens of their society. It is within the bounds of such definition that the intellectuals are both the guardians of traditions and the vanguards of change. Intellectuals explain and interpret the reality of the existing order, because they are more able to construe and see the nature of things, thus contributing to the preservation of the order of things, better known as "tradition." At the same time, far better than anyone else, it is they who comprehend the needs for accepting changes and modifications in the existing order or the prevailing tradition. In a way they are entrusted with the double functions of preserving tradition when it is necessary, and encouraging changes and modifications, when and where contingencies deem it necessary.

Intellectuals in the life of a civilization

How do the intellectuals perform this paradoxical role? In the life of every society one can identify at least three different situations, and in each the function of the closing of the gap between tradition and change may take a different form. The first situation refers to the life of any civilization in its normal course; the second when the culture of a society is in contact with another society on equal terms, at least in the mind of those who are intellectuals; and the third refers to the situation where the interaction between the two cultures is unequal and the intellectuals of both cultures encounter each other with superior and inferior attitudes, even though this might be quite unintentional and unconscious. In the case of the second situation, the two cultures interact and as a result gain from one another, and the third occurs when a superior culture presents a great challenge to the inferior one. The intellectuals of the third world operate within the latter situation, i.e., under circumstances where a "progressive, universal, self-augmenting, self-generating, and aggressive" culture of modernity challenges the more traditional and prevailing culture of their societies. This constitutes the greatest dilemma. To understand this dilemma, one should be clear about the function of intellectuals in these various situations.

Regardless of the economic structure of the society, or the prevalence of religious or secular *Weltanschauung*, the intellectuals perform the dual function of preserving the "eternal yesterday" and encouraging the smoother emergence of the "eternal tomorrow." They make the first happen by making sense of the existing way of life in society or providing, to quote Mannheim, "an interpretation of the world for that society." In so doing, they perform the second by initiating changes and innovations which take society one step closer to the present. They do both in conformity with the collective conscience of society, otherwise they will not be understood, let alone be effective. Thus, their method centres around the two concepts of explanation and initiation. Through the first, the intellectuals preserve tradition and through the second, bring changes. To put the argument in perspective, I will cite two examples: The first is Ibn Khaldun (1332–1406), prominent historian, sociologist, and philosopher of history in Islamic Egyptian civilization, and the second is Visnugupta (433–?BC), better known as Kautilya, priest and political thinker in the cultural milieu of ancient India.

Abd-ar-Rahman abu Zayd ibn Muhammad ibn Muhammad ibn Khaldun fits the above-mentioned definition and function of an intellectual perfectly. He was well versed in the Islamic tradition and trained as a jurist. Not only did he teach jurisprudence in the best contemporary colleges, but also achieved the highest office in the legal establishment in Cairo to become Chief Justice (*Qadi-al-Qadat*). In his masterpiece, *The Muqaddimah, an Introduction to History*, he laid down his philosophy of history as to the nature and process of any civilization.[7] As Chief Justice, it was his main task to preserve the traditions of Islam, which he did effectively, and in his writings he expounded on the fundamentals of Islamic tradition. For example, he defends the orthodoxy in the face of challenges in his homeland, the western part of the Islamic world, from the extremist Kharijite and Shi'i heterodoxy.[8] In this capacity, he does present the function of the guardianship of the tradition.

More interesting, however, is his awareness of the fact that it is not enough to expound on existing tradition. In fact in his time, he criticizes the older scholars for merely imitating the past. For example, he writes:

> The later historians were all tradition-bound and dull by nature and intelligence, or did not try to avoid being dull. They merely copied their predecessors and followed their examples. They disregarded the changes in conditions and the customs of nations and races that the passing of time had brought about.[9]

Then he sets for himself the task of not only explaining the past so as to free the reader from the "blind trust in tradition" but also invents a new science, i.e., the science of culture. He is well aware that he has introduced the unfamiliar. As he himself puts it, "this book has become unique, as it contains unusual knowledge and familiar, if hidden, wisdom."[10] In this capacity he served as the vanguard of change. He founded philosophical history in Islamic tradition and introduced the notion of "group solidarity" (*Assabiya*) without any help from religion. Of course, as a Muslim, he emphasized that any political order based on religious solidarity is preferable.

While ibn Khaldun invented the science of culture, Kautilya established the science of politics and government (*Arthasastra*). Considering that before his time the most prominent way of thinking was that of Brahmanism, according to which the centre of politics and worldly life was the dharma as understood and explained by the Brahmans, Kautilya established that "the source of the livelihood of men is wealth, in other words, the earth inhabited by men. The science which is the means of attainment and protection of that earth is the Science of Politics."[11] He has written his masterpiece as to what the contents of such science should be. But he is well aware that any introduction of change could only bear fruits when it is done through modernizing tradition. Thus, he begins his book as follows:

> This single treatise on the Science of Politics has been prepared mostly by bringing together the teachings of as many treatises of the Science of Politics as have been composed by ancient teachers for the acquisition and protection of the earth.[12]

Moreover, in many sections he ends his discussions with "thus say the ancient teachers." And in this capacity, Kautilya ranks among the prominent guardians of the past and tradition.

At the same time, it was Kautilya who redefined the components of the political society of his time. He ended his treatise by stating the reason for the composition of this work. "Seeing the errors of the writers of commentaries on scientific treatise, Visnugupta (Kautilya) composed the text and its commentaries."[13] When he enumerates the constituent elements of the state, it is the king who ranks at the top. He writes: "The king, the minister, the country, the fortified city, the treasury, the army and the ally are the constituent elements of the state."[14] This is a novelty. The king at the centre of politics means defining politics in terms of power and the glory of the kingdom.

Indeed, the book presents insight as to the way power of the kingdom is maintained and glorified, just as Machiavelli wanted to restore the power and glory of Italy. The ends and means of politics are defined in terms of the above-mentioned elements. The six measures of foreign policy, elaborated in Book VII of Arthasastra reflect these generalizations. Other countries are categorized according to their attitudes towards the power and glory of kingship. These constitute a rather new way of looking at politics, but no one considers it a heterodox view or an alien interpretation within the Indian tradition. Thus, Kautilya is both a guardian of tradition and a vanguard of change.

By explaining the existing tradition, the intellectuals help preserve it, and by initiation update it, but also bring about changes and progress for their society. Thus, they preserve the balance between the past and the present. What about the time of interaction between civilizations? While ibn Khaldun and Kautilya were able to preserve the balance between the pressure of the "eternal yesterday" and the demands of the "eternal tomorrow," the intellectuals in time of interaction do the same but use such concepts as distinction and selection. Because they are equipped with theoretical and practical wisdom, they are able to explain which aspects of the contribution of the other civilization is not culture bound and, therefore, could be selected and which aspects are culture and place bound and should be rejected. By enlarging the distinction, they facilitate the selection process. In a way, here also the intellectual acts both as the guardian of his own tradition and at the same time the vanguard of change. The distinction process points to the impurity of the other culture and the selection enriches and updates the internal development. The necessary condition is that the interaction must take place on an equal basis or at least perceived equal.

The following two examples illustrate the process. Abu Nasr Farabi (AD 870–950) and St. Thomas Aquinas (AD 1225–1274), within a framework of the interaction of Islamic and Christian world view with that of Greek philosophy, respectively, both learned from the Greeks that the processes of distinction and selection not only enriched their own culture but contributed to human understanding in general. Farabi is one of the greatest thinkers of the Islamic world who has written treatises on logic, physics, metaphysics, ethics, and politics as well as commentaries on the works of great Greek philosophers like Aristotle and Plato. Farabi is considered in the West as the second teacher, and within the Islamic world as the founder of

Islamic philosophy.[15] This dual appellation is very interesting, because it implies that he is accepted in both his own cultural milieu and within the culture which claims to be the inheritor of Greek philosophy. In other words, he has successfully been able to take from the other culture and then synthesizes it with his own. His founding of Islamic philosophy is a great achievement but at the same time an innovation as well as an introduction of change.

The way in which Farabi has been able to achieve this exalted position is through distinction and selection. He distinguished between what was Greek in the thought of Plato and what constituted human achievements. He dehellenized Plato and brought him within the Islamic world. Thus, his explanation of the Greek world for his fellow Muslims made it possible for them to learn from the Greeks without feeling threatened by them. He also made the selection of that thought easier. He mixed the idea of the philosopher/king with that of the prophet/ruler. Like Plato, he believed in the special qualities of the ruler and like him he dictated that the ruler should know both theoretical and practical wisdom, but like the prophet of Islam he will be given revelation and thus become qualified to rule the city. The ruler has the best natural environment, but also the fullest development of rational faculty.[16] And in that condition, such a person will receive revelation. "The rule of this man is the supreme rule; all other human rulerships are inferior to it and are derived from it."[17] Thus, with this combination he has also played the dual function of guardianship of tradition as well as the vanguard of change.

Just as Farabi brought Greek and Islamic world view together in a harmonious fashion, so did St. Thomas Aquinas by bringing Christian world view close to that of the Greeks. He is seen "as the most illustrious of all Christian Aristotelians."[18] He distinguished between what was Greek in the thought of Aristotle and what constituted the great contribution of Aristotle to human understanding. He took Aristotle's greatest insight, namely, the fact that man is a political animal by nature.[19] Man participates in social life due to his natural inclination. This was contrary to the Augustinian view that man is sinful and forms a society in order to avoid original sin. But this selection from Greek thought was accepted by contemporary Christians because according to Aquinas man's natural inclination to form a society is endowed on him by God. Thus, he performed the function of a vanguard of change and innovation. At the same time, he played the role of a guardian of tradition by defining human excellence in terms of Christian ethics and as product of the conditions of political life.

The best regime is the kingdom of God and not the work of man or of practical reason guided by philosophy. The laws of society come from the notion of natural law as promulgated by God.[20]

The interaction of Greek philosophy and that of Christianity in Aquinas's mind constitute a harmonious process. He feels neither inferior to the Greek culture nor superior to it. Aquinas feels confident enough to tackle Aristotle, write a commentary on his work, and not feel intimidated. Thus, he is able to understand the distinction and guide his audience as to which part to adopt and which to give up altogether. In so far as Aquinas adopts the Aristotelian notion of the political nature of man, he has introduced change and that may cause further and broader change in the future. But in so far as he emphasizes the sanctity of divine legal order, he is operating within the realm of tradition.

In short, through the use of the four concepts, analysed above, societies ensure balanced development and progress. The content and meaning of development and progress is culture and place bound. When certain values are to be adopted, and new ideas and processes are to be incorporated, these four concepts will guarantee that it is done smoothly without threatening the existing framework. At the same time, they will encourage additions and advancement. But how do they relate to the third world today? The societies of the third world wish to prosper and progress. Considering the present challenges of modernity and one of its major components, i.e. democracy, how could these concepts help them preserve their traditional values while coping with the demands of democracy? These are some of the questions to which we will now turn.

The dilemma of third-world intellectuals

An interesting situation appears when a given civilization is in a state of unequal encounter with another. Third-world societies today face such a civilization in their encounters with the West. The technical aspects of modernity has enabled the contemporary civilization of the West to become global. Its massive products have in turn undermined the normal process of life in the societies in which it has arrived. One observer has compared this disruption with the function of a prism in the path of a ray of light.[21] Such societies under the impact of modernity can no longer operate at a traditional pace. At the same time, they are not original and do not contribute players within the context of world civilization. One contradiction relates to the successful way in which the West has been able to equate technical advancement with the modern secular world view and value system. It is commonly held that technical advancement would be achieved only through complete adoption of Western ways. Thus, while the critical circumstances of this unequal encounter demand a greater role for intellectuals, they cannot perform the four above-mentioned functions without difficulties. The four key concepts of explanation, initiation, distinction, and selection take new meanings and connotations. In encountering cultural arenas these functions display a different meaning than the ones suggested earlier.

Now, I will consider each in this new situation. If and when an intellectual tries to explain tradition, he is viewed in his own society as a traditional reactionary, and in superior civilization as a fundamentalist. That is how the traditional *ulama* are viewed in any of the Islamic countries. If and when an intellectual sees the solution to the problems of his society in initiating a reformist interpretation, he will be considered as a heretic in his own environment, whereas within the cultural milieu of a superior civilization as a non-indigenous imaginary. Any attempt to distinguish between the human contribution of the other civilization with those of its aspects which are place and culture bound, will be considered as apologetic in both cultural milieux. And finally, any selection on the part of the intellectual will earn him the label of eclectic. He will be seen among the people of his own tradition as not having enough purity or loyalty while in the aggressive culture as being too rigid. In short, in this situation, the intellectuals are damned in every step they might take.

Third-world societies suffer from this unfortunate fate at the present time in their interaction with the cultural milieu of modernity and technical culture. Their intellectuals operate in this very difficult situation. They face these undesired and unresolvable dilemmas, even when they want to adopt certain aspects of technic and technical ways, let alone when they confront an ambiguous and almost incomprehensible notion such as that of democracy. In other words, the intellectuals of the third world today not only have to perform the four tasks enumerated above, but also play the role of greater restorers of lost confidence. First, they have to close the gap between the normal mental state of their citizens with their actual state and then act as the bridge between the pressures of "eternal yesterday" and the demands of "eternal tomorrow." One is immediately reminded of many of the nationalist leaders of the third world who led nationalist resistance movements for independence. Many of them had understood that the root of their problems lies in the lack of self-assertiveness which had been lost to colonial experience and they thought could be restored through political independence. They made remarkable contributions and their achievements left greater marks on the political life of these societies. While perhaps that solution made sense at the time, it is no longer enough to emphasize the political aspects of lost assertiveness. The challenge no longer is limited to the lack of political sovereignty.

Considering the close link between modernity and the West, the logic of the argument here leads to the conclusion that the present intellectuals of the third world should de-Westernize – following the path of Farabi or Aquinas – the thought of the major Western thinkers, and distinguish between their contribution to human history and that which is culture and place bound. But even that does not suffice. The reason lies in the fact that the encounter between the two societies of the West and the third world is taking place in what is now known as the "global village." It is much harder to make the distinction between what is eternal and what is culture and place bound. The all-encompassing nature of modernity which has raised the level of consciousness among even the least literate people in the far corner of the world warns that while the "eternal yesterday" may be exclusive to a particular culture and place the demands of the "eternal tomorrow" is an inclusive, global, and universal phenomenon. The closing of the gap between the two is much more difficult today than for a Farabi or an Aquinas. The pressure of the "eternal yesterday" is much more acute than it was at the time of those great thinkers. The new movement within the third world known as "the return of the indigenous self" no longer preoccupies the mind of the intellectuals, rather it has grown to a mass demand; the constant re-emergence of the so-called "fundamentalist movements" is its more obvious sign. On the other hand, the demands of "eternal tomorrow" is also much more obvious. Development, democracy, open society, higher standards of living, greater demand for mass participation, even a more intangible issue such as the environment, are no longer demands of a luxurious nature which is recognizable by the intellectuals only. They have proved to be part of the necessary condition for a decent life. The amazing breakdown of the Soviet empire proved that the social engineering of a particular type of society no longer constitutes a viable response.

In other words, it seems that democracy, in the special form of an open society, and development in terms of better living conditions have become part of the "eternal yesterday" already. While the intellectuals of the third world must be aware of the four tasks of explanation, innovation, distinction, and selection, they should pay more attention to their task of providing "an interpretation of the world for their society" to repeat the words of Mannheim. But, the world has become much more sophisticated than ever before; thus, it requires a more sophisticated mind than those of their predecessors. They operate in a sensitive realm. They should avoid the role of "reactionary or fundamentalist, heretic, or non-indigenous dreamer, apologetic, and finally eclectic." They should present a workable explanation for their society which would make its citizens feel it will preserve the tradition as well as make possible any change.

Notes

1. I wish to express my gratitude to the United Nations University for providing the opportunity to write this essay. My mentor, Prof. K.W. Thompson, was kind and gracious to discuss with me the idea for the essay. The fellow contributors to this collection made insightful comments in Indonesia during the meeting of the authors of the present collection.
2. John Hall, *Powers and Liberties; the Causes: The Causes and Consequences of the Rise of the West* (Oxford: Basil Blackwell, 1985), p. 20.
3. Edward Shils, *The Intellectuals and Powers and Other Essays* (Chicago: The University of Chicago Press, 1972), p. 3.
4. Karl Mannheim, *Ideology and Utopia* (London: Routledge & Kegan Paul, 1936), p. 9.
5. Ibn Balkhi, *Farsnameye Ibn Balkhi*, ed. Seyyed Jalal ed-din Ashtiyani (Tehran: Mehr, 1313/1935), pp. 24–25.
6. Compare with Mannheim, op. cit., p. 10.
7. The introduction was translated from Arabic into English as follows: Ibn Khaldun, *The Muqaddimah, an Introduction to History*. Three volumes. Translated by Franz Rosenthal (New York: Bollingen Foundation, Inc., 1958). Later an abridged version of the same translation appeared as follows: Ibn Khaldun, *The Muqaddimah, an Introduction to History*, translated by Franz Rosenthal, edited and abridged by N.J. Dawood (New Jersey: Princeton University Press, 1969). The quotations cited in the present essay are from the latter work.
8. The historical background to this challenge is found in the classic work of Mahdi on Ibn Khaldun. Muhsin Mahdi, *Ibn Khaldun's Philosophy of History* (Chicago: The University of Chicago Press, 1957), pp. 27–62.
9. Ibn Khaldun, op. cit., pp. 6–7.
10. Ibid., p. 9.
11. *The Kautilya Arthasastra*, translated into English by R.P. Kangle (Delhi: Motilal Banarsidass, 1972), Book 15, chap. 1, section 180, 1 and 2.
12. Ibid., Book 1, chap. 1, 1.
13. Ibid., the last paragraph in Book XV.
14. Ibid., Book VI, chap. 1, section 96, 1.
15. See, for example, Reza Davari Ardaakani, *Farabi No'assesse Falsafeye Islami* (Tehran: Cultural Studies and Research Institute, 1362/1983), particularly pp. 47–73.
16. Farabi, *Ara'e ahle Madineye Fazele*, translated from Arabic into Persian by Ja'far Sajjadi (Tehran: Tahuri, 1361/1982), p. 269.
17. Quoted in Muhsin Mahdi, "Al-Farabi," in *History of Political Philosophy*, eds. Leo Strauss and Joseph Cropsey (Chicago: The University of Chicago Press, 3rd edn, 1987), p. 213.

18. Ernest Fortin, "St. Thomas Aquinas," ibid., p. 248.
19. Thomas Aquinas, "On Princely Government," translated by J.G. Dawson. In: Thomas Aquinas, *Selected Political Writings*, ed. A.P. D'Entreves (New York: Barnes and Noble, 1959).
20. Thomas Aquinas, *Treatise on Law*, translated by English Dominican Fathers (Chicago: Regnery, n.d.).
21. Fred Riggs, *Administration in Developing Countries: The Theory of Prismatic Society* (Boston: Houghton Mifflin Company, 1964).

3

Economic democracy: What can the intellectuals do?

Mine Eder

"To define the king," wrote French playwright de Montherlant about one of his characters, "amounts to erecting a statue with the water of the sea."[1] The same could be said of this omnipresent figure in all social settings that is the intellectual. The figure of the intellectual had obviously been invested with all kinds of attributes without, however, reaching a final portrait. If each attempt at defining the intellectual seemed a new kind of failure, it is probably because every historical period, every cultural space, appeared to create its own intellectuals.

For the ancient Greeks, the term intellectual was an equivalent of "the philosopher," "the lover of wisdom." Pythagoreans referred to the philosophers as those who were not tied by the temptations of the body and the material world, those who preferred, instead, to cultivate and exercise their intellect in the pursuit of knowledge and science. These philosophers related to the game of life as mere spectators, but in doing so they also sought "wisdom," in order to purify their souls. Such wisdom, however, as Heraclitus asserted, lay neither in erudition nor in the mere acquaintance with facts, but in the clear insight into the meaning and essence of reality as a whole. Wisdom, thus, differed, for the Pythagoreans, from the "opinion" of the Sophists, or the "illusions" of the masses, which deal only with appearances.

In Plato's *Republic*, the philosopher acquires a new responsibility. He now has to place his insights into the service of mankind, for:

> Cities will have no respite from evil, nor will the human race, I think, unless philosophers rule as kings in the cities, or those whom we now call kings and rulers genuinely and adequately study philosophy, until, that is, political power and [philosophy] coalesce, and the various natures of those who now pursue the one to the exclusion of the other are forcibly debarred from doing so.[2]

Thus, the philosopher-king who really knows the truth must transmit that knowledge to his fellow men.

Aristotle, though as firmly convinced as Plato in the philosophers' commitment to truth, points insistently to the contingency of human existence. No individual, he suggests repeatedly, is able to know the truth in its totality, and, accordingly, one's ability to convey parts of the truth is obviously conditioned by the specific situation in which one finds oneself. The philosopher has, then, to work within the limitations of his or her own nature and society. And, of course, Aristotle, too, considered the intellectual life, or what he calls "the life of contemplation," as the highest and the most intrinsically worthwhile way of life for any human being. "If reason is divine in comparison with the rest of man's nature," he wrote in *Ethics*, "the life which accords with reason will be divine in comparison with human life in general."[3]

This glorification of the life of the mind can be found in many different cultural and historical settings with, however, a new meaning for each one of them. The ancient Chinese, for example, also placed a strong emphasis on wisdom, but particularly on its application to civic duties. The development of a class of Confucian "scholar-officials" which were the precursors of the mandarins in feudal and later monarchical China, points to this civic tradition. In fact, the Chinese term for intelligentsia, *chih-shih fen tzu*, meaning "they who know," indicates that the intellectuals were distinguished as a separate and powerful group very early in China. When asked by a student, by the name of Fan Ch'ih, what it meant to be wise, Confucius answered:

> He who devoted himself to securing his subjects what it is right they should have, who by respects of the Spirits, keeps them out at a distance, may be termed wise ... By raising the straight and putting them on the top of the crooked, one can make the crooked straight.[4]

Thus, the wise man in the Chinese context, needed to know both "what is" and "what ought to be." He needed to be virtuous and, again, most importantly, he needed to be loyal to his civic duties.

In yet another context, that of medieval Europe, the life of the mind was indeed divine but in a sense different from Aristotle's, just as the intellectual was loyal there too, but not quite in the sense of the loyalty advocated by Confucius. With the rise of Christianity in Europe, the intellectual began to assume a religious role. The term cleric, which meant the intellectual or the expert in Latin, referred then to those who mastered and interpreted the sacred writings, those who sought divine wisdom. The opposite, "the layman," included both those who were ignorant and uninitiated. As the church, which monopolized all intellectual activities, became the most powerful institution in feudal Europe, the clergyman enjoyed an unchallenged authority and legitimacy as the interpreter of the Holy Law. He became the middleman between God and the people, the one who knew the way to the "City of God."

At the same time, even though in a slightly different geographical area, the intellectual tradition of the *ulama* was also founded, in the Muslim world, on religious authority, built on the principles of Islam. Ulama, which means "scholars" in Arabic, or more precisely "those who possess knowledge" (in Arabic, *ilm*) came to signify quite early in the Muslim era those who possessed *religious* knowledge in particular. Educated in special institutions called *madrasas*, the ulamas too, studied and interpreted the Sacred Law (the *sharia*), and enjoyed a moral authority over the rest of the believers.

Renaissance, to come back to Europe, and the rise of humanism secularized this religious intellectual tradition to a large extent. The authority of religion came to be replaced with the authority of Reason. Renaissance intellectuals are well known: In poetry, the Italians Dante, Boccaccio, and Petrarch wrote in a laic vein by cultivating a taste for the classics; in the visual arts, da Vinci provided first examples of humanism, which is an interest in the human dimension as opposed to the divine dimension, for instance; in the sciences, Galileo, Copernicus, and Kepler surpassed earlier conceptions of the physical world and nature, while in political science Machiavelli and Bodin brought in initial formulations of secular politics. But it is probably in Montaigne, and in his *Essays*, that the sceptical Renaissance intellectual is best represented. In this era of unprecedented challenge to all philosophical dogmas and accepted sciences, Montaigne wrote in *The Education of Children*:

> Let the tutor make his pupil examine and thoroughly sift everything he reads, and lodge nothing in his head upon simple authority and upon trust.... Let the diversity of opinions be propounded to and laid before him, he will himself choose, if he can; if not he will remain in doubt. (I love sometimes to doubt as well as to know.) For if he embraces the opinions of Xenophon and Plato, by exercise of his reason, they will no longer be theirs, but become his own.[5]

To doubt and to reason: such were the advice Montaigne, and the Renaissance through him, gave the following generations of the modern age.

Of course, the works of Spinoza and Descartes cheered this celebration of human reason and logic in the seventeenth century. But it was in the eighteenth century, however, that the notion of the unlimited powers of the human mind found its widest appeal. The ideas of the intellectuals, for the first time, went beyond the walls of the church, the universities or the coffee houses to reach a wide, anonymous audience. The works of Rousseau, Saint Simon and the encyclopedists, for instance, were a source of inspiration for the American and French revolutions. As de Tocqueville aptly describes in his analysis of the intellectual foundations of the French Revolution:

> The men of letters did not merely impart their revolutionary ideas to the French nation, they also shaped the national temperament and outlook in life. In the long process of moulding men's minds to their ideal patterns, their task was all easier since the French had training in the field of politics, and they had a clear field. The result was that our writers ended up giving the French men the instincts, the turn of the mind, the tastes and even the eccentricities of the literary man. And when the time came for action, these literary propensities were imported into the political arena.[6]

Thus, the intellectuals of the Enlightenment became the agents of radical social transformation and "progress." With their ideas diffusing faster than ever, they came to define and change the political, social, and moral tone of their era. They were then social critics, criticizing society and its institutions from the vantage point of broad and ideal conceptions which were assumed to be universally applicable.

Such was also the role of the intellectuals in nineteenth-century Russia. The term "intelligentsia" first coined by a Russian author, Boborykin in 1860, referred to a particular self-conscious stratum who were living on the margins of society and who were opposed to all forms of authority.[7] Influenced by German idealism and romanticism, this intelligentsia had a sense of a collective mission, that of affirming the necessity to reconstruct a society based on rationality, progress, and justice. Such was the mission of the intelligentsia that eventually brought about the revolutions of 1905 and 1917 in Russia.[8]

The origin of the term intellectual in France, also exemplifies his or her socio-political and critical function. Clemenceau first used the word in an article which appeared in *L'Aurore*, in 23 January 1898, entitled "Manifesto of the Intellectuals," to refer collectively to the most prominent Dreyfusards protesting against Dreyfus's imprisonment. For this group of writers, poets, and professors, the intellectuals were the articulators of dissent or those who not only mirror but also question and challenge the values, the customs, and the assumptions which are taken for granted in society. Although opposing the establishment has always been a function of the intellectuals in the past, as was the case with Martin Luther, for example, or the French revolutionaries, it now became, at least in France, the very definition of the modern intellectual.

But this definition of the intellectual does not go without a certain number of objections. Why should an intellectual be a perpetual dissenter? Can one not conceive of an intellectual disinterested in the social and political issues of his or her time? When Leonardo da Vinci was asked why he was indifferent to the misfortunes of the Florentines, he simply replied "the study of beauty has occupied my whole heart."[9] Goethe, on the other hand, persistently advised other intellectuals "to leave politics to diplomats and soldiers," while Flaubert considered politics as the "poison of the arts." The European aesthetic movement, particularly *l'art pour l'art* cult in France, was also based on the idea that the search for truth and beauty had to be divorced from politics and the unsophisticated public, or what the Germans called *Bildungspöbel* (the cultural mob). Later, Julien Benda went so far as to call the political involvement of contemporary intellectuals a treason. By bringing partiality and political passions to their works, Benda argued, the modern "clerks" have betrayed their true function, which consists in finding the universal truths alien to the laymen.[10]

Yet, an entirely disengaged intellectual is, obviously, an illusion, since every intellectual has an implicit or explicit position (including that of indifference) to politics, in relation to the society they live in. Being engaged, on the other hand, does not necessarily imply that an intellectual should become a political activist or assume a direct political role in society, though the two are not mutually exclusive. But it does suggest that every intellectual activity has a socio-political implication, since the intellectuals are the ones who produce ideas, and ideas are always "engaged." Although the intellectuals might not be politicians, they are the creators of political ideas; though they might not always enact it, they are the creators of language and political discourse.[11]

But what exactly is the role of the modern intellectual in society? Some scholars have implicitly or explicitly equated the function of the modern intellectual with his or her profession. Such an equation is, however, problematic. For, as we reviewed early in this essay the status of the intellectuals in different historical and cultural settings, we found them assuming a great variety of professions, ranging from philosophers, theologians, civil servants to clergymen, writers, and artists. Given our modern era, defined by extreme diversification of social functions and modes of life, attributing a particular profession or set of professions to the intellectuals is, of course, even tedious. It is safer to say that each cultural context emphasizes one particular profession, or group of professions, as opposed to the others, in referring to their intellectuals. While they are more or less equated with writers in France, for instance, the intellectuals have historically been university professors or *Akademiker* in Germany. While the intellectuals are the experts in the United States, including consultants or the so-called "brain trust," i.e., lawyers and specialized professors, the intelligentsia in the Soviet Union have been roughly equated with those who fulfil technobureaucratic functions. And the intellectuals' functions in the Muslim world include the sheikh who is specialized in law, philosophy and theology, while the intellectual professions in India include astrologers and practitioners of medicine (Vaidyas and Hakims). Clearly, the cultural relativity of intellectual activity impedes the argument equating the function of the intellectual with his or her profession.

Defining the function of the modern intellectual, on the other hand, has itself been a highly politicized issue. Fabian socialists, Katusky, and Lenin have argued, for instance, that the main function of the intellectual lies in raising the revolutionary consciousness of the working classes. Gramsci has developed the idea of the "organic" intellectual of the working classes whose main function is to demystify the ideology of the bourgeoisie. The false intellectuals of the bourgeoisie, he argued, are the "legitimizers" presenting the particularistic bourgeois interests as universal goals and values. The true intellectual, Gramsci claimed, is one who continuously unmasks this false universalization, becoming thereby organically linked to the lower, or the working, classes.

Other scholars have been quick to point out that this particular role, i.e., raising the consciousness of the working classes, contradicts the social position of the intellectuals who, most of the time, belong to the dominant classes themselves. Pierre Bourdieu, for instance, called the intellectuals "cultural capitalists," who constituted a subordinate faction of the dominant classes. Accordingly, the intellectual depended on the moneyed bourgeoisie for his survival but was part of it as well, since he or she shared the same interest: that of preserving their privileges at the exclusion of other classes.[12] Waclaw Machajski, a Polish-Ukrainian anarchist, has raised a similar criticism in reference to the intellectuals in the former socialist countries. Machajski argued that rather than working for egalitarianism and the workers' emancipation, the intellectuals sought to monopolize state power. They were a self-serving class, consolidating their power based on the monopoly of knowledge.[13] Alvin Gouldner also argued that a new class has recently emerged in modern capitalist societies, constituted of managers, technical experts, professionals, and intellectuals. Seeking to monopolize power, this "new cultural bourgeoisie," as he called it, aims at undermining the legitimacy of the old ruling classes in order to replace it with their own.[14]

The theorists of the modern post-industrial societies and the proponents of the "end of ideology" thesis also developed arguments along similar lines in the early 1970s.[15] Highly influenced by positivism, these theorists claimed that improving living standards and major technological changes have eliminated the usual conflicts of the industrial societies between labour and capital. New post-industrial societies, where every conflict can be solved through science and technology, are, therefore, more dependent on their intellectuals. The "critical" intellectuals who do not accept the role of "social engineers" create, obviously, in this perspective, a major problem for modern societies by challenging the very structure and stability of the social and political order.[16]

All the arguments over the function of the intellectual presented above are based on various political assumptions and norms. The socialist view which limits the function of the intellectual to that of raising the consciousness of the working classes, for instance, is based on the conception of an ideal socialist society. But the proponents of the "new class" theorists, who point out the growing significance of intellectuals in modern societies, assume an inherent élitism of the intellectuals based on the power of knowledge. Finally, propounded on the ideal of technocratic society, the theorists of "post-industrial" society, assume that the "critical" function of the intellectual is necessarily disruptive and socially destabilizing. Reducing politics to pragmatism and valuing order over change, these theorists think that intellectuals are dogmatic ideologues who condemn everything that doesn't fit their ideal concept of society.

Clearly, as in any historical period, these assumptions and norms are founded upon various visions of an ideal society. Just as the philosopher-king was a product of Plato's ideal society, for instance, so were the Chinese mandarins and Muslim ulamas in their respective societies. While the clergyman was guide to the "City of God," the function of the Renaissance intellectual was based on the principles of a humanist society. Similarly, the function of the Enlightenment intellectual was to sketch the map of a society based on Reason. Thus, the role of the intellectuals in society has been shaped not only by the social and political context they live in but also by the ideals and ideas of their time.[17]

Every discussion of the function of the *modern* intellectual is bound to be based then on a conception of an ideal modern society. On an ideal of a *democratic society*, this essay proposes that the major function of the intellectual in modern societies is that of democratization. This involves making the society "self-conscious," through continuous criticism. As Sartre described in his discussion of the role of the writers:

> If society sees itself and, in particular, sees itself seen, there is, by virtue of this very fact, a contesting of the established values of the regime. The writer presents it (the society) with its image; he calls upon it to assume or to change itself. At any rate, it changes; it practises honesty; thus the writer gives society a *guilty conscience*; he is thereby in a state of perpetual antagonism toward the conservative forces which are maintaining the balance he tends to upset.[18]

This means that intellectuals serve as a mirror for their society. By continuously asking questions, relativizing all forms of power, and doubting what appears to be obvious, they enhance democracy by becoming the consciousness of the society they live in.

But social criticism is not a value-free "science" either, as some scholars would like it to be. Clearly, what the intellectual chooses to criticize in a society is contingent; it is obviously produced by a history. It can even be argued that in most modern societies, just as in any society in history, what the intellectual *can* criticize has already been defined by the existing political and economic structure which are themselves based on established norms and values. If the most "critical" function of the intellectual is that of expanding the democratic space, then the intellectual needs to create new concepts and languages, redefine old ones and go beyond the "controlling gazes" of modern societies.[19] He or she paradoxically needs to escape his or her history.

This democratizing function can start with setting aside, to the best of one's ability, the limitations of current ideological discourses and redefining the very concept of democracy itself. In our era of radical change characterized by rapid transition to democratic regimes in the developing countries, the fall of the Berlin wall, and the opening up of the Eastern bloc, the task of defining and redefining democracy appears more and more necessary, even though more and more difficult. "We have frequently printed the word democracy" wrote Walt Whitman, "yet I cannot too often repeat that it is a word the real gist of which still sleeps, quite unawakened.... It is a great word, whose history, I suppose, remains unwritten, because that history has yet to be enacted."[20]

Current discussions over this sleeping beauty have been based on two different ideological discourses: liberalism and socialism. The liberal conception of democracy stemmed from the discourse of natural rights based on natural laws which date back to Locke, Mill, and Smith. The rights to life, liberty and property, form the fundamentals of liberal democracy. Based on the distinction between private and public, between the political and the economic, liberal democracy involves the limitation of public and political authority, and the expansion of individual rights in the realm of the "non-political" civil society. Respect for law, freedom of speech, institutionalizing of electoral procedure, separation of powers, and multi-party politics ensure – the liberals argue – the accountability of the Government and individual liberties. Furthermore, the State – no matter how liberal and democratic it might be – is regarded in this perspective as the "realm of unfreedom." Limiting the power of the State amounts, therefore, to expanding individual liberty and democracy. In order to become free, these theorists claimed, "citizens" who exercise their political rights equally through their votes, need – in Berlin's words – only "to keep the authority at bay."[21]

This particular concept of political authority and the State contrasts sharply with the republican tradition which dates back to Aristotle. The individual, argue the classic republicans, realizes her *telos*, her full potential, only in and through the state. Rousseau carried this tradition even further by arguing in his *Social Contract* that man becomes free, or more precisely man is "forced to be free," through his participation in the general will. Similarly, Hegel argued that the individual can only find his true self, his true identity, in the spirit of the State. This republican tradition can be found, incidentally, in various political forms such as French Jacobinism, English Chartism, or American Jacksonianism.

The socialist conception of democracy is also founded on this republican tradition. In sharp contrast to the "liberal democrats," the "socialist democrats" regarded the State as a positive agent of social change. Emphasizing the significance of collective action, these theorists criticized the individualist and utilitarian basis of the liberal democratic theory. Most importantly, they rejected the line drawn by the liberals between public and private and pointed out the different forms of domination that are at work in the supposedly non-political private sphere. The liberal democrats, according to these theorists, overlook the major inequalities which are continuously being created by the capitalist system in the private realm. Although all citizens might be politically equal exercising similar political rights, they are, for the socialist democrats, hardly equal economically. Thus, according to them, defining democracy only in terms of political rights and liberties, is entirely insufficient and contrary to the very concept of democracy itself.

Though based on a sound criticism of the theory of liberal democracy, the theory of socialist democracy has its theoretical problems as well. First of all, the socialist theory of democracy neglects the centrality of individual rights and political liberty in human emancipation, concentrating too much instead on collective action and organization of the "masses." It underestimates the importance of political liberties and political equality by regarding them as the tricks of the bourgeois democracy.[22] Moreover, by focusing more on exploitation and class domination, they, in turn, neglect the non-economic forms of domination based on gender, race, and ethnic differences. This theoretical deadlock and even the dogmatism that have resulted from the liberal and socialist discourse originated from the failure of *both* conceptions of democracy to address the intricate linkages between political liberty and economic equality. While the theorists of liberal democracy see the two mutually encroaching on one another, the socialist theorists emphasize the latter mostly at the expense of the former. While the theorists of socialist democracy were reluctant to admit the significance of political liberties in achieving economic equality, the theorists of liberal democracy, such as Mill and de Tocqueville, treated individual liberties as incompatible with excessive equality and justice. They believed that freedom and liberty, being the most valuable achievements of modern societies, had to be protected under all circumstances from the threats of an egalitarian mass society. Too much equality and justice for these theorists was, then, a barrier to the expansion of liberties.

Yet liberty is necessarily a function of equality. Without political *and* economic equality, liberty is not possible. As Harold Laski puts it:

> It is because political equality does not permit the full affirmation of the common men's essence that the idea of democracy has spread to other spheres.... In the absence of economic equality, no political mechanisms will, of themselves, enable the common man to realize his wills and interests.... Economic power is the parent of political power. To make the diffusion of the latter effective, the former must also be widely diffused.[23]

Economic equality is, therefore, the expansion, not the limitation, of individual liberties. Economic and political liberties and equality are the two sides of the same coin.

Furthermore, although absolute economic equality is more an ideal than a reality, some degree of minimum economic justice, i.e., a fair distribution of economic resources, is essential for the maintenance of a political democracy. In her comparative work on India, Costa Rica, and Turkey, Zehra Arat demonstrated, for instance, that the breakdown of political democracy is more likely to occur in less egalitarian societies. Clearly, in the absence of economic justice, even the democratic institutions and, indeed, political democracy itself, might be threatened since the very legitimacy and the durability of these institutions are dependent on some degree of perceived or real economic equality.[24]

The false dichotomy created by political freedom and political equality on the one hand, economic liberties and economic justice on the other, have also generated continuous debate over the compatibility of our existing economic systems, which are becoming predominantly capitalist, with the concept of democracy. One view has been that capitalist development and democracy are mutually reinforcing. The proponents of this view emphasized the importance of capitalism in the rise of democracy and argued that a minimum level of capitalist industrialization is necessary for the development of democracy.[25] Indeed, capitalism and democracy have risen together historically. The fact that democracies, defined in terms of representative institutions, exist today mostly in advanced capitalist countries have also reinforced this view. Most recently, the socio-economic changes in the ex-Soviet Union and Eastern Europe have also brought about arguments equating capitalism, sometimes defined simply in terms of free markets, with democracy.

The opponents of the above view argued instead that capitalism and democracy are a contradiction in terms. They pointed out that capitalism existed for extended periods without allowing democracy even to start, let alone flourish. Property rights of capitalism have generated only inequality and economic injustice which mean that democracy cannot exist. Nehru raised the same issue when he wrote:

> Real democracy has had no chance to exist so far, for there is an essential contradiction between the capitalist system and democracy. Democracy, if it means anything, means equality; not merely the equality of possessing a vote, but economic and social equality.[26]

Thus, put in Rousseau's terms, property rights, once established, have become the very source of inequality challenging, thereby, the core principle of democracy.

Not surprisingly, the proponents of these two opposing views also had substantial differences over the issues of democracy and development in the so-called third-world countries and the related role of the intellectuals in these societies. Taking the Western democracies as an ideal, the proponents of the first view, which considered capitalism and democracy as mutually reinforcing, tended to see the difficulty of establishing and maintaining democracies in the developing countries as a consequence of problems of modernization. As these countries pass from traditional to modern societies, as their backward economies catch up with the advanced industrialized countries, and as they eliminate the "residual" autocratic and nepotistic sources of power, argued these theorists, they will gradually democratize. The absence or failure of democracy should thus be attributed to so-called growing pains which find their origins in the lack of institutionalization, political corruption, too many rising expectations, and the absence of a democratic culture.[27] The role of the intellectuals in this context should be that of helping their societies develop economically, ease these growing pains and act as "modernizers" during this eventual transition.

The proponents of the opposite view have, naturally, rejected this notion of gradual democratization as a function of modernization. Any true democratic movement in the developing countries, they argued, should be based on the mobilization of the masses against unequal development and capitalism. On the three examples of revolutionary moments in modern history, i.e., French, Russian, and Chinese, these theorists claimed that democratization is only possible as a result of sudden radical social transformation. The role of the true intellectuals in these crucial moments is to act as the brain and the catalyst of the revolutionary process. This process should include the elimination of private property and capitalism as an economic system without which a true democracy based on equality cannot be possible.

It is indeed true that capitalism has historically exhibited and still exhibits considerable economic and social inequalities. Among the advanced industrialized countries, this problem has been partially remedied at the national level through rigorous government welfare programmes.[28] But in the less developed countries, where resources are usually limited and the national economy is increasingly vulnerable to, if not dependent on, the changes in the world economy, the inequalities are much more acute and visible. Brazil, for instance, where the richest 20 per cent of the population consumes approximately two-thirds of the national income, provides a grave example.

Furthermore, in a period when the boundaries between the national, the international, and the transnational are becoming ever more blurred, the ability of governments to ameliorate the problems of social and economic inequality have seriously declined. This growing transnationalism has also led to concentration of economic power in the hands of giant multinational corporations where most strategic decisions are being made. The natural consequence of these developments have been the deepening of inequalities between the North and the South and the increasing peripheralization of the developing countries in what has recently become a truly global capitalist economy.

Yet, since the dreams of non-capitalist development have, at least for the moment, been abandoned, does this antagonism between capitalism, which clearly generates inequality, and democracy necessarily suggest that democracy is a futile dream? Is it indeed impossible to synthesize what Bowles and Gintis called democracy's "expansionary logic of personal rights," and capitalism's expansionary logic of property rights or production where "the capitalist firm's ongoing search for profits progressively encroaches upon all spheres of social activity leaving few realms of life untouched by the imperatives of the accumulation and the market"?[29] Where can one draw the line between these two rights? Are the young democracies in Latin America, Africa, Asia, which suffer from the worst consequences of capitalist development, including uneven and underdevelopment, necessarily doomed?

All these questions provide good examples of the theoretical and practical impasse generated by the current political and economic discourses. These ideological discourses do not allow for the formulation of alternative strategies to development and democracy which would transform the existing political and economic structure so as to promote economic justice as well as political liberties. Economic justice has clearly not been achieved through the "invisible hands" of market capitalism. But the long-awaited socialist revolution based on the elimination of property rights has not occurred either. This is why modern intellectuals, both in the developed but particularly in the developing countries, are now faced with the difficult task of going beyond the existing liberal and socialist discourses, redefining "development" and "democracy" and promoting economic and social justice.

Distribution and accountability of economic and social power, i.e. economic democracy, can be an important initial step toward achieving this economic justice upon which every stable democracy is based. The concept of economic democracy is indeed a synthesis, however uneasy it might be, of liberal discourse based on the expansion of personal liberties and choices with the socialist discourse based on economic equality. It refers to the devolution of economic decision-making from the few to the many.[30] It also involves the elimination of the distinction between public and private, subjecting all the individual and collective actors in the economy to democratic accountability. Economic democracy is founded on an understanding that economic decision-making is a "political" process and that individuals in democratic societies should have the right to determine their economic future as well as their political one. As Carnoy and Shearer put it:

> The principle of one person/one vote in the political arena confronts the reality of unequal economic rights and unequal distribution of economic power. The two cannot be separated. The "free speech" of a General Motors is obviously greater than that of any individual. . . . Economic democracy is a crucial ingredient of political democracy and vice versa.[31]

Economic democracy is, therefore, based on the recognition of both the heterogeneity of power, political or economic, and the existence of different patterns of domination at various "sites" in society, particularly in the economic realm.[32]

How can this economic democracy be developed and what can the intellectuals do? Perhaps the most difficult task here of the modern intellectual is, as Kenneth W. Thompson pointed out in the context of international relations, to bridge the gap between theory and practice.[33] Always thinking in terms of abstract principles and universalities, the modern intellectual is indeed faced with the problem of linking the concept of economic democracy to praxis, to political and economic strategies. Although no final solution to this perennial problem will be given here, several possible propositions can still be made.

As has already been suggested, promoting economic democracy involves understanding the political aspects of economic decision-making and providing alternatives to diffuse economic power. But in most of the capitalist societies, be it developed or developing, economic decisions which involve investment and production are increasingly being monopolized or oligopolized by major business corporations. Indeed, as Schumpeter rightly pointed out in his criticism of the liberals, "reducing the tasks done by the State and other public bodies makes no or little difference if they merely get assumed by private corporations whose bureaucracies are sometimes even more extensive.[34] Furthermore, these corporations are seldom socially or politically held accountable for the decisions they make. Although some attempts have recently been made to hold private corporations accountable for socially irresponsible decisions which resulted, for instance, in environmental pollution, health hazards, or nuclear disasters, these corporations, with almost unlimited access to legal and financial resources, have suffered minimal damages. Meanwhile, small entrepreneurs who have neither the money nor the scale of production of the corporations have gradually been pushed out of the market. This concentration of economic power in a small number of firms is hardly compatible with the vision of economic democracy. As Charles Lindblom stated in the conclusion to his *Politics and Markets*, "The large private corporation fits oddly into democratic theory and vision. Indeed, it does not fit."[35]

Nationalizing these private corporations, as has been proposed by many socialists, hardly advances economic democracy if power gets simply concentrated in the hands of the state élite. To paraphrase Schumpeter, it also makes little or no sense to transfer the tasks of the private corporations if they are simply assumed by the state élite. There is indeed no evidence, furthermore, that the state-owned enterprises promote more egalitarian distribution of income or allow more democratic penetration. Economic democracy, in this respect, involves restructuring of both state and corporate power.

Economic power of the large corporations both at the national and international level along with big state-owned enterprises can indeed be diffused through allowing multiple ownership and management. By converting these corporations to workers/consumers/community-owned enterprises, it is possible to achieve a heterogeneous and pluralist pattern of ownership which would be a significant step toward economic democracy. Multiple ownership will expand individual rights into the economic realm. The individual can now participate not only as a citizen in the political realm but as a consumer, as a worker, or simply as a member of the community. No doubt this expansion of participation in different aspects of social life constitutes the basic principle of democracy.

Another site where economic democracy can be developed is at the workplace. So far, organization of production in capitalist as well as socialist countries has been based on the separation of the control of work from work itself where an élite management has carefully safeguarded their rights over investment and production decisions. This process of exclusion has been defended in terms of effective decision-making and based on the assumption that managers are better informed than workers. Yet, equipped with firsthand experience and knowledge of production, workers' participation in investment decisions and worker control over production will improve not only labour productivity but also help further the economic democratization process. This process will also help shift the focus from pure profits to workers' income and welfare, which is crucial in bringing economic justice.

But the concentration of economic power in the hands of a few, as with political power, has been often justified in terms of dynamic efficiency. This argument was based on the assumption that the lesser the number of people involved in the decision-making, the more effective, rapid and efficient will the firm or the State become. In fact, the recent economic success among the so-called newly industrializing countries (NICs) have easily been attributed to the profitable state and big business alliances and labour exclusionary policies.[36]

Such arguments have been accompanied by suggestions that an authoritarian or exclusionary regime might indeed be necessary to provide political stability which is a prerequisite for efficient accumulation and economic growth.

The implicit assumption behind these arguments is equating both political and economic democratization with instability and inefficiency. Yet there is no reason to assume that the authoritarian and élitist regimes are inherently more stable than their democratic counterparts.

On the contrary, authoritarian regimes are more likely to face "legitimation crises," which breed long-term instability.[37] Arguments based on efficiency are also unfounded. There are many examples of inefficient authoritarian regimes which are unable to carry out economic and political decisions. There are also corporations which, despite their élitist decision-making process, suffer from inefficiency and hoarding.[38] Thus, there is no inevitable trade-off between stability and efficiency on the one side and democracy on the other.

Finally, the critics of economic and political democracy fail to address the fundamental question, namely, how high a price should society pay in terms of human costs and rights for economic growth and efficiency? The answer to this question requires a clear distinction between economic growth and development. National economic growth is meaningful if and only when it is generated by and shared equally among its citizens; when it guarantees to *all* its citizens basic rights to an economic livelihood and offers them opportunities to participate in all those political *and* economic decisions that shape their lives. The process of development, then, should involve *both* economic growth and democratization at the same time.

Economic democracy is only an initial step towards economic justice and true development process. Redistributive policies such as significant land reforms, carefully directed subsidies for small enterprises, individual initiatives, and emphasis on community and welfare programmes can clearly be helpful in promoting economic justice. To transform continuously the concept of economic democracy and justice into effective concrete policies will be, indeed, difficult. It is in this particular area that the contribution of the intellectual is most crucial and needed.

The first and far most important task of the intellectual in bringing about economic democracy is that of education. Education empowers individuals by sensitizing them to the various forms of power structures that exist in modern societies. It allows the expansion of the people's capacity to govern themselves by questioning all forms of power and authority. Thus, ironically, the main function of the intellectual is to eliminate herself, or himself, and her, or his, social distinction based on knowledge by turning the entire society into a "society of intellectuals."

Similarly, the intellectual, as the creator of language and political discourse, can act as a synthesizing force to generate collective action. This function is particularly important in the initiation of popular movements. Popular action and continuous social mobilization are not socially disruptive and destabilizing processes, as Huntington and his followers have continuously argued in the context of developing countries.[39] In fact, social unrest and threats to democratic institutions rarely originate from social mobilization *per se*, but from extreme social and economic inequalities. Social mobilization can be, instead, an effective instrument of struggle against injustice and inequality and a valuable learning experience in self-organization and self-development, both of which are essentials of economic democracy. This would also help eliminate the concentration of political and economic power, be it corporatist or bureaucratic. Furthermore, social mobilization is particularly important for the intellectual since it is only through people and popular movements that ideas can become socially relevant. Without an audience, the intellectual can still perform, but cannot become an agent for social change.

Finally, it is crucial for the intellectual to continue to give society a "guilty conscience," for it is only through continuous criticism and dialogue that a society can improve itself. Perhaps only then will the intellectuals stop being "free floating" individuals, as Mannheim called them, and find their true role in modern societies.[40]

Notes

1. Henry de Montherlant, *La Reine Mort* (Paris: Gallimard, 1947), p. 90.
2. *Plato's Republic*, translated by G.M.A. Grube (Indianapolis: Hackett Publishing Company, 1974), Book V, 473d.
3. Aristotle, *The Nicomachean Ethics*, translated by J.E.C. Welldron (London: Macmillan Press, 1912), Book X, chap. VII, p. 337.
4. Arthur Waley, *The Analects of Confucius* (Pennsylvania: Franklin Library, 1980), Book VI, no. 20, p. 43, and Book XII, no. 22, p. 97.
5. William Hazlitt, *The Works of Michel de Montaigne*, 3rd edn (Philadelphia: J.W. Moore, 1851), chap. XXV, p. 88.
6. Alexis de Tocqueville, *Old Regime and the French Revolution*, translated by Stuart Gilbert (New York: Doubleday Anchor Books, 1955), pp. 146–147.
7. As Louis Bodin wrote: "*Professeurs sans chaire, écrivains et artistes sans moyens, nobles déclassés, ecclésiastiques sans bénéfices, etc., ces 'vagabonds de la terre russe' marqués par*

l'influence du romantisme et de idéalisme d'allemands, ressentent vivement la condition 'd'humiliés et d'offensés,' selon le titre de Dostoievsky, faite à leurs compatriotes. Les Intellectuels (Paris: Presses Universitaires de France, 1964), p. 62.

8. See the works of Richard Pipes, ed. *The Russian Intelligentsia* (New York: Columbia Press, 1961) and Cyril E. Black, ed. *The Transformation of Russian Society: Aspects of Social Change since 1861* (Cambridge: Harvard University Press, 1967).
9. Quoted by Archibald Macleish, "The Irresponsibles," *The Nation* (18 May 1949), p. 618.
10. Julien Benda, *La trahison des clercs* (Paris: B. Grasset, 1927).
11. See Mohamed B. Taleb-Khyar, "The Languages of Literary Criticism" for the elaboration of this idea, *Callaloo*, 14.3(1991):611–618.
12. P. Bourdieu, *Distinction: A Social Critique of the Judgment of Taste*, translated by Richard Nice (Cambridge: Harvard University Press, 1984), pp. 114–125. Also see his *Reproduction in Education, Society and Culture* (London: Sage Publications, 1977).
13. See Machajski, "Selection from his writings," *The Making of Society*, ed. V.F. Calverton (New York: Modern Library, 1937).
14. See A. Gouldner, *Future of the Intellectuals and the Rise of the New Class* (New York: Seabury Press, 1979), particularly pp. 18–20.
15. For the best representatives of this argument, see Thorstein Veblen, *Engineers and the Price System* (New York: B. W. Huebsch, 1921), Daniel Bell, *The Coming of Post Industrial Society* (New York: Basic Books, 1973) and *The End of Ideology* (New York: Free Press, 1962). Also see Kenneth Galbraith, *The New Industrial State* (Boston: Houghton Mifflin, 1978), and Raymond Aron, *The Industrial Society: Three Essays on Ideology and Development* (New York: Praeger, 1967). Implications of this transformation in modern societies have also been carefully analysed though from a different perspective by the Frankfurt School. See, for instance, Herbert Marcuse, *One-Dimensional Man: Studies in the Ideology of Advanced Industrial Society* (Boston: Beacon Press, 1964) and Theodore Adorno, *Negative Dialectic* (New York: Seabury Press, 1973).
16. For a good discussion of this point see Seymour Martin Lipset and Richard B. Dobson, "The Intellectual Critic and Rebel: With Special Reference to the United States and the Soviet Union," *Daedalus*, 101. 3 (Summer 1972): 137–199. Similar arguments also appear on the role of intellectuals in Eastern Europe. See, for example, G. Konrad and I. Szelenyi, *The Intellectuals on the Road to Class Power* (New York: Harcourt Brace, 1979).
17. For an excellent discussion of this point, see J.P. Nettl, "Ideas, Intellectuals and Structures of Dissent," ed. Philip Rieff, *On Intellectuals* (New York: Anchor Books, 1970), pp 57–137.
18. Jean Paul Sartre, *What Is Literature?* (New York: Philosophical Library, 1949), pp. 81–82 (parenthesis added, emphasis original). See also his *Plaidoyer pour les intellectuels* (Paris: Gallimard, 1972).
19. For the elaboration of this point, see Michel Foucault, *Discipline and Punish: The Birth of the Prison* (New York: Pantheon Books, 1977).
20. Walt Whitman, *Complete Poetry and Selected Prose* (Boston: Houghton Mifflin Company, 1959), p. 477.
21. I. Berlin, *Four Essays on Liberty* (London: Oxford University Press, 1969), p. 126.
22. This is not true for the post-Marxists who concentrated on the politics of Marx. See, for instance, the following passage of Ralph Miliband, "Bourgeois is crippled by its class limitations.... But the civic freedoms which, however, inadequately and precariously form a part of bourgeois democracy are the products of centuries of unremitting struggles. The task of Marxist politics is to defend these freedoms and make possible their extension and enlargement by the removal of class boundaries." *Marxism and Politics* (Oxford: Oxford University Press, 1977), pp. 189–190.
23. Harold Laski, "Democracy," *International Encyclopedia of the Social Sciences* (London, New York: Macmillan Press, 1931), vol. 5, p. 77.
24. Z. Arat, *Democracy and Human Rights in the Developing Countries* (Boulder: Lynne Rienner Publishers, 1991).

25. See, for instance, Max Weber who argued that "early" capitalism and the ethical, cultural values that came with it, was crucial in fermenting democracy. He also, however, pointed out to the threat that modern "high" capitalism as the embodiment of "rational impersonality" poses for democratic freedoms, *Archiv für Sozialwissenschaft und Sozialpolitik*, 22.1 (1906):346–347. More recently see M. Lipset, *Political Man: The Social Bases of Politics* (New York: Doubleday Company, 1960) and D. Usher, *The Economic Prerequisites to Democracy* (Oxford: Basic Blackwell, 1981).
26. Quoted from Z. Arat, *Democracy and Human Rights in the Developing Countries* (Boulder: Lynne Rienner Publishers, 1991), p. 103.
27. For the best examples of this modernization theory, see the works of W.W. Rostow, *The Stages of Economic Growth* (Cambridge: Cambridge University Press, 1960) and Daniel Lerner, *The Passing of Traditional Society* (Glencoe: Free Press, 1958). On the role of intellectuals, Edward Shils' work can also be considered in this context, *The Intellectuals and the Powers and Other Essays* (Chicago: University of Chicago Press, 1972).
28. The United States and to some extent Britain constitute an exception here where the welfare programmes are considerably weak in comparison, for instance, to Denmark, Sweden, or Germany.
29. Samuel Bowles and Herbert Gintis, *Democracy and Capitalism* (New York: Basic Books, 1986), p. 29.
30. For the elaboration of this concept from which the following analysis is heavily influenced, see Bowles and Gintis, *Democracy and Capitalism*, Martin Carnoy and Derek Shearer, *Economic Democracy: The Challenge of the 1980s* (New York: Sharpe, 1980). Also see David M. Gordon, Thomas E. Weisskopf, and Samuel Bowles, *Beyond Waste Land* (New York: Anchor Press, 1983) and *After the Waste Land: A Democratic Economics for the Year 2000* (New York: M.E. Sharpe Inc., 1990). Also see K. Cowling, "Economic Obstacles to Democracy," *Economy and Democracy*, ed. R.C.O. Matthews (New York: Macmillan Press, 1985).
31. M. Carnoy and D. Shearer, *Economic Democracy: The Challenge of the 1980s*, p. 131.
32. The term is borrowed from Gary Wickham, "Power and Power Analysis: Beyond Foucault," *Economy and Society*, 12.4 (1938):468–498.
33. See Kenneth W. Thompson, *Theory and Practice in International Relations* (Washington, D.C.: University Press of America).
34. Quoted from Richard Bellamy, "Schumpeter and the Transformation of Capitalism, Liberalism and Democracy," *Government and Opposition*, 26.4 (Autumn 1991):507. We should point out, however, that Schumpeter's main concern in his *Capitalism, Socialism and Democracy* was to delineate the self-destructive patterns of capitalism through concentration and centralization of economic power and his theory of democracy is quite different than the one suggested here.
35. Charles Lindblom, *Politics and Markets* (New York: Basic Books, 1977), p. 356.
36. This view is particularly popular among the proponents of the so-called strong state thesis who argue that an authoritarian regime might be necessary for rapid and efficient economic growth. See, for instance, Frederick Deyo, *Political Economy of East Asian Industrialism*, 1987, and *Beneath Miracle: Labour Subordination in the New Industrialism* (Berkeley: University of California Press, 1989).
37. See Jurgen Habermas, *Legitimation Crisis* (Boston: Beacon Press, 1973). Also see, for an excellent analysis, Nicos Poulantzas, *Crisis of Dictatorships* (New York: New Left Books, 1979).
38. Most of the African and Latin American authoritarian regimes have become a source of hoarding and corruption.
39. See Samuel Huntington, *Political Order in Changing Societies* (New Haven: Yale University Press, 1968).
40. Karl Mannheim, *Ideology and Utopia*, translated by Louis Wirth and Edward Shils (New York: Harcourt, Brace Company, 1936), pp. 155–162.

4

Culture, development, and democracy: The role of intellectuals

Sulak Sivaraksa

I should like to define intellectuals as a tiny group of people who provide for their society – be it the world or the nation state – the most articulate, persuasive, precise, and perhaps accurate definition of the society from their experience. They also have a serious commitment to improve that society. Often, they are major living writers, educators, technocrats, members of parliament, and intellectual leaders of their religious institutions. They dare to write and speak openly against current public opinion, especially against the policy and administration of the ruling élites. Scholars and academics and journalists who do not perform such function cannot claim to be intellectuals. In the Northern hemisphere, intellectuals enjoy a large degree of freedom, but in the South, they are often oppressed by the regime currently in power.

Intellectuals feel, perhaps wrongly, that they have replaced the priests of the older generation, who had done too much, perhaps, to maintain the status quo. Their vote is like that of the prophets, but, however much they try, they cannot manage to solve the most fundamental problems of society, in order to bring about social justice as they perceive that it should really care for the welfare of the com-

The views expressed in this paper are solely those of the author and are not necessarily those of the UNU and the Indonesia Social Sciences Foundation (YIIS).

mon man and decrease the exploitation of the world's natural resources.

While they were alive most intellectuals felt that they had failed in their objective to improve the lot of humankind, politically, socially, ethically, aesthetically, and ecologically. Select any name from Rousseau, Voltaire, Karl Marx, Lord Acton, Bertrand Russell, George Orwell to Soedjatmoko. They all feel frustrated that their intellectual ability had somehow been wasted.

The reason for this sense is obvious, because by definition intellectuals are independent thinkers and those who control the Church, the State, the media, or multinational corporations do not like intellectuals to tell them or the public that those in power tend to be corrupted. In a more open society, they have no absolute power; hence, they cannot corrupt absolutely. Yet, the power they hold behind the scenes can also make life for any intellectual difficult, especially if he or she does not toe the line of the prevailing political climate or policy.

In the European context, one can see very clearly why Marx could not even live in Germany, France, or Belgium. Luckily, he was allowed in Britain. Yet, in England itself, Bertrand Russell was not only jailed, but was not even allowed to teach at Cambridge University because he disagreed fundamentally with the British government on the virtue of entering the First World War.

In the Spanish Civil War, beginning in 1936, it was clear to most Western intellectuals that the fascist movement in Europe was threatened with a serious set-back, because the common people like the Spanish workers had taken up arms to oppose General Franco's revolt against the nation's elected government. Up to that point, the fascist powers had been enjoying a long string of fairly easy successes, including Mussolini's conquest of Abyssinia and Hitler's reoccupation of the Rhineland. Hence, many committed intellectuals of socialist persuasion not only wrote and spoke for the cause of democracy and freedom against totalitarian regimes but went to fight in Spain. Yet, the elected Spanish government compromised with the Soviet Union – another dictatorial regime, which claimed to be socialist.

George Orwell had a hard time fighting in Spain. He was shot and nearly died. Yet the Spanish government believed the Russian KGB that he was Franco's spy. Luckily, he escaped back to England with his wife, where he wanted to tell the world the whole truth of the messy war, that the government of the Republic "has more points of resemblance to fascism than points of difference." He was not allowed by respectable magazine editors and publishers like Kingsley Martin of the *New Statesman* and Victor Gollancz of the Left Book Club, because left-wing opinion was too accustomed to thinking of the Republic as a victim of fascism to accept this, and not many people were prepared to see the element of truth in the broad generalization, namely, the Republic was wrong to think that it could use fascist methods to achieve socialist aims. This same mistake was repeated over and over again in China, Viet Nam, and Cambodia.

This classic example could be cited almost anywhere in the world – be it in China or Thailand. In the case of Soedjatmoko, he fought the Dutch for Indonesian independence and supported Sukarno for democracy and socialism, but when the guided democracy of the father of the nation became more and more oppressive, he could no longer serve the government in which he painfully helped to create. Again, when Suharto toppled Sukarno in 1965, he was called on to serve as Indonesian Ambassador to the United States, to gain recognition for the nation to pursue her development towards democracy and decency. Yet, he must have felt frustrated that the new president and his henchmen are perhaps even worse than the Sukarno period.

The case of Soedjatmoko illustrates that intellectuals do not need to be outside the corridor of power all the time. But when they are with the powers that be, if they themselves are not corrupted by the authority and glory they enjoy, the best they can do is improve the economic conditions of the country a little, not the cultural aspects or fundamental development towards equality, freedom, and fraternity. The case of John Maynard Keynes with the British government and Puey Ungphakorn with the Thai government are clear examples of intellectuals with moral courage who tried hard to use their economic expertise to guide the Government towards a sound financial policy which could benefit a large majority of its citizens. But generally speaking, both failed in their mission.

In the case of Puey, like Soedjatmoko, he had to serve under a dictatorial regime. Then it was not possible even to look for the rule of law or freedom of speech. In the case of Keynes, who served under the Labour government which had swept to power after defeating Churchill and the Conservatives in the general election after the Second World War, we may ask what changes were made in the administrative personnel even though there had been a change of government? Did the police officer, who had a vague notion that "socialism" meant something against the law, carry on just the same when the government itself was socialist? The Labour Party, with a lot of intellectual backing, could pass all the new laws it wanted, but that would mean little if the changes were not accepted wholeheartedly at the bottom of the system – by the policeman on the street, for example – as well as at the top.

Britain prided herself on being the mother of modern democracy, and with the Industrial Revolution, she claimed to have so developed society economically and culturally that eventually Britain ruled the waves, with the English sense of justice and fairness. They felt other countries should develop in the British image, e.g., the Indians were forced to sell their wool to British industry and Ceylon was made to grow tea instead of rice so that the price of tea was settled in London. Yet, before the Second World War, Orwell wrote *The Road to Wigan Pier* describing the social condition of British mine workers in the north. His research in the public library revealed that miners were suffering from a phenomenally high rate of accidents. He learned that nearly 8,000 had died in the mines in the period from 1927 to 1934. He calculated that "every year one miner in about 900 is killed and one in about six is injured equalling the whole of the casualties sustained by the Gallipoli Expeditionary Force." To be sure, many of the non-fatal injuries reported by the mines were insignificant compared with the wounds inflicted on the troops in the disastrous Gallipoli campaign. Nevertheless, this reference helps us see that there was a kind of war being waged in the north of England at that time – and that only one side was taking casualties.

This very fact is still relevant in the third world, for instance Thailand; the Buddhist kingdom has 300,000 monks but more than one million prostitutes. It is known as the rice bowl of Asia, yet 60 per cent of its children now suffer from malnutrition. Most of its farmers have left home for the Bangkok slums or to work in the Arab world with a social guarantee less than those enjoyed by the British miners in the 1930s. Similar cases are found in Malaysia, Indonesia, and the Philippines. Do our Asian intellectuals regard these phenomena as a war within our country, which our political leaders do not know widely, while they themselves lead luxurious lifestyles not unlike those of the élite leaders in the West? Do they allow multinational corporations, as well as the great economic powers like Japan and the United States, to exploit their national resources, use cheap labour, produce polluted industrial complexes, while exploiting our common people with consumer goods through advertising in our mass media?

A lot of political leaders mean well for their country. Their rhetoric is for the welfare of the people, but at the same time they want to maintain the status quo. As Tolstoy once said, "I shall give you all the things you want, except that I won't get off your back."

Quite a few political leaders are honest and some think that they are intellectuals as well as technocrats. At least, they are rationalists and are often optimistic that they can cure the social ills if they are in power. They even compromised by serving totalitarian regimes. The discovery of truth satisfies their self-esteem. They believe it will light the way to a wiser, happier future, and this fires them with such ardour and eloquence that they are popularly supported. They, too, have a vision: the vision of the present forging the shape of the future. Yet in reality their vision is tragic. For if they are honest, they know that their hopes will be dashed. The crassness of human stupidity, the evils corrupting society, the dreary aimless course of peoples and governments exasperate and frustrate them and whisper that tyranny, misery, and calamity are the eternal lot of man. Thus, unable to remould the scheme of things nearer to their hearts' desire, they work on, now in this vineyard or in that, trying to bring order into one small corner of the chaos to which they inescapably belong. The belief that order can be created and the realization that their own efforts will change little in the world are the two central facts in their experiences that dignity enables them.

Thus, British socialist intellectuals – ranging from Beatrice Webb, Harold Laski, Stafford Cripps to Maynard Keynes – did their best to bring about the Labour victory after the Second World War. Yet, it did not necessarily mean the beginning of fundamental change in British society. That victory, through the democratic process, reflected merely a drift towards socialism, not accompanied by any strong revolutionary yearning or any sudden breakup of the class system. The majority of people who voted for Labour were not really for real change, but wanted only the adoption of a certain specific improvement. In the popular mind, the Labour Party was the party that stood for shorter working hours, a free health service, day nurseries, free milk for school children, and the like, rather than the party that stood for equality and fraternity in the true sense of the word.

It is true that the Labour Party helped in granting independence to India. The Indian masses, however, have not been able to improve as have their counterparts in Britain.

If the intellectual really cared about the destitute people whose suffering he shared and wanted to help them, there should not be any national boundaries to divide humankind. By joining the Government, the intellectual must compromise so that at best he can only remain independent and hope he is able to do a little for social justice, not being able to eliminate the cause of suffering altogether.

For the intellectuals who really care for humankind, it is a question of sticking to essentials, and the essential point is that all people with small insecure income or the landless labourers are in the same boat and ought to be fighting on the same side. If the intelligentsia could talk a little less about "capitalist" and "proletariat" and do a little more about the "robbers" and the "robbed," socialism could then offer a way for the robbed to protect themselves from the robbers, but it can only work if its base support is broad.

The people who have got to act together are all those who cringe before the boss and those who shudder when they think of others' problems, as well as those who oppose the gigantic dams that will destroy their environment for the benefit of the electricity board and the super rich who care more for golf courses than rice fields and forests. This means that the smallholder must ally himself with the factory hand, the typist with the coalminer, the schoolmaster with the farmers. There is some hope of getting them to do so if they can be made to understand where their interest lies.

Unfortunately, in many countries, the schoolmaster wants to become a member of parliament by lying with political propaganda or betraying the farmer once they are in the corridor of power. They are even willing to kowtow to the military which controls "democracy" behind the scene.

The problem is that practical men have led us to the edge of the abyss, and the intellectuals in whom acceptance of power politics has first killed moral sense, and then the sense of reality, are urging us to march rapidly forward in the name of development without changing direction – hence, the catastrophe of modern development, where the rich get richer and the poor become poorer, while no one is happy, and all suffer at the expense of environmental degradation.

In the minds of active revolutionaries, at any rate, for the intelligentsia who "got there," the longing for a just society has always been fatally mixed up with the intention to secure power for themselves.

One has seen so many revolutions in the USSR, China, Viet Nam, Burma, and Cambodia, which claim to be on the left. Everyone has a violent conspiratorial revolutionary led by unconsciously power-hungry people. Likewise, the *coup d'état* of the Thai, Indonesian, Pakistani, or Bangladeshi varieties are essentially the same, i.e., they can only lead to a change of masters. During the struggle for home rule, Parnell was hailed by a labourer who built roads and shouted "Independent Ireland." The great politician replied to him that "Yes, Ireland shall become independent, but you will remain building roads as you are doing now."

The revolution may effect a radical improvement when the masses are alert and know how to check their leaders as soon as the latter have done their jobs.

About *Animal Farm*, Orwell wrote:

> The turning point of the story was supposed to be when the pigs kept the milk and apples for themselves. If the other animals had had the sense to put their foot down, then it would have been all right. If people think I am defending the status quo, that is, I think, because they have grown pessimistic and assume that there is no alternative except dictatorship or *laissez-faire* capitalism ... what I was trying to say was "You can't have a revolution unless you made it yourself, there is no such thing as a benevolent dictatorship."

In *1984*, he went further, that under Big Brother's rule, it is certainly true that public opinion has no power, but that is because the common people have not awakened to the fact that they have always had the power to make their voice heard.

Without this power, dictatorship can win the day very easily, whether in Singapore, Malaysia, Indonesia, or Thailand, most of which claim to be or prefer to be democratic. Fascism, after all, is only a development of capitalism, and the mildest democracy, so called, is liable to turn into fascism when the hitch comes.

Intellectuals who join any government can pass many laws for the benefit of the people – to have the law on the side of the people is better than the law that oppresses the people – but, even so, the good law is no sure protection. If a large number of people are interested in freedom of speech, there will be freedom of speech, even if the law forbids it. If, however, public opinion is sluggish, inconvenient minorities will be prosecuted, even if laws exist to protect them. Hence, those minorities who dare to speak out, denounce the regime, will have to suffer. To avoid suffering means compromise, which may end up in the worship of power.

Indeed, the worship of power for its own sake is not limited to any particular group of people. Its appeal is widespread, and once a leader begins to exploit it effectively, it can grow by great leaps until it encounters another force which can meet its power with equal power.

Intellectuals who serve dictatorial regimes anywhere have the tendency to become functionaries or technocrats who go along with whatever regime they claim they can influence – hence, the Berkeley mafia in Indonesia and the Cambridge mafia in Thailand, because power worship blurs political judgement. It leads almost unavoidably to the belief that present trends will continue. Whoever is winning at the moment will always soon be invincible. Yet if one looks at a long-range view, one can see clearly that the great power that is feared one year is often destroyed by its own overreaching ambition within a few years and inevitably loses its aura of invincibility, if not its actual force.

When Correlli Barrett wrote *The Collapse of British Power* in 1972, he had this to say:

> The power of a nation state consists not only in its armed forces, but also in its economic and technological resources; in the dexterity, foresight, and resolution with which its foreign policy is conducted; in the efficiency of its social and political organization. It consists most of all in the nation itself; the people; their skills; their energy, ambition, discipline, and initiative; their beliefs, myths, and illusions. And it consists further, in the way that all these factors are related to one another. Moreover, the national power has to be considered not only in itself or in its absolute extent, but relative to the State's foreign or imperial obligation – it has to be considered relative to power of other states.

If the intellectuals want to have any role in culture, development, and democracy, their role is not to bow down to the dictatorial regime of the left or right and take the above quotation in mind. They should have a long-range view. They should have a firm belief in the common man – not in Superman or Big Brother. As early as the 1930s, Orwell said: "The Russian regime will democratize itself or it will perish ... one way or another the regime will die because ... the common man will triumph in the end."

The key thing is to bring the restraining force of public opinion into play. As long as the public has a chance to make itself heard, the State will have to curtail its appetite for power.

Even a multinational corporation, with its power over advertisement and the mass media to brainwash the people to be addicted to consumerism, will have to confront the fact that this development for a luxurious lifestyle is harmful to all concerned and is wasteful as well as exploitative to the environment.

The whole society fails when the people of that society allow the State, the mass media and the multinational corporation to strip them systematically of their rights to be individual human beings, to be sentimental and trivial, to take away their rich language and indigenous culture, and replace it with an ugly, utilitarian one – with fast food, Coca-Cola, jeans, and plastic and foam, denying them the ordinary pleasure of a private life – beyond the decadence of television programmes.

If people are willing to fight for such things, and are willing to see that freedom to enjoy them means more than any "ism" or any leader, then there will be hope for the future.

The role of the intellectuals is not that of the prophets of doom. Though they may criticize the regime in power and the wrong direction of development which gears for technical and material advancement at the expense of social justice and ecological balance and the prevailing consumer culture, they must have hope for the future and have their complete trust in ordinary men and women.

For those of us who write, in a peaceful age, we might have written an ornate or merely descriptive book, and remained almost unaware of our political loyalties. But in the circumstances of our time, while the "robbers" and the "robbed" face each other mercilessly everywhere, it is necessary for us to choose between the life devoted to those "ornate" books or one devoted to political literature.

If the intellectual cared about the destitute people whose suffering he shared and he wanted to help them, he must be aware of his limitation, i.e., he cannot ignore the fact that he is not one of them. He has talent, education, family, and friends willing to help him, whereas they have none. The best that he can do for those who are less fortunate is to speak out for them, to articulate their aspiration, to remind the rest of the world that they exist, that they are human beings who deserve better, and that their pain is real. They should not be robbed. And he should also remind those in power – in Church, State, military and civilian, as well as the commercial sectors – that we, himself included, are often "robbers," who should re-examine our lifestyles thoroughly and develop our critical self-awareness to be less greedy, less hateful, and less deluded.

The intellectual must not play God, i.e., he is not able to shape the culture or development of his society or his age – even the many brands of democracy he may know may not lead to any – he can, however, propose alternative models to the prevailing ones. Since he is not in power, however, he can only criticize and persuade. His moral courage must be strong.

He need not be apolitical as Blake was, but there is more understanding of the nature of the capitalist society in a poem like "I wander through each charted street" than in three-quarters of socialist literature.

Good novels are not written by the orthodox, nor by people who are conscience-stricken about their own orthodoxy. Good novels are written by people who are not frightened. As Aung San Suu Kyi said, "People are usually afraid, but I have no fear." Hence, this little woman, locked for over two years in Burma, is a real intellectual with strong moral courage.

Those with strong moral courage can make moral criticism, which may prove more revolutionary than some politics or the economic criticism that is fashionable at any given moment.

Whatever he or she stands for, the foremost should be cultural freedom, i.e., any man or woman must have the liberty to lead his or her own life, and have the right to decide his or her own destiny – with dignity.

There must be a place in the modern world for things which have no power associated with them, things which are not meant to advance someone's cause, nor to make someone's future, nor to assert someone's will over someone else. There must be room for beauty, for goodness, for spiritual development, as well as for trees, animals, paperweights, and fishing rods.

The intellectual's role is to help society to achieve this, i.e., he must articulate enough and have enough moral courage to speak out. If liberty means anything at all, it means the right to tell people what they do not want to hear.

By saying so, the intellectual may face grave consequences. He must pay for it, and society will not be any better while he is alive. But he will not be a failure, if the light of truth prevails even in the dark corners of the globe where there are believers.

With such a light, people's power will certainly dawn and it will be democratic in essence, not in form. The Chinese people, the Tibetan people, the Burmese people, etc. will certainly have a democratic future, while those who control them will sooner or later be doomed and disappear.

With this democratic essence, the people will develop their culture and society to be non-exploitative and peacefully co-existent. This certainly is not wishful thinking or a dream, but it will be a reality – otherwise human beings will not be able to maintain this global village meaningfully into the next century.

What the intellectual wants to envisage is that in the future we must be able to choose our political leaders from an unworldly type, without being saintly, unambitious without being inactive, warm-hearted without being sentimental. Through good and ill report, such men and women work on, following the light of truth as they see it, able to be sceptical without being paralysed, content to know what is knowable and to reserve judgement on what is not. The world must be driven by such men and women, if we want our culture, development, and democracy to be meaningful, for the spring of action lies deep in ignorance and madness. But it is they who are the beacon in a tempest; they are more, not less, needed than ever before.

Yet, even with these men and women in power, there must always be freedom of speech and system to counterbalance them for the posterity of mankind.

II. Reflections on the role of intellectuals

5

Technology and Dr. Faustus

Alexander King

I greatly welcome the choice of culture, development, and democracy as the substance of our essays in homage to Soedjatmoko. These topics were central to his concerns and I have often witnessed his brilliant exposition of the importance of the cultural features in development, changing the direction of international debates between people who had never before taken the cultural dimensions of world change into consideration.

But these three interwoven subjects are themselves in interaction with other aspects of world development. We of the Club of Rome have coined the term "the world problematic" to describe the massive and untidy mix of intertwining and interrelated difficulties and problems that form the predicament in which humanity finds itself. In our present case, the nexus of culture, development, and democracy is clearly influenced by demographic increase, political events, technological developments, environmental constraints, and many other elements which must necessarily impinge on our discussion. My background as a natural scientist encourages me to introduce some thoughts on the impact of science and technology on society into the argument, since these have had great influence on society for both good and evil, which I perceive as a sort of Faustian drama now being formed on the planetary stage; hence, the title of my paper.

As a consequence of my origins and conditioning, my approach must inevitably be somewhat Eurocentric, but I hope that this is tempered somewhat by world concern. I start with the assumption that we are in transition towards a global society, but not, I am sure, towards a unitary world government. We seem to be in the early stages of the formation of a new type of world society which will be as different from today's as was that ushered in by the Industrial Revolution from the society of the long agrarian period that preceded it.

The three environments of man

Following the publication of *The Limits to Growth* in 1972, a series of discussions took place in many countries on what was termed "the outer limits" of the environment, namely, the extent to which the exosphere is capable of supporting the growing demands of an ever-increasing world population with its needs for raw materials and energy as well as its accumulation of industrial and urban wastes. Subsequently, the concept of "inner limits" was evoked, the capacity of our social and political systems and their inventiveness to master the evolving situation of uncertainty that has invaded our economic and social structures. To these two zones which clearly demand continued exploration, I would plead for priority attention to be focused on the investigation of the "innermost limits" within each human individual, which are finally determinative of the collective human performance and the future of society and the planet.

It seems to me that each one of us humans exists simultaneously in three different but linked environments, and that a projection of this concept to the collective level can be used to describe the workings of society. There is, firstly, the external environment of the planet, the earth, the waters, and the atmosphere. At the other extreme is the internal, secret world within each individual, highly subjective, and of which we are only partially conscious. Somewhere between and connected with both is the social environment, the arena in which individuals interact with each other, forming a vast spectrum of alliances ranging from marriage and the family all the way through to the United Nations, involving common action for security, prosperity, and individual fulfilment.

To the external environment belong the environmental issues and the controversial but simplest question as to whether increasing economic growth – the wishful hope of nearly all governments – can continue indefinitely. These grave issues are beyond the scope of our present meeting and will not be pursued here. The inner environment of society, on the contrary, embraces all the relationship of culture, development, and democracy. However, the forces that mould society arise from the actions and attitudes of countless individuals and are determined by their value systems, aspirations, and motivations. In fact, the "innermost environment" can only be explained and explored in terms of human nature, its capacities, potentialities, and limitations, about which we know so little. It is my conviction that fundamental understanding of social forces and societal evolution cannot be achieved unless deep consideration is given to the play of individual motivations which underlie the life of society.

Yet these matters seem to be taboo by general unspoken consent. In international and national debates, economic or political, these matters are avoided, we are well aware of extreme forms of selfishness, which the media expose as scandals in the case of gross corruption, financial fraud, extortion, drug dealing, and the like. We understand well that much of politics, democratic and otherwise, is based on power struggles between individuals and parties. We realize that the patriotism of individuals within nations encourages chauvinism, expansionism leading to war and domination. Nevertheless, political dialogue takes place in terms of a spurious rationalism which refuses to recognize the irrationality and motivational struggle which underlies it. I feel, therefore, that it is necessary to say a few words about human motivation, before proceeding to the discussion of development.

The common enemy of humanity is man

It would seem that the cohesion of a society is assured, or at least reinforced, by the existence of a common enemy. How easy it was for France, Great Britain, and their allies to mobilize against their common Nazi enemy, with their citizens closing ranks and willing to endure hardships and mortal danger. How easy it was also, during the period of the cold war, for the capitalist countries to find cohesion in the face of the "communist menace" and for the Soviet Union to rally against "American imperialism." Again, freedom fighters, despite tribal and ideological differences, were able to find unity in the struggle against the common enemy, the colonial power. With the disappearance of the opposition of the two ideologies which have dominated the century, we find ourselves in a vacuum and are left only with crass materialism. The present fragmentation of the Soviet Union may well have resulted, at least in part, from the disappearance of their common enemy.

Can we then invent a world enemy to reinstate the lost cohesion of the nations? Some have suggested the complex of problems represented by earth warming, population explosion, water shortages, famine, and the like, in their totality and their interactions, constitute a common threat which necessitates a solidarity between all the people. But in designating them as the enemy we are dealing merely with symptoms, because all these dangers are caused by human intervention and it is only by changing human behaviour that they can be overcome. The real enemy is humanity itself.

What then, is the place of our behaviour within the contemporary *Weltanschauung*? Dennis Gabor, the Nobel laureate and inventor of holography, has remarked, "Our present civilization is based materially on an extraordinarily successful technology and spiritually on practically nothing." This is a trenchant indictment of Western culture. Both the workings of society and the being of the individual are seriously out of balance; the emotional, spiritual, and intellectual elements of our nature have been overwhelmed by the sheer weight of our physical triumphs. The establishment of a sane equilibrium, the formation of the whole man, and, hence, of the whole society can only come through a full awareness of our motivations, with honest recognition of both their positive and their negative aspects. The problems of individuals and society reside deep within human nature and, until this is fully appreciated, solutions to problems, the causes of which are dimly understood, will continue to be attacks on symptoms of diseases imprecisely diagnosed.

Egoism is a manifestation of the "life force" as it was called in the first flush of Darwinism, a property shared by all biological species, providing the primeval urge to survive; to reproduce, to prosper, and to excel. It is the driving force of innovation and progress. But it also manifests itself conspicuously in selfishness, greedy and antisocial behaviour, brutality, lust for power, however petty, exploitation, and dominance over others.

The struggle between the positive and the negative aspects of egoism is the eternal Faustian drama in which we all perform, the establishment of a dynamic equilibrium between the two sides is the central, but seldom admitted, objective in formulating social policy. Too much liberty given to the egoistic urge may well give rise to a dynamic society, but one with features of exploitation, brutality, lack of social justice, and discrimination. Egoism, too much controlled, leads to apathy and stagnation.

We are haunted by our biological inheritance. The negative aspects of human nature – such as greed, vanity, anger, fear, and hatred – are manifestations of the force of our egoism. Through the long process of organic evolution, they have served our species well in achieving dominance over all the other species of creation. And over weaker strains of *Homo sapiens* which have long since disappeared. Having reached our present state of consciousness, aware of our own mortality, and capable of looking into the future as the generational continuum of life, these negative futures are of much less use to us in the struggle upwards. But they persist and harass us and have to be allowed for in personal and collective behaviour. For centuries and perhaps millennia, simple people have been disciplined and their negative features held in check to some extent by fear of Hell and hope of Paradise, but with the widespread loss of faith in religion and, indeed, of political ideologies and institutions, restraints have dissipated and respect for the law has diminished, with mounting terrorism and crime. Our present generation feels an absence of a sense of self and knows not where to seek it.

These features, projected from the individual to the collective level, operate correspondingly in the social environment. National egoism is equally ambivalent; it can express itself as a natural and desirable love of country or ethnic community or it can be whipped up to chauvinism, xenophobia, racism, and finally to war. In international negotiations it often surfaces as advocacy of narrow self-interest against the wider harmony and well-being of a group of nations including its own and appears to sacrifice long term self-interest to score immediate tactical points.

These considerations are carefully avoided in public and private life, but if the arguments are at all valid the taboos should be lifted and a candid assessment of the negative and positive aspects of human behaviour made with regard to personal and collective decisions.

Concepts of development

Ideas of development are relatively new. Over the ages, the flow of life has been interrupted by the incursion of new concepts introduced by teachers such as Buddha, Jesus Christ, and Muhammad. Also, there have been innumerable wars, invasions, and the destruction of civilizations, often in the name of religion. Nevertheless, during long periods life has been seen as a continuity subject only to incremental change. In the West, this attitude was demolished by the enlightenment with its concept of progress, and reinforced by incursion of technology and industrialization, ushered in by the Industrial Revolution.

The years following the end of the Second World War saw a great upsurge of hope for the creation of a better world and, despite the debasement of the concept of progress by many intellectuals, development became a main theme, especially in relation to the needs of the poorer countries and those emerging from colonialism. This was largely conceived in the Euro-American mode. Development usually meant economic development or at times reluctantly as socio-economic development. Cultural and traditional aspects were seldom evoked. True, anthropologists were brought in to advise, but usually with the object of helping to find acceptance of the Western brand of development to traditional societies regarded as "backward."

During the successive development decades of the United Nations, aid to the poorer countries was delivered mainly in terms of the Anglo-Saxon perspective and based on the three following assumptions:

- Despite the failure of the rich countries to abolish poverty completely, the fact of their overall prosperity, unique in the history of the world and achieved through the systematic pursuit of a technology-based economic growth, has been taken to indicate that this is the unique and, hence, inevitable path to be followed by all countries.
- It is assumed that economic benefits "trickle down" from the rich to the poor; in the case of presently industrialized countries, decades of social reform have been necessary to ensure a reasonable distribution of wealth and many would say that now, two centuries after the beginning of the great generation of wealth created by the Industrial Revolution, the trickle down is far from complete; there are few signs that most third-world countries are being more successful.
- That technologies designed for a particular industrial, social, and cultural environment can be transferred smoothly and advantageously to quite different environments. It is taken for granted that sociocultural changes caused by the transfer of technology are self-evidently beneficial.

With the relative failure of the development decades of the United Nations and, as a consequence, search for new approaches, these assumptions are increasingly being questioned. For those near to subsistence level, economic improvement is the first necessity for the alleviation of hunger, poverty, and disease, but this is far from saying that the Northern pattern of economic growth is the most appropriate way to achieve it. Again, in stimulating the growth of the economy of societies with very different traditions and circumstances, the optimum path may be very different from that which has been followed by countries already highly industrialized. For example, demographic pressures combined with already very high rates of unemployment and underemployment may call, in many places, initially for agricultural improvement and the use of technologies which are inherently labour-intensive. These will usually come from local initiative, because technological innovation in the North is essentially directed toward increased labour productivity and, hence, means high per capita employment of capital. In the developing countries, capital is usually the scarcest of commodities.

Development in the third world, then, has aimed at achieving high rate of growth, necessitating the adoption of huge infrastructural and industrial projects involving high construction costs on the capital-intensive Northern model. It has also encouraged the building of huge modern cities quite out of touch with the rural communities. This approach has seriously neglected the well-being of the many poor, rural communities; it has benefited urban minorities at the expense of the masses of the poor. Furthermore, many of these large investments have failed to achieve their objectives. Policies which emulated those of the Northern industrialized countries have often clashed with local customs and structures and induced rejection from the very people they were supposed to help. This path to development resulted from the desire of leaders to achieve unrealistically rapid transformation of their economies and societies and has been supported and proposed by the international agencies and the North-South aid agencies. In Africa particularly, neglect to encourage and finance agricultural development in favour of industrial and infrastructural investment in the cities has resulted partly from the fear by insecure administrations of opposition and overthrow by urban mobs; it is very difficult for peasants dispersed over wide areas to organize rebellion. They, therefore, tend to be neglected by the central power. The result has been marginalization, famines, and deterioration of the land.

Such policies have resulted in a long series of projects which have plunged many countries into debt and financial disorder with too little benefit. Outstanding has been the construction of many large dams, of which Aswan on the Nile is a leading example, although many others can be cited throughout the developing world. There has been a catalogue of major and minor disasters; hundreds of thousands of people have been displaced without any previously prepared settlements to receive them; water-borne epidemic diseases have been disseminated; local environments have been destroyed, and all in all these large projects have caused unprecedented financial waste.

It must be admitted, nevertheless, that in some instances, particularly in the NICs (newly industrialized countries of Asia), the Northern, industrialized model has been successful. These are, however, somewhat exceptional cases. Some of them, such as Hong Kong and Singapore, were already important banking and trading centres, with accumulated capital, while Singapore, South Korea, and Taiwan were able to emulate the Japanese model and base their development on the basis of high educational standards and the building of sound science and technology infrastructures. Such conditions do not exist throughout most of the developing world, which greatly lacks a capacity for science and technology.

Existing development policies have led to many countries being crippled by large external debts. The payment of interest on these and the often huge sums spent on the import of arms constitute a considerable flow of wealth from the poor to the rich countries which has inhibited the development possibilities of the latter. It is also of prime importance that a way be found to correct the existing situation, in which commodity prices are fixed by the international markets, strongly to the advantage of industrialized countries.

These circumstances demand a rethinking of development strategies, more people-oriented and less exclusively economic. Much greater priority needs to be given to the needs of the marginalized and forgotten millions of the rural poor in all parts of the developing world. Such areas are off the economic map. Production and trade in the vast rural zones do not show up in the statistics. The traditional economic growth objective is meaningless in these circumstances; the immediate needs are for growing more food, improved health and hygiene, clean water, and the availability of basic education and training facilities, as well as a vast improvement in the situation of women and their role in the development process.

Assistance on rural development is not popular with the so-called donor countries. It is difficult to administer because of the need for funds to be widely dispersed in relatively small amounts. Successes are difficult to quantify and are less impressive to the donor country taxpayers than are large dams or steel works. Also they are unattractive to corrupt leaders on the lookout for plunder for repatriation to the banks of Europe.

In these circumstances, it is remarkable and encouraging that, throughout the developing world, groups of determined men and women have banded together and begun work for the improvement of the situation of the rural poor based on their own efforts. Assistance to this movement comes, in varying measure, from central governments, international agencies, domestic and foreign non-governmental organizations (NGOs). Large numbers of small development projects in agriculture, health, education, etc., have sprung up in the poorest parts of Latin America, Africa, and Asia, initiated by the Southern NGOs, independent bodies, farmers' groups, and village communities. A report, "The Barefoot Revolution" of the Club of Rome, estimated that in 1985 over 100 million farmers were already involved in development projects of this type. This approach is helping villagers to realize the precise nature of their problems and take responsibility for their own development.

Parallel initiatives with regard to the creation of home industries, handicraft enterprises, and small business firms in cities and urban outskirts are also spreading, giving rise to new production and hence new modest incomes.

Such movements demand high priority within the new development strategies; they need greater cohesion and, as they spread, to become incorporated within government policies to provide roads, markets, small hospitals, and schools to support them.

Rural development is, of course, only one element of development strategy. The concept of the "three worlds" – that of the advanced industrialized countries, the central economy countries, and the third world of the poor nations – is already obsolete, if indeed it has ever been valid. In the future, development of the poor countries will have to be seen as one element of global development and tackled possibly on the basis of various regions of the world, each of which may contain advanced industrial, semi-industrialized, and under-developed countries. With present attitudes, such a system would be too asymmetric to operate without forcing the poorer countries into the position of colonies. A prerequisite to success must be a recognition on the part of the industrial countries that massive help to their neighbours wisely given in partnership is a matter of their own self-interest. At present most of the citizens of the North regard aid given for development as charity and resist its increase to anywhere near the necessary level. At the same time, many in the South consider the aid they receive as guilt money in expiation of the "crimes" of the former colonial masters. Until both sides recognize that it is in their common interest to become partners, the present disparities will continue to grow. There is little public recognition in the North of its dependence on the South in terms of raw materials and other commodities, energy, debt servicing, arms sales, etc. For example, the European Union imports 70 per cent of its raw materials from the developing countries. But beyond all this, unless the North is willing to diminish its economic growth mania and tighten its belt in the interest of world harmony, the South in its desperation and bitterness and with its exploding populations will overwhelm it.

Science and technology – Culture and development

Culture has been defined as the total pattern of human behaviour and its products embodied in thought, speech, action, and artifacts. However we define it, it is impossible to exclude science and technology from culture. Science is an element of the intellectual component of culture, technology of the practical. While the two are distinct in method and function, they are intimately related. Technology in the past arose from empirical invention, but with the advancement of science its development now relies almost exclusively on the offerings of the research laboratories. Indeed, the economic growth drive now more and more dictates to science in the lines on which its search for new knowledge should be focused. There has long existed a dichotomy of opinion as to the relative value of material culture, i.e., technology, and of the intellectual and artistic culture, within which science belongs. The roots of this can be found in classical times when many of the Greek philosophers expressed their contempt for those whose pursuits were other than the intellectual. It can be argued that these attitudes, coupled with the ethical and aesthetic bias of Plato and Aristotle, were the reason why, despite the rich intellectual atmosphere of the Hellenic culture, science was crippled, and, indeed, science and technology were held back in the West for some 2,000 years until interest in them was reawakened by the Renaissance. Even then the dichotomy continued, Galileo being the father of modern science and Bacon, with his practical interests, of modern technology. Even in the nineteenth century we find Clark Maxwell, the famous physicist, decrying Graham Bell's invention of the telephone as merely a simple device using elementary principles. This élitist attitude to science still persists in the form of ivory towerism.

In the fundamental transition from *Homo erectus* to *Homo sapiens*, during the period from 50,000 to 30,000 years ago, the evolution of the brain was inextricably associated with the use of tools and fire. It may well be that the skills the hands and eyes of primitive man began to acquire with the onset of cultural life made demands on intelligence and hence encouraged the evolution of a larger brain. Thus, it can be argued that the first shaping of tools was a critical point in the biological evolution of man. This was the beginning of technology and the first case of technological advances influencing the nature of society. With the use of tools and weapons it became useful and necessary to introduce an important social mechanism, the division of labour. The men went hunting and the women gathered seeds and berries and cared for the young. Within this situation some clever woman discovered that plants could be propagated and domesticated. This, aided with the new tools, was the beginning of a settled agriculture which, over a period of perhaps several thousand years, spread throughout the world. The food gathering society began to change to become a food producing society. This led, in due course, to major social developments and eventually to tribal organization and eventually to the building of cities.

Relative security of food supplies, and later the technological innovations of bronze and still later of iron smelting, provided some leisure which allowed men and women to contemplate the mystery of existence, of the sun, the moon, and the stars; from this the primitive religions arose and men began to find means to exercise their imagination in painting, the telling of stories, the construction of buildings, and many other ways.

From the beginning of human history then, technology has been the main agent in the long struggle upward from subsistence and imprisonment within nature; it must be regarded as an essential instrument of man. From earliest time it could be used for good or evil; it richly feeds the Faustian attributes of humankind. The impact of innovations in military technology has been particularly important in providing superiority in battle to those tribes or nations that were the first to adopt them; replacement of the longbow by the crossbow, the use of gunpowder, the atomic and later the hydrogen bomb are examples. It must be admitted also that with some exceptions such as the alphabet, the printing press, and later forms of communication, technology has mainly enhanced the physical properties of man; the aeroplane gives us wings; the automobile provides our seven-league boots; the intercontinental ballistic missile is an extension of our arms, just as was the primitive club or spear. The tragedy of technology is that it has done so little to enrich aspects of human existence other than the directly material.

With every stage of technological advance there are criticisms that it is bringing about a deterioration in the quality of life. This is inevitable in that new inventions, however useful, are necessarily disturbing to the settled habits and traditions of people, the more significant the innovation the more disturbing. Each generation tends to look back nostalgically to the golden years of the past. This is no new phenomenon. Hesiod, writing in the eighth century BC, bemoans the deterioration of society, citing the terror brought by the new race of men with their implements and armour of shining brass, and hints the worse was still to come with the "dark iron," the latest technological material, "sleeping within the mines." This attitude still persists, perhaps with good reason, because of the inability of society to adjust and evolve to make the best human use of the enormously rapid development of technology. Furthermore, a nuclear holocaust or earth warming allowed to envelop too far in the service of technology could lead to the destruction of our material civilization or even the death of the planet.

It is clear that earlier technological changes had an important role in the moulding of societies, but it was not until the Industrial Revolution that the role of technology became visibly dominant. The use of energy, first by means of the steam engine, and later through oil, electricity, and nuclear energy, greatly augmented the puny muscular power of men and animals without, alas, increasing knowledge and wisdom to master their use. While the force of industrialization is still by no means exhausted after 200 years and may well spread further in the underdeveloped regions, we are already faced with a new and socially challenging wave of technology which is shaping the so-called information society. We are witnessing today, in the wide application of micro-electronics, the possibility of embodying both mind and memory in virtually any machine or equipment devised by man. This development, which is penetrating society very rapidly, has already changed the pattern of employment towards the service sector, is modifying education and training needs, and has a great potential for the liberation of humankind from the curse or maybe the blessings of work; at the same time it could be a further step towards dehumanization, depending once again on our wisdom in its use.

Parallel to this, we are experiencing radical developments in the new biology. Molecular biology, with the breaking of the genetic code and other discoveries, holds promise of many significant applications pertinent to the biological functioning of humans, other animals, and plants, many of which pose difficult ethical problems.

With the emergence of an ever more sophisticated technology, lifestyles and aspirations in the industrialized countries have gradually adapted so as to permit the enjoyment of what we perceive as material progress. This process has greatly increased the prosperity of a wide range of the citizens of such countries, reducing most of the grossest forms of poverty, improving health conditions, extending life expectancy, providing general if not always appropriate education, and introducing many social amenities. Recognition of the role of technology in world development is relatively recent. Does technology arise spontaneously from scientific research and stimulate growth or does high economic performance make possible the funding of research and development, leading to further growth? The economic system which relies heavily on technology in the solution of problems has not fully come to terms with it. It is still implicit in the thinking of many economists, that technological development arises in response to the interaction of economic forces and is, as it were, one of the muscles in Adam Smith's invisible hand. This is, no doubt, partly true; however, more and more technological opportunities arise from discoveries in the research laboratories, that cannot be foreseen. Hence, technology or at least the science on which it is based can be regarded as an autonomous force in creating new products and systems and, hence, new demands.

Some words should be added concerning the problems of science and technology in the development of the poor countries. Economic disparities are paralleled by scientific disparities. With the exception of a few countries such as India and Brazil, the scientific activities of developing countries are quite marginal. What is more, most of the scientific work which is undertaken is in pure research in the universities. As most of the industrial enterprises in such countries are too small to afford to do research, applied research and technological development are virtually absent. Absence of a scientific and technological infrastructure and suitable training facilities makes effective transfer of technologies from outside quite difficult. The establishment of an indigenous capacity for science and technology in such countries is a very complex affair which cannot be delved into in this paper. Help in the establishment of such a capacity is undoubtedly one of the most important developments to which the countries of the North could contribute.

The struggle of the cultures

We have already stressed the spiritual poverty of the exultantly triumphant industrial societies and this troubles many thoughtful people within these societies and has led to much questioning concerning the dominant role of technology and the use of science for negative ends. The success of science in determining the outcome of the Second World War, which produced penicillin and DDT, the computer, the jet engine, and the nuclear bomb, persuaded governments that scientific research leading to technological development could contribute decisively to the peacetime recovery in creating wealth and well-being. Hence, enormous increase in resources are given to such activities. This was the high period of euphoria for science and the scientists. Parallel with this and related to it, the 1950s and 1960s witnessed a period of exceedingly high economic growth in the industrialized countries.

By 1968 doubts had crept in. Unwanted side effects of these movements could no longer be ignored. Growth had certainly generated affluence and had aroused expectations of its endless increase, yet much poverty and inequality remained; the effects of environmental pollution became visible to all; the threat of nuclear annihilation hung above us as a sword of Damocles; the young could see no future and general affluence enabled them to demonstrate their frustrations and to rampage and riot; alienation diffused into society; millions of line workers were bored by uninteresting repetitive work, and all in all there was the sentiment that quality was lacking from life. Nevertheless, despite the triviality of the rewards of consumerism, the pressure of people for more money and more and more material goods persists within an economic system which is driven by the stimulation of consumer spending and credit availability. The luxuries of yesterday become the necessities of today; planned obsolescence speeds up the turnover of goods; the waste products of society accumulate and become more toxic as scientific sophistication diffuses into the everyday products of the material bonanza.

There is, of course, another side to the coin. Contemporary capitalism has moved far from its earlier, exploitative phase, influenced greatly by fear of the spread of Marxism. Considerable proportions of the wealth coming from economic growth have been diverted to the creation of social goods including national health schemes, unemployment benefits, education and training, as well as many welfare measures for the alleviation of poverty. Indeed, in a number of countries this development has been so strong as to evolve the so-called welfare state which has psychological costs as well as benefits. In some of the affluent countries of the North with low fertility rates, and hence with ageing population, the ever rising costs of health and welfare are approaching levels difficult to maintain. It is also felt by many that the welfare state approach encourages an over-reliance on the State by its citizens with an unhealthy decrease of individual responsibility and initiative. The paternalism of employers, so much resented in the past by workers and their trade unions, has been replaced by state paternalism, whose huge bureaucracies are now resented as being faceless, uncaring, and impersonal.

The great materialist culture is spreading throughout the planet, threatening to interpenetrate if not to submerge the multitude of rich cultures and traditions scattered over the world. How has this happened and how can we account for its success? My own view is that it originated with the Industrial Revolution. This had its beginning in Scotland and the English Midlands. Entrepreneurs were able to see the significance of James Watt's improvement of the steam engine, which not only led to the mechanization of manufacturing processes, but made it possible to pump water from mines dug to exploit conveniently located coal. This not only provided the energy to run the engines but also a seemingly inexhaustible source of reducing agent which transformed the metallurgical industries. Scottish Presbyterianism, with its feeling for the work ethic and worldly success, as well as the nonconformism in England, made the most of the propitious local conditions and the revolution succeeded. Emigration to America took the process a stage further. The vast resources of the new continent nourished the entrepreneurial spirit; huge fortunes were made and the mighty dollar became the idol of the United States and later most of the world. Returning to our discussion of human motivation, one could say that the success of the materialist society has been largely due to its appeal to individual selfishness.

The spread of materialism has been greatly assisted by the film and television. Images of a quite unrepresentative wealth and elegance have been brought to the eyes of the multitudes of the poor and underprivileged throughout the world for whom improvement of the physical basis of life is the primary necessity. Resentment is inevitable together with "we want some of this too." The appeal is especially great to local élites. Indeed, even the most rigid, traditional, and fundamentalist societies, while denouncing the corruption of Americanism, find it difficult to resist the promise of wealth, power, and influence which the materialist culture seems to offer.

At the same time there is a growing feeling, even in materialist societies, that a diversity of cultures must be maintained and stimulated if our children are to inherit a sane world. Indeed, it may well be that cultural diversity is as important for our future as generic diversity. Recent events seem to vindicate this. The disintegration of the Soviet Union into many diverse ethnic groups suggests that the unity of this extremely large and heterogeneous country could not continue under an alien political dogma once brutal enforcement was relinquished.

What about the future? Will the difficulties of the technically advanced world, with the environmental and other constraints which its excesses are generating, make it possible to change its ways and its self-interest to seek a new understanding with the rest of the world? And will the diverse cultures of the planet find the strength to resist the materialistic take-over from the North, while at the same time grow sufficiently to alleviate poverty and cross their various development thresholds? It may be that many of them may follow the example of Japan and acquire a sort of cultural schizophrenia, in which successful growth-based economy still permits the traditional culture, the writing of poems, the pride in calligraphy, ikebana, and all the other refinements of the past to continue.

Globality and ethnic autonomy

Our present period is witnessing an ever-increasing recognition of the interdependence of nations and, beyond that, what seem to be the birth pangs of a global society. Interdependence has long been recognized in the economic field. One has only to remember how quickly the Wall Street crash of the 1930s spread to become a world depression, or how mass unemployment tends to appear simultaneously in many countries and seems to resist the remedial measures of the individual countries. A more recent feature of the geopolitical scene is the recognition of an increasing number of issues which are essentially global in nature and cannot be usefully tackled by individual countries in isolation. These range from environmental problems to "law of the seas" negotiations and international financial and monetary problems.

The situation is clearly illustrated by the macro-problems of the environment such as acid rain, the depletion of the ozone layer, and earth warming, through the "greenhouse effect," resulting from the ever-increasing combustion of fossil fuels. These difficulties, unless tackled by the concerted action of all countries, could have an influence on the lives of every inhabitant of our planet.

There are, in addition, many other trends which favour the growth of interdependence. Most obvious is the evolution of huge industrial and trading blocs such as the European Union, the North American Free Trade area, and the cooperation among the countries of South-East Asia, ASEAN (Association of South-East Asian Nations). Furthermore, the immense expansion in communications and the activities of the transnational corporations link the nations and encourage uniformity. This is true also of the inexorable spread of technology which demands common standards, codes of agreed practice, agreed distribution of radio wavelengths, and a thousand other technical agreements which represent in their totality a spreading web of interdependence and a de facto erosion of national sovereignty, the extent of which is not yet fully recognized.

The very concept of sovereignty, proclaimed as sacrosanct by all governments, is being challenged not only by the emergence of regional communities. Many of the smaller countries have already a diminished control over their own affairs as a consequence of decisions taken outside their territories, such as the establishment of interest rates or commodity prices, or as a consequence of the need to modify their economic policies to obtain support from the International Monetary Fund.

A new concept of potential significance has emerged in the recent Gulf war, namely "the right to interfere" by strictly defined interventions in the internal affairs of a country – in this case Iraq. On a proposal which was supported by the allies, a humanitarian operation was mounted in favour of the Kurdish minority. Were this precedent followed, it would represent a considerable evolution in international law, which for once would be more a reflection of humanitarian considerations and for the general good than of constitutional rules and national self-centredness.

This brings us to an apparent paradox in world political trends. On the one hand, as we have seen, there is a strong trend toward the formation of larger economic units increasing understanding of the "spaceship earth" and the "planetary village" concepts and the need for concerted international action in the face of planetary problems. At the same time, there is a widespread public dislike of what is seen as excessive centralization and the dominance of large faceless bureaucracies which appear to be insensitive to the needs of individuals and local communities.

This situation is particularly acute where the dominance of a central bureaucracy appears to disregard the needs of various ethnic or cultural minorities and threatens their sense of identity. Thus, all over the world we see ethnic groups becoming vocal and active in their demands for autonomy and independence. In Europe, the Catalans and the Scots are asserting their nationhood with moderation, while the Irish, Basques, and Corsicans have resorted to terrorism. Yugoslavia, an uneasy federation of republics with complicated distribution of ethnic mixes, has descended to a particularly brutal and senseless civil war. Collapse of central authority in the Soviet Union and evaporation of the Marxist ideology which gave at least a semblance of communality is precipitating a complete fragmentation of this impossibly large country, with possibly very dangerous consequences. The Soviet Union sought cohesion through a sense of universality which Marx has inherited from the Enlightenment. When, after 70 years, the pressure of tyranny was released, all pretence of universality vanished and a confused kaleidoscope replaced it. Armenians, Georgians, Uzbeks, and the rest began resurrecting their buried pasts. The process of breakaway continues within the breakaway republics with their own ethnic minorities such as the Tartars and Ossetians clamouring for autonomy in their turn.

It seems that the human being has a deep need to belong to a family, a group, or a nation with which he or she can identify. To be human is to feel at home somewhere with others who share the same collective historical experience. This belonging brings cohesion to the group and induces loyalty to it. Without a sense of belonging, the individual slips into a state of alienation towards the milieu in which he lives. The materialist society generates alienation, as do human and geographical distance from the centre of power, as well as "modernity" and the encroachment of technology. In large modern cities, lacking a feeling for community, the individual is lured by advertising into finding a fragile loyalty to McDonald's, IBM, or the local football team. In fact, the transnational corporations offer a new but spurious brand of universality.

The situation of ethnic groups is especially difficult in sub-Saharan Africa. The new countries of that continent, formed on independence from their former colonial masters, are inherently artificial. The colonies were formed by agreements in the last century between the British, French, German, Portuguese, and Belgians, often by drawing straight lines on the map without any recognition of tribal boundaries. The recently independent African countries often consist, therefore, of uncomfortable groupings of tribes which are in reality nations. A country such as Chad is politically a state, but it is unlikely ever to become a nation. The matter is further complicated by the fact that important nation-tribes are often distributed over several states. This makes for their distribution between two or more of the new states. This accounts for much of the instability of Africa since independence, including wars such as those in Uganda and the Biafran war in Nigeria, which were in reality tribal wars. This precarious situation forces the leaders of Africa to do all in their power to enhance the sovereignty of their states to protect their fragile cohesion. Much of the real power in Africa seems to rest with the tribal leaders and the existence of dual power systems does not augur well for the future of the continent. It is unrealistic to hope that the boundaries of the many African states could be redrawn, however much readjustment could take place, if a number of regional regrouping of countries could take place towards the formation of economic communities with, perhaps, a more distant aim of federalism. This is in any case necessary, because many of the existing African states are too small to be viable.

These two seemingly opposed trends, towards a global society on the one hand and Balkanization on the other, are, in reality, compatible. The apparent conflict arises from the difficulty of reconciling them within the present political system which is rigidly set on the model of the nation state. What is needed is a fundamental reformulation of appropriate levels of decision-making to bring the points of decision as near as possible to those who enjoy or suffer the consequences. This, together with the shaping of more effective mechanisms, is necessary in the movement towards a global society – a rejection of universalism and centralized bureaucracy.

Degrees of democracy

We start with an assumption of principle that the legitimacy for those who govern is the consent of the governed and with a prejudice which is well expressed by Churchill's famous quip that democracy is the worst of all political systems – except for the others.

The number of countries that operate on a more or less real democracy is still rather small, but there is, as it were, a general consciousness that democracy is a prerequisite for legitimacy. The recent changes in Eastern Europe, caused by the failure of the centrally planned economy, have caused these countries to accept the need to adopt the market economy and, with it, to establish democracies. However, there has been many instances in the past in which high economic performance has been achieved without democracy, and today we need only mention the Republic of Korea or Pinochet's Chile.

The concept of democracy stems, of course, from the Hellenic culture, but was dormant until the Renaissance, with a few sporadic stirrings such as the Magna Carta and the parliament of the Icelandic Vikings. It was not until the eighteenth century that democracy became a political process and not merely an idea in Europe and North America. These stable and relatively successful democracies evolved quite slowly. Their stability and acceptance depended initially on a strict limitation of suffrage to numerically small groups of land-owning notables. In this they followed the Hellenic situation. In the Athens of Pericles there were only some 43,000 land-owning citizens in a population of 315,000. Throughout the nineteenth century in Europe, franchise was gradually extended to the middle classes, more or less parallel to the increase in educational standards. It was only in the early years of the present century that Britain achieved universal suffrage when it granted women the right to vote. This gradual process has much relevance, as we shall see later, to less developed countries with high illiteracy levels such as many of those in Africa and Latin America.

Democracy is spreading quickly throughout the world. It is desirable but is not a panacea. To be wise and effective, it demands a well-informed and involved citizenship. The necessity for deep consultation with the public tends to make it slow and uncertain in times of crisis; indeed the temptation is to suspend some of its freedom when the state is threatened. It is also open to overthrow by populist movements.

The striving towards a full democracy is thus a slow, difficult, and uncertain process. Democracy must evolve within a country; it cannot be thrust upon it. It is particularly important that this be realized at this time when a democratic consciousness is so widely spread and when so many countries, both in the ex-communist world and within the developing world, have started out on the road to its achievement. Examples of the imposition of democracy by introducing a series of radical measures for the restructuring of society are rare. More often, uncertain and divided societies have been drawn together in creating totalitarian regimes through the actions of remarkable leaders, either of the left or the right. Examples are Lenin in 1917 and Mustafa Kemal in 1922. Such leaders tend to hang on to and perpetuate themselves in power. However, for specific reasons they may be willing to make way for democratic change or prepare for it on their departure. An outstanding example was that of de Gaulle who, by assuming authoritarian power, replaced the floundering Fourth Republic of France, restructured the state, and allowed it to return to the democracy of the Fifth Republic. Even repressive leaders such as Franco in Spain and Pinochet in Chile, after a period of brutal repression, gradually adopted competent and rational although still authoritarian methods of administration which eventually produced conditions which permitted the introduction of democracy by their successors. It may well be that the shock of the sudden disruption of communist authoritarianism, together with acceptance of the democratic consciousness, will enable the East European countries to restructure radically and rapidly. But the transition is necessarily difficult psychologically as well as politically.

Introduction of democracy is extremely difficult for countries at a low economic-cultural level, where people are illiterate and live in poverty. In most cases, the countries are governed by autocratic and often military regimes; there is a very small middle class and a wide gap between the governed and the government. Often such regimes are broken by insurrection, incited by leaders who, affronted by the intolerable conditions of life of the ordinary people, may well have a genuine social concern. However, the populist regimes that take over are usually forced to introduce measures which are irrational in terms of the immediate economic realities and, as conditions deteriorate still further, are then removed by military coups. The military governments may well attempt to overcome the lack of legitimacy of their power by attempting to provide good government and better living conditions. Usually due to arbitrary behaviour and corruption, they themselves may be swept away by popular uprising and the result may be a long period of dialectic alternation, leading in some cases to a gradual improvement in the economic-cultural situation and a slow build-up of a political class with sufficient integrity and capability to introduce gradually a rational and democratic situation.

A few words have to be added concerning the limitations and difficulties of the democratic process in our present conditions of rapid change. Democracy as practised now is not fully suited to the tasks ahead. The complexity and technical nature of many of today's problems do not always allow the elected representatives of the people to make competent decisions at the right moment. Few politicians in office have a detailed awareness of the nature and linkage of the global problems. Informed discussion on the main economic, social, and political issues seems to take place more on radio and television than in the chambers of parliaments. Moreover, the party system is based on confrontation, and televised proceedings of parliamentary debate expose the absurd antics of the party confrontation to the public. The impression given is that more time is spent in the power game between the parties than serving the best needs of the nation, and this becomes ever more incomprehensible with the shrinking of the distinction between left and right. A consequence of this is a loss of interest in the formal political system, loss of confidence in individual politicians, apathy, and an ever-diminishing fraction of the electorate bothering to vote.

The crisis of the contemporary democratic system in the countries of the North must not be allowed to serve as an excuse for rejecting democracy as such. Rather it must be taken as an urgent warning that new and better methods must be sought, particularly towards consensus-seeking and opening the system so as to ensure access to expert advice.

The role of the intellectuals

In the above I have deliberately refrained from discussing how the intellectuals can assist in guiding the present world transition and helping to design a new global society. I have felt it best to leave this to other members of the panel and rather sketch some of the main trends as they relate to development, culture, and democracy. It is obvious that the rate of change in the world is so great that the need for new thinking and innovation in all fields is greater than ever before in human history. Science, in the wide sense of the word which equates it with knowledge, is also undergoing a change. New paradigms are appearing in most sciences, determinism is fading, multidisciplinary approaches both to solving problems and proving the frontiers of knowledge is gaining ground. We are looking at society in terms of systems, at bifurcations in evolutionary process, and concepts of self-organizing systems arising from chaos. The richness of the intellectual product in symbiosis with the wisdom of the past offers limitless possibilities which will eventually have a revolutionary impact on society and world governance – and will inevitably generate a new batch of problems!

One of the immediate issues is how the contributions of the intellectuals can best be brought to the points of decision-making. There are many difficulties. Firstly, intellectual perfectionism often prevents ideas from being brought forward at moments of critical decision. Then again, as is inevitable in intellectual debate, divergent views are often pressed enthusiastically, leading to complete confusion on the part of simple-minded politicians and others who make decisions mainly on intuition based on experience and who dislike advice, however rational, because it goes against their prejudices. Again, the very richness of studies and recommendations, and the number of reports which decision makers have no time to read, greatly slows up the absorption of new ideas and concepts. The functions of policy analysis, alternative scenario assessment, and advice to ministers and other decision makers are of obvious importance but as yet insufficiently developed. However, the basic benefits that intellectuals can contribute to society remain unchanged amidst the movement, complexity and uncertainty of the contemporary scene – the extension and transmutation of knowledge into understanding and, at times, wisdom. It is not normally their task to attempt to put their ideas into practice, but to act as the ferment of the brew, the catalyst of change.

Coda

In conclusion, I return to my initial theme. Science has penetrated global cultures and, through technology arising from scientific findings, has provided wealth and economic dominance to the materialistic cultures of Europe and North America and later Japan. However, even in these countries, there is a wide recognition of the positive and negative aspects of technology, its power to create material riches, and destruction as dramatized by the nuclear bomb. This duality reflects the two tendencies within the nature of every human being – the eternal drama of Dr. Faustus continues.

6

The changing role of intellectuals in Indonesian national development

Selo Soemardjan

As is common in the social sciences in the past and also today, it is not an easy matter to construct a definition of a concept in such a way that it can carry general agreement among social scientists and, at the same time, offers a correct clarification and delineation of the principles included in the concept. The same difficulty applies to the definition of the words intellectual and intelligentsia. As is usual in social science literature, every writer has his own way of coining the definition of a concept, in this case the concept of the intellectual. It is true, though, that the definitions create largely the same understanding of the subject, but with the emphasis on different aspects. But, nevertheless, the reader is left to determine for himself what to take of the various explanations of the word and then try to check in his mind the validity of the interpretation in the framework of his social and cultural environment.

For the sake of exactness, the present paper would like to take the Oxford Advanced Learner's Dictionary as a starting point. This dictionary defines the adjective "intellectual" as having or showing good reasoning power, while being interested in things of the mind, such as the arts and ideas for their own sake. It further determines that the concept of "intelligentsia" should be understood as that part of a community which can be regarded or which regards itself as intellectual and capable of serious independent thinking.

On the basis of these interpretations, the concept of "intellectuals" in the sense of those who are regarded or regard themselves as intellectuals should be taken as identical with the word "intelligentsia."

What distinguishes an intellectual in the present sense from a non-intellectual is not his ability to use his reasoning power, for every normal individual is endowed with that ability. It is rather his ability of independent thinking, as distinct from placating the opinion of others, which makes the intellectual stand out from the non-intellectual.

The concept of independent thinking in this respect includes careful observation of phenomena in the intellectual's environment, his understanding of the causes of those phenomena and their correlations with other phenomena, and ultimately the formulation of a conclusion which can be communicated to other individuals in clear language.

Whether the process of independent thinking is coloured by established belief systems or ingrained ideologies, and whether the outcome can be accepted as objective or subjective, does not affect an individual's quality as an intellectual. After all, every individual socialized in a living culture can hardly escape the power of that culture which shapes his world of feeling and thinking, or, in other words, which determines the network of values and norms that envelops his basic way of life.

Few people, if at all, can build up their capacities for independent thinking without systematic and purposeful training, generally obtained in formally organized educational institutions. Even there it requires a long, arduous, and disciplined process of learning and training before one arrives at a point where the mind can operate autonomously from the thinking of others. It should be mentioned here that not everybody enjoying the highest level of education can make such an accomplishment. In commenting on the role of university graduates who have joined village communities in a volunteer rural programme of development, a *Kompas* correspondent in 1946 remarked pointedly that the people in the rural areas do not need university graduates as much as they do intellectuals.

As pointedly as this article heading has expressed the felt needs of village communities for real intellectuals above the needs for individuals carrying university degrees only, to help in rural development, it should be admitted that in a society where higher education is not yet institutionalized, formal symbols stand in higher esteem than the actual qualities of an individual which those symbols are supposed to stand for. In this social situation, it is therefore understandable that formal regulations render a high rank to those carrying a university degree when entering government service without submitting them to any test or examination of their actual capabilities. It was also until recently a common attitude of university diploma owners to be satisfied with no less than a job with leadership requirements even if they do not have a single day of experience in real working life.

A student of the economic faculty of the Universitas Indonesia in Jakarta, involved in a discussion with business managers, was heard saying in complete honesty that before too long he would carry his doctorandus degree (equivalent to an M.A.) and that therefore nobody would then be able to fool him in matters of economics and business.

That student can hardly be blamed for bragging or consciously overestimating his knowledge and capacities, for large sectors of the population do believe that a university diploma is a guarantee of supremely trained intellect, and therefore supersedes all other faculties in society. In fact, it can even be said without exaggeration that a university degree in modern Indonesian social life functions in the same way as did the now desocialized aristocratic titles before the 1945 revolution for national independence and democracy. It gives the bearer a status of distinction, although not necessarily one of social usefulness.

The quality of this status symbol, however, is declining in the last two or three decades, particularly in large urban areas, although less so in the countryside. The rapid increase of university graduates, inadequately matched by an increase in employment possibilities, has created inflationary pressures which cause considerable damage to this university-generated symbol of social prestige. Sharp competition for jobs between them is forcing many of the less fortunate to accept employment below the level considered due to them by social stratification standards.

The position of intellectuals in relation to other social groups

Until 1945, when the people successfully started an armed rebellion against foreign colonial regimes, there were three different indigenous social groups which concurrently competed in the exercise of influence on the population in Indonesia. Neither of the three groups has been able to gain a position on, what now can be termed, a national level. Their sphere of influence was always local, limited in many instances by physical boundaries created by nature, but more often by the differences in culture between numerous ethnic groups.

A man, a group, or a dynasty, in power in a specific territory over a specific ethnic group, could not expect to be of much significance in an adjacent area but with a different ethnic group.

The oldest group, emerging since the dawn of Indonesian history, were the aristocrats, members of the extended royal family which, in the course of time, developed into an institutionalized dynasty. Such a power dynasty could be so firmly integrated in the local society that its roots penetrated deeply into the entire network of social institutions. The stratification system of the population, its system of values and norms, and its set of customs were organized in such a way that they accorded the most favourable position to the ruling dynasty. There used even to be a standard cultural belief system which proclaimed the monarch in power as an indispensable link between the world of human beings and the cosmological powers which rule the universe.

Modern democratic observers may find such a social system feudal and irrational, but as a reality it has socially and culturally survived all major political and other changes and, even in the present new order in Indonesia, one can observe its manifestations, of course in modified versions, all over the country. It is worth mentioning that this feudal aristocracy was through the policy of indirect rule kept by the Dutch colonial administration in controlled power to exercise the administration over the population.

The second group, generated after the introduction of Islam in Indonesian society, comprises the religious leaders. The overwhelming part of this group is made up by Islamic cadres, since more than 95 per cent of the population regards itself as Muslims. But where another religion is locally dominant, like Hinduism in Bali, and Christianity in a number of islands in East Nusa Tenggara, the priests or other recognized office holders enjoy an unchallenged confidence of the congregation.

Although these world religions have been superimposed on the previously existing native belief systems, the fact that through a long drawn process of mutual influence both factors became inextricably integrated, has made those religions an integral part of the culture. On this basis, the prestige and influence on the population of the respective religious leaders became institutionalized. The process of institutionalization is continuously reinforced among others through socialization in the family and by way of religious education and training in *langgar*, *madrasah*, *pondok*, and *pesantren* from the large urban centres to the most remote villages in Indonesia's sprawling archipelago. The strength of Islam and the power of its leaders over the population is convincingly evidenced by the failure of the Dutch after their efforts of more than three centuries to submit the province of Acheh, the country's stronghold of Islam, under its effective colonial regime. Other evidence is offered by the Darul Islam movements in West Java and South Sulawesi, which challenged the secular national government of Indonesia in favour of an Islamic state. This armed and political movement started in 1948, and only after 14 years of incessant political and military operations did the Indonesian government manage to capture its top leaders and suppress the religiously inspired insurgency.

Religion-based political parties, particularly those with exclusive Muslim membership, were strongly influential under President Sukarno's administration. With the introduction of the state philosophy, *Pancasila*, by President Suharto as the only legal basis for all political and social organizations, the religion-oriented political parties were dissolved. The Muslim parties retreated from the political to the social arena, where their influence is no less considerable.

The last group to come into being is that of intellectuals. This group developed largely as a product of formal secular education.

Starting in the first half of the seventeenth century, although this kind of education was introduced, under the Dutch colonial regime, with great hesitation and very sparingly among the population, it managed in some way to enhance the training in rational thinking. In Thailand, Malaysia, and other foreign-ruled colonies in South-East Asia, education was organized primarily to train indigenous young people for administrative functions below the policy-making level. In other words, it was the purpose of the colonial system to train them for clerks and other low-ranking office or field personnel who were only required to carry out orders and were not supposed to do any independent thinking. The haunting fear was, of course, that government-sponsored education would create a critical intellectual class which would endanger the ruling foreign regime.

In order to prevent this from happening, the Dutch designed a policy whereby popular education, primarily for the rural population and the lower class in urban settlements, was kept on a three- or five-year primary school level. A seven-year language of instruction was maintained in towns, but largely for the children of loyal government employees. The best of the graduates, whose parents were able to afford to pay the cost, could be admitted to junior and perhaps later on to senior high schools, which until the 1930s numbered fewer than 10 for a population of 60 million.

Senior high schools provided, for a very long time, the top-level type of education for Indonesians, since only in the 1920s was higher education inaugurated in the form of three separate colleges of engineering, medicine, and law.

Needless to say that where students were mostly selected from dependants of government employees and where in the near absence of an indigenous private middle class the Government was the largest, and under the existing system the most prestigious, employer, the most logical way for graduates to seek employment was to enter government service. Only a relatively small number of them, who for some reasons could not join the Government, remained in low-earning private employment. Enforced by colleagues with university training in the Netherlands, this group had more liberty than their associates in government service to develop nationalist political movements which ran counter to the Dutch colonial regime.

Summarizing the positions of the three groups at the time of the pre-war colonial dominance, we find the traditional aristocracy under the firm control of the Dutch. Being predominantly Christian, the Dutch were not effective in keeping the Islamic population in their administrative network. The group of educated intellectuals was partly kept in discipline as government employees, whereas the other part remained in critical attitudes outside the Government.

The group of intellectuals at the time of the Netherlands East Indies occupied diverse social roles in their relationships with the other groups and the colonial government. Their status and role at that time was to a large extent influenced by the social dichotomy between the ruling group and the non-ruling group. At the summit of the ruling group were the Dutch, the indigenous aristocracy, and the Dutch-speaking Indonesian intellectuals in the Government.

To be included in Dutch social circles was considered the ultimate of an Indonesian's social status. As a consequence, adequacy in mastering the Dutch language, the most important instrument for relationships with the Dutch, was a much-used yardstick for measuring an individual's position in social life. Since the language could only be learned in Dutch-controlled formal educational institutions, and since college education was considered of unequalled supremacy, it was only logical that people accorded the highest social esteem to college degree holders, particularly if the degrees were earned in the Netherlands. This esteem could only be matched by the aristocratic titles of the indigenous nobility, who understandably looked at the intellectuals as rivals in their search for social prestige.

Other intellectuals, also those who were in good command of the Dutch language, who did not occupy a position in the government bureaucracy, were placed in the next lower group, on account of their detachment with the ruling group and their distance from the Dutch, and eventually from aristocratic circles.

In this stratification system one can understand the low social status accorded to the million non-Dutch-speaking Indonesians, including the formally non-educated Muslims. Social interaction between the Dutch-speaking intellectuals and this group was friendly, but never intimate and with a minimum of mutual respect. The former were proud of their knowledge of and eventual orientation to Western cultures, whereas the latter could not help to feel socially and intellectually ill at ease, even if they maintained strong allegiance to their traditional or religious way of life.

It was from this non-intellectual group that the aristocracy enjoyed recognition as their social superiors within the same social structure and native culture. Relationships between the outstanding aristocratic personalities and religious leaders were usually imbued with mutual understanding, respect, and a spirit of cooperation. Unfortunately, however, there were many occasions whereby local aristocracies, favoured by the Dutch as their administrative intermediaries with the population, assumed positions more in compliance with Dutch policies rather than protecting the people in case of conflicting interests. These occasional attitudes were instrumental in creating the image among the people that the aristocracy everywhere functioned as loyal associates of the colonial regime.

In this respect, there was a better integrated system of relationships between the non-government intellectuals and the leaders of the religious group. Both occupied positions outside the administration, and for that reason they felt that they had a common platform for cooperation, especially on the political level. Being no part of the ruling group they both integrated themselves with the people to become popular leaders. The most outstanding political leaders at the time inevitably emerged from their ranks, much to the dismay of the Dutch colonial government. It seems that the Dutch were more afraid of anti-Dutch intellectuals rather than anti-Dutch Muslims, for more prominent intellectual leaders like Sukarno, Hatta, Ratulangie were exiled than were Islamic politicians.

The period of the Japanese military occupation

In March 1942 the Dutch surrendered to the Japanese armed forces and Indonesia was put under the Japanese occupational forces. There was no doubt that Japan, under the disguise of an East Asian Co-prosperity Sphere, wanted to settle in Indonesia as the new colonial master.

The aristocracy was kept in charge of local administration, but under strict Japanese control. However, in order to gain popular support for their war efforts, they secured the cooperation of both intellectual and Islamic leaders. Some sort of national leadership was put together comprising four members: three members were recruited from the most respected anti-Dutch intellectuals and one from the prominent leaders of the Islamic group. It should be mentioned in passing that the three intellectuals were all Muslims, but their political influence on the Indonesian people originated primarily from their being intellectuals, while their religious affiliation was only a supporting factor.

To organize the youth for military support the Japanese created an army called "The Defenders of the Fatherland," armed with only light weapons and trained in Japanese style by Japanese officers. The commanding officers of this hurriedly organized army were almost without exception Islam leaders.

When the Japanese announced that Indonesia would be made independent, and a committee was formed to make the necessary preparations, members of this committee were carefully selected exclusively from the intellectual and Islamic groups.

The prohibition of the Dutch language both in school and for use in the administration opened the opportunity for non-Dutch speaking intellectuals to rise in the government bureaucracy by learning Japanese. Through this language vehicle they hoped to come closer to the Japanese ruling class and thus secure a better social position which they had no hope of occupying under the Dutch regime. Unfortunately, the chance they had achieved did not last long. While the Japanese army command on the national level in the island of Java took every major effort to win the support of Indonesian influential intellectuals, the Japanese naval command in charge of the occupation of the island of Kalimantan seemed to maintain quite a different policy. Indonesians who were able to run away from that island could tell of the apparently systematic and persistent killings of local intellectuals by the Japanese military. The Japanese, most probably working under military orders, summoned their prospective victims from their homes or offices, to which they never returned. Among the victims were medical doctors, lawyers, engineers, and many prominent officers of the civil administration. It was not clear what motives drove the Japanese naval command to enforce such a policy, and so far no documented evidence can be produced on the number of victims, but rough estimates run into the hundreds all over the island. Considering the scarcity of educational facilities in Kalimantan, this purge of the local intellectuals deprived the people of potential modern leadership which they so badly needed for their development in the coming years.

Intellectuals in the post-independence period

When the Second World War came to an end in 1945 with the defeat of the Japanese armed forces, the Indonesian intellectuals were very quick in choosing the right moment for their popularly supported proclamation of national independence. So the Republic of Indonesia was born.

What then followed in the way of building a new nation, organizing a national government, and at the same time defending the proclaimed independence against powerful armed and political attacks by foreign colonial forces, was of truly gigantic dimensions. The entire population of 80 million was mobilized and moved under the leadership of a small number of anti-Dutch intellectual and religious political leaders.

The group of aristocrats in almost all levels of the population were politically, and on a number of occasions also physically, swept away in the upsurge of democracy that accompanied the revolution of independence. So far, they never had the chance to re-emerge and it seems most unlikely that such a chance will ever come again in the near future.

This left the group of intellectuals and Muslims with the tremendous task of creating substance to the national revolution. The religious leaders, with their institutionalized role as solidarity makers, supplied all their authority and experience to keep the masses organized as their followers. Specific aspects of the religious teachings were used to keep the revolutionary spirit burning and channel the movement into active participation in the revolution.

The group of intellectuals was faced with the multiple task of organizing the entire state bureaucracy and educating the people in the basic principles of theoretical and operational democracy. The intellectuals, being an active and selective part of the Western-educated section of the population, were widely expected to play the role of modernizing agents in the changing society.

It was a mission silently assigned to them by the people as a logical consequence of the revolution which had quickly reached the point of no return.

A constitution, drawn up by the preparatory committee for national independence during the last weeks before the collapse of the Japanese war machine, was announced and, perhaps for lack of other competing concepts, unconditionally accepted by every individual in the country as the basic infrastructural institution in the ensuing process of building the new Indonesian nation. Strangely enough, this constitution, which is now popularly referred to as the 1945 Constitution, and which preamble includes the Pancasila, or five basic principles of the state, has gained, in the course of time, a sacred recognition by the people, far beyond the intentions of its original framers.

It was conceived in a tumultuous situation of war and under incalculable pressures of time. Therefore, and to the best of Western democratic legal theories, a provision was made in the body of the constitution itself which opens the way for making amendments and additions. Once, in 1950, this constitution, which calls for a unitary Republic of Indonesia, was set aside and replaced by an intellectually more correct institution of a federal structure of the republic. The people in their spontaneous actions refused to accept the federal republic and its constitution, both considered as a result of some Dutch-sponsored conspiracy to re-establish colonial power in the country. Eight months after its inception, the federal republic was dissolved, its constitution abandoned, and the original unitary republic was reinstalled with the re-acceptance of the 1945 constitution and its inherent Pancasila.

Since then, 12 armed uprisings rocked the country, some of them originating from Islamic parts of the population and demanding the transformation of the Pancasila republic into an Islamic state. Communist-sponsored rebellions, the most serious being those of 1948 and 1965, violently attempted to mould Indonesia into a "democratic republic" or a "people's republic." But the country's intellectual leaders were able to warn the people against the anti-1945 constitution and anti-Pancasila nature of the insurgencies. After this was successfully done, the national government had a firm political platform to destroy the insurgent movements with the strength of the armed forces.

The proven effectiveness of the 1945 constitution and Pancasila to help the country over so many political military crises has lent to both institutions a sacred nature which resists any attempt, legal or illegal, of amendment, addition, and let alone replacement. In fact, the two concepts have now been made, as President Suharto has repeatedly enforced, the unalterable cornerstone of the anti-communist and development-oriented new order in his policies.

In their efforts to design a political system suitable to an independent Indonesia, the intellectuals in the 1950s and early 1960s, guided by agile President Sukarno, split themselves into two broad factions, the nationalists and the communists, which together with the religion-oriented group formed what was then known as *Nasakom* (nationalism, religion, and communism).

President Sukarno, a master orator and politician, who in 1959 successfully seized all powers of state by dissolving the conflict-ridden constitutional assembly and parliament, decided that the best pattern of political education and reconstruction was the mobilization system, by which the whole population was expected to rally around him as President for Life and the Great Leader of the Revolution.

The intellectuals, being part of the population, were also expected to render full "support without reservation" to the leader.

In this respect, many academics at the universities, particularly at Universitas Indonesia in Jakarta, who were trained to do independent and critical thinking, underwent severe pressures from the president and communist-influenced political groups. In his speeches for mass rallies President Sukarno ridiculed them as bald-headed nonpolitical individuals and textbook-thinking teachers. The politically passive attitude of the academics at that time was even called by the communist group "intellectual prostitution," which did not deserve a place in the revolution.

The mobilization system at that time called for the highest priority for political education in the national development. It was determined by the national leadership that what the country needed most of all was nation- and character-building. For the attainment of this overriding objective, loyal politicians were given stronger preference over educated and trained intellectuals. When the President in 1960 decided to have a national development plan drafted, he recruited representatives of the Nasakom group and functional groups to form a national development council, but no experts in any academic discipline were called to render their services, not even as staff members or consultants. There were, of course, among the council members, those who were experts in specific fields, but they were selected on the basis of their political affiliations rather than for their expertise.

Typical of the social atmosphere in those days was the great significance accorded to the physical aspects of the planning product which covered 17 sectors of the development, comprising eight volumes containing 1,945 paragraphs. The figures 17, 8, and 1945 symbolized the proclamation of national independence on 17 August 1945. The plan failed to reach even initial programming because of its overambitious objectives and inconsistencies with the economic and social realities in the country.

The succession of President Sukarno by General Suharto marked a radical change in the state policies which guided the development of the nation. It also pushed the educated intellectuals from the dark corners of the past to the limelight of development in all procedural aspects from data collecting, planning, programming, implementation, and evaluation. The focus of national development was shifted almost overnight from the political to the economic.

Communism was banned and the communist party dissolved as a result of an unsuccessfully attempted *coup d'état*. Other political parties were reduced in number and their activities diminished to make way for political and social stability. National ambitions, previously elevated to make Indonesia a towering lighthouse in the political development of all nations in the world, were scaled down to realities and operational feasibilities. An era of rationalism and realism set in to replace a long period of romantic idealism.

The armed forces came into power to save the country from falling into the hands of the communists and further economic deterioration. Perhaps because of the fact that President Suharto and many of his close associates come from a Javanese ethnic group where the culture is known to show strong humanitarian overtones, the regime of the armed forces presents itself in only mildly military concepts in the administration, although an irreconcilable attitude is retained against the communists in the country.

The military, by its own nature harbouring a high value on organization and discipline on the basis of a rational and realistic way of thinking, quickly realized that for the further development of the country, a well conceived plan was needed that would reflect the true need of the country on the one hand, and on the other hand could effectively make the best use of available resources both on the domestic and international levels. For this purpose, it was recognized that the services of the intellectuals in the country were indispensable.

A development planning agency, *Bappenas*, was organized, manned exclusively by professors and other university graduates, and working with consultants from international development organizations. Fifteen out of the 22 members of the first Suharto cabinet, excluding the president and vice-president, were technocrats, professors who for a large part were still active at their universities. In addition, the policy-making management of each ministry, particularly those concerned with economic affairs, was entrusted to other university-affiliated intellectuals.

To prepare the first and second five-year plan, 1969–1973 and 1974–1978, frequent and intensive bull sessions were held by selected intellectuals on various subjects of development. Participants in these sessions came from both government and private circles, and the views they expressed were highly valuable as building stones in development planning.

Universities and other research institutions were widely utilized to do surveys and research to supply reliable data and systematic analysis thereof. Each ministry is now equipped with a department of research and development, run by intellectuals with appropriate training. Wherever local expertise falls short, foreign experts are called in to help, but decisions are made by Indonesians themselves.

To help governors in drafting provincial development plans, an instruction was sent by the national government to governors and university rectors in the region to organize close cooperation in that endeavour.

In the present system of administration there is no parliamentary approval required for a national development plan, neither is there a provincial plan to be submitted to the regional representative councils for debate and decision. The signature of the president, or that of the governor in the regions, is all that is needed for a development plan to start operating. There are, in fact, two occasions which can be used by the elected representatives of the people to exercise some influence on development planning. The first occasion is in the five-yearly session of the People's Assembly – the nation's supreme power assembly – where the broad outlines of the republic's policies for the next five years are determined. In this respect, it should be known that many intellectuals, employed or not employed by the Government, have been instrumental in drawing up the draft outlines.

The second occasion is the debates on the annual budget in parliament, which includes, of course, debates on the development budget for the forthcoming year. So far, however, no major changes have been made either by the people's assembly or by parliament in the draft policy outlines and the annual budgets.

This system of state development planning has been continued until today and is very likely to be applied in many more development periods in the foreseeable future.

Not only publicly financed development, but the private economic sector makes also extensive use of Indonesian intellectuals, perhaps more successfully because of the considerably higher wages they can pay than the Government.

The demand for intellectuals to work in private business has steeply increased since the influx of foreign capital investments following the foreign investment law of 1967, which was in fact an open invitation with facilities and guarantees for foreign capital to enter the country.

There seems at present to be a strong desire for further economic and social progress among large parts of the population in Indonesia, so that people can hardly tolerate any event which hampers the process of development.

In this respect there is a tendency to overexpect the intellectuals, especially in the academics, to solve all development problems. The commander of the second defence territory, on the occasion of the twelfth anniversary of the Purwokerto University in Central Java, said that if social scientists could fully work like a medical doctor through examination of the patient, followed by diagnosis and therapy, then society could be saved from unnecessary suffering, pressures, and destruction. The commander, however, forgets that the role of social scientists is limited to the study and analysis of society and social problems, and they have no authority themselves to take actual measures which would intentionally affect the course of development. Such measures require political decisions, which can only be taken by top executives in either public or business administration.

But whatever their arguments, intellectuals in less developed countries cannot ignore the mission assigned to them by society to utilize their trained intellect for the development of the country and the people.

The role of intellectuals in various stages of cultural development

There is, in the culture of the Javanese people on the island of Java, a concept of social leadership that provides a system of adaptation in the changing relationship between leader and society. This concept has spread all over Indonesia and is accepted in almost all ethnic groups in the country. In the Javanese language, it says:

Ing ngarso sung tulada
Ing madya ambangun karsa
Tut wuri handayani.

Liberally translated, it means:

Front leaders, give an example
Central leaders, build up a social will
Rear leaders, watch the people (for social disruptions).

To grasp the significance of this leadership concept in Indonesian society and, at the same time, find the role of intellectuals in their specific cultural environment, one should be aware of the cultural diversity of the society.

The Indonesian nation, scattered on 17,000 small and large tropical islands, comprises more than 400 different ethnic groups. Each group has its own indigenous culture with a language, *adat* (tradition), mores, and values different from those of other ethnic groups. Many ethnic groups live as tribes and clans in isolation, physically and culturally, in almost impenetrable jungles and swamps, or on small islands in the wide ocean. They have lived there for many centuries, devoid of regular contacts with other communities. Their culture is ages behind those of other more open ones. Here, adat that rules supremely in both public and family life is perpetuated by all members of the community.

Democracy is exercised in public life in its peculiar form: from the tribal elders, by the people, and for the people. Since a tribe or a clan is relatively limited in its numerical membership, hence informal intercommunications take place every day among families. The elders of the community are always well informed of the problems and needs of the people. Individual needs and interests are socially subordinated to communal ones. In this way, opinions and suggestions which are present in the meetings of the elders can have no other qualification than those of the people, who are undiversified in their social structure. Decisions from the elders, if they concern the interest of the community, have to be carried out by the people collectively and without any doubt for the people's benefit.

In discussing problems of the people, the elders, including the tribal chief, have to follow the rules and values of adat, which are known to everybody in the community. In most cases, problems are presented *post facto* to the council of elders, who are expected to find solutions and restore peace for the social unrest or tensions which arose out of the problems.

On account of the fact that the elders act after problems emerged, they can be categorized as rear leaders, who watch their community to restore peace and tranquility among the people.

The intellectuals, if any, have no role in such a small and adat-oriented community. All that is needed in the management of the community is to apply the fixed adat rules to bring disrupted social situations back to normal.

Moving away from the isolated tribes and clans, one finds village and small town communities, where adat still functions as the basis of the communities' culture, but where information from outside sources also seeps into the culture through formal education, government channels, mass media, and physical contacts through trips and travels to, as well as from, other communities. Shortages of electric power to operate radio and television receivers and underdeveloped reading habits, combined with limited household funds, severely curtail the introduction of written mass communication. These shortages soften the impact of the modern flow of information from other and presumably more advanced culture and have a confusing effect on village and small-town communities. This effect is in its strength conversely related to the age brackets of the population. The older generation generally takes a conservative attitude in their evaluation of news from outside. The younger generation, however, tends to be more receptive to everything novel, including new styles of behaviour, dress, music, and inexpensive consumer commodities.

This intergenerational divergence slowly, at times also rapidly, generates an uneasy feeling in the relationships between the old and the young. But both are on the receiving end of cultural penetration. What comes to them, however, is information only. However great the influence of the incessant flow of information is on the people, it affects only their mind, but very seldom generates constructive action. To arrive at this stage of information contribution, the people need the services of the intellectuals to develop a social will.

Local intellectuals, recognized by others as members of their community, are called upon to identify the social processes emanating from the information flowing into the community. They are expected to explain to the people, through the existing local information channels, the significance of the incoming information and the advantages the people may be able to gain from it, as well as the possible disadvantages that may confront the community. To lead the people towards some action, either for the acceptance or rejection of information effects, a social will has to be formed. This is the mission of the central leader, who in most cases is an intellectual. Non-intellectuals, however great their power in a community, will hardly be able to predict the ramifications of new social facts, determine in a rational way their interfactual correlations, and ultimately arrive at objective conclusions. They may be able, in their own way, to arrive at conclusions, but these may not be objective and therefore contain a certain degree of bias. Such a biased conclusion, especially if it is deceptive, has its dangers if used as a basis of action for the benefit of the people. Conclusions must be objective if they are to be used as a starting point for action. Whether the action will be launched for the benefit of all, or of a group, or of an individual, is another matter beyond the responsibility of the intellectuals who made up the conclusions. Decisions for action are either politically, economically, or socially subjective.

In a tradition or adat-oriented community, decisions for action may be made by the elders collectively. But in many instances guidance leading towards a decision is accepted from the *panutan*, who is the *primus inter pares* among the elders. The panutan is the most respected person in the community because of his cultural and moral integrity. He is, in sociological language, the informal charismatic social leader, whose words, attitudes, and behaviour are taken by the community as a guidance for their lives.

When the decision has been arrived at to enter into action, the moment has come for the front leader to give his examples. A community, or for that matter a society or a nation, which has decided to get into action as a response to social stimuli, shows a social will to determine its own destiny, however small the scale covered by a particular decision. If that decision is not to confirm a lifestyle of the past, but is meant to shape a new style, a breakthrough has been made which opens the road to the future.

The more social decisions are made which affect life in the future, the more diversified the community's lifestyle becomes, and more specialized knowledge in developing parts of life is needed. Specialization is the field in which intellectuals have the greatest potential to excel. Where development takes place, the role of the intellectuals is enhanced. They are charged to understand with reliable objectivity the situation of the present. They are expected to know the real forces which can change that situation for the better. Finally, they are obliged to make plans for the future even if that future is only of an immediate nature.

The mission for development cannot be carried out by wishful thinking only. It needs the disciplined way of reasoning of the trained mind and the ability to accept realities in its natural, social, and cultural environment.

This has been convincingly proven by the failure of the 1960 development council of wishful thinkers as compared with the success of the Bappenas with its full staff of university graduates as planners.

The Bappenas intellectuals stand as economic and social planners ahead of national development. As front-line leaders they were expected to give examples to the people of how to develop the country and the nation. The way they lived up to popular expectation was not only by hard and honest work, but also by institution building. New social institutions were built for the implementation of the development plans like provincial development planning offices, research and development bureaux in government departments, rural banks, and Indonesian-foreign joint ventures.

In a modern culture which gives high priority to development in general, it is not the social quality of the individual which makes him accepted as a leader, but people are more prone to accept intellectual expertise and social achievements as leading principles to guide them towards the future. In a modern society no leader can survive without achievements.

Summary

Intellectuals, as referred to in this paper, distinguish themselves from others in a society by their ability and consistency to reason rationally and realistically, independent from the ways most people think. In that way they may deviate from general opinions, but at the same time they may create new ideas which help others look at things differently. This creative thinking, if accepted by society at large, paves the way for social development.

The role of the intellectuals in a society, like that of any other group, cannot escape the influence of dominating social forces and culture in general. The short history of the Republic of Indonesia, which came into being through a proclamation of independence on 17 August 1945, suggests that in a newly developing country Western democracy may be nominally accepted by the people, but it is in fact the ruling élite which determines how that democracy should be actualized. This role of the ruling élite determines in large measure the effective role of the intellectuals in society. And since in such a country non-governmental social and political forces are generally too weak and not well organized, there is not much chance for intellectuals to come forward if they are not accepted by the ruling élite.

Indonesia under President Sukarno exercised, after its successful revolution of independence, a liberal parliamentary democracy. But because of the people's inexperience in matters of borrowed Western democracy, national politics was filled with never-ending interparty conflicts until the president inaugurated Guided Democracy with nationalism, religion, and communism as its principal components. In this threesome combination, the communist party cleverly propelled itself into a leading position in alliance with Sukarno as the Great Leader of the Revolution.

Intellectuals who did not agree with this political development had no way of playing a public role. In spite of the formal democracy in the country, only those intellectuals who were in support of the ruling élite could make themselves known to the people.

Another reason why at that time only intellectuals of the ruling group could play a social role was the fact that national development was almost exclusively focused on the political level. Consequently the accepted ideology bearers were more in demand, rather than intellectuals with a critical attitude.

In 1965, the communists who tried to launch a *coup d'état* were defeated by the national army led by General Suharto. The military came into power and Suharto succeeded Sukarno as president of the country. The Guided Democracy was replaced by a New Order Democracy which was aimed at political and social stability as a prerequisite for an overall national development with emphasis on the growth of a market economy. Ideology bearers were by law required to accept the constitutionally determined state philosophy of Pancasila as the sole basis for their political and social organizations.

The intellectuals all over the country, and particularly those of Universitas Indonesia in Jakarta, were mobilized for development planning and implementation. This active role of intellectuals has been maintained since the inception of the first five-year development plan of 1969–1974 until today.

This experience in Indonesia gives ground to a conclusion that democracy should give equal chances to everyone, including intellectuals, to play a role in society. But in real life it is only the dominating ruling group which determines the social roles its citizens can play. Intellectuals are not excluded from the influence of the dominating force.

With regard to culture, there is in Indonesia a multiplicity in stages of development existing side by side until today. There are the isolated jungle tribes who still live by hunting and food gathering. On the next stage of cultural development are the millions of small farmers. The third stage includes the communities in modern cities with an electronic way of life and a searching eye on a better future.

Every community has its particular group of social leaders in accordance with the specific stage of their cultural development. The Javanese has a cultural typology of leadership which says: Front leaders, give an example. Central leaders, develop a social will. Rear leaders, watch the community (for social disruptions).

Primitive jungle tribes, living almost entirely in the hold of adat, honour rear leaders. There is no place for rational intellectuals.

Small farmer communities, primarily adhering to adat, but feeling the impact of modern life from other communities, still hold their rear adat leaders in high esteem, but at the same time accept the role of village intellectuals to guide them in their encounter with modernity.

Modern urban communities, living in an atmosphere of modern technology and with a mind towards a better future, are highly appreciative of the role of intellectuals as social modernizers.

In sociological terms, the leadership patterns in the various stages of cultural development show a corresponding change from an ascribed leader status of adat elders in a primitive culture to an achieved leader status of intellectuals in modern urban communities.

Bibliography

Anderson, Benedict. "Reflection of the Origin and Spread of Nationalism." *Imagined Communities*. Revised edn. London, New York: Verco, 1991.

Benedict, R., Anderson, O.G. "Explaining Political Cultures in Indonesia." *Language and Power*. Ithaca and London: Cornell University Press, 1990.

Fals-Borda, Orlando (ed.). *The Challenge of Social Change*.

Geertz, Clifford. *The Interpretation of Cultures*. Basis Books, a Division of Harper Collins, 1973.

Gorbachev, Mikhail S. *The Coming Century of Peace*. New York: Richardson and Steirman, 1986.

Haferkampf, Hans (ed.). "A Collection of Gorbachev's speeches before the abortive coup." *Social Structure and Culture*. Berlin–New York: Walter de Greyter, 1989.

Johnson, Paul. "The Private Lives of Jean-Jacques Rousseau, Shelley, Karl Marx, Henrik Ibsen, Tolstoy, Ernest Hemingway, Bertold Brecht, Bertrand Russell, Jean-Paul Sartre, Edmund Wilson, Victor Collanez, Letion Hellman." *Intellectuals*. New York: Harper and Row, 1988.

Kisenstadt, S.N. "Cultural Traditions, Power Relations and Modes of Change." *Socialist and Sage Studies in International Anti-capitalist Sociology* 32, 1985.

Wilhelm, Donald. *Global Communications and Political Power*. New Brunswick (USA) and London (UK): Transaction Publishers, 1990.

7

Culture, development, democracy: In the eyes of the little people

F. Sionil José

Whenever academics and writers from the South gather, I am somehow saddened because I know that among us there is a lot of goodwill, that we are all for justice and democracy. But somehow, our ideas and ideals never seem to influence the power structures of our societies.

I looked around me in my own country, for instance, at a president who boasts of having restored democracy in February 1986 – in what they call the EDSA revolution – but I know only too well that it was not a revolution. It was a restoration of the oligarchy which Marcos had emasculated.

I cannot but be nostalgic about that event; for three glorious days, the masses, the *hoi polloi*, the great unwashed – the common people – were there, in equality with the middle class and the radical chic from the elegant Makati housing areas.

I know these people, not only because I came from their ranks but because, although I am comfortable now, I have never left them or betrayed them. There was real democracy in EDSA – it was heady, it was real, but it died soon after, for there was no transfer of power from the oligarchy to the people.

In saying this, I am explicitly questioning the relevance of so-called democratic institutions like free elections, freedom of the press, speech, and thought, when the larger masses of our people have no recourse to justice.

It should come as no surprise then why we are witnessing in the Philippines today, a secessionist rebellion on one hand, and, on the other, peasant unrest and rebellion that are a continuum from the days of the Spanish conquest.

But, at the same time, I ask why a revolution has succeeded. Who will come to the succour of our people? Is there another Ramon Magsaysay on the horizon? Or will it be a man atop a tank?

The Philippines was comparatively better off than all South-East Asian countries in the 1950s and 1960s, and was certainly ahead of Taiwan and Korea at the time. Why are we now left far behind?

One can easily blame Marcos for our plight; he had, after all, plundered the country for 20 years. Or because we are prisoners of a feudal agrarian culture, or that we are not serious enough given as we are to fiestas. These are reasons real enough but too simple.

Philippine conditions – The role of the intellectual

I will now define Philippine conditions, the reasons for our poverty, and the culture which this poverty has spawned. I will also try to define the role of the artist, the intellectual in such a society. I will be doing a lot of wishful thinking in doing this, for in the Philippines our creative people – the writers and the artists and those involved in what we loosely term the humanities – shun politics. If they don't, they do not always make good administrators. They cannot seem capable of truly leaving the sanitized world of the mind for the harsh everyday world.

If other Asian countries have a shame culture, we Filipinos have a blame culture. We have a tendency to blame everyone except ourselves.

There is a lot of truth, however, in our belief that we are poor because we are victims of the imperial order. This old bogey is still very real, not only in the dominance of multinational corporations and foreign banks in our commerce, but also in the US military presence. Even in terms of education, Filipinos, myself included, continue to send their children to the United States for higher learning. When they return, they are often conditioned by American methods which do not always conform with native resources and aspirations.

On the economic level, the logic of trade persists, and this logic, in its simplicity, means that the strong take advantage of the weak. Thus, if a country is strong, it expands, and if it is weak, it contracts. A country with a booming economy looks for raw materials, and one with a weak economy looks for markets.

This is the history of empires, and this logic dominates our relationship not only with the United States but also with Japan. Ideology makes exploitation more palatable, particularly if the colony swallows it, and this ideology can be Christianity, socialism, or even democracy.

Even after the imperialist has departed or dismantled his instruments of direct control, his influence and the ties that bind remain in the attitudes of the native élite, which owes its existence to alliances with the former overlords.

Now, the native élite wants the whole cake. Conditioned by the values of the imperial order, the native élite now masks its objectives with such slogans as building a new society for restoring democracy to draw the masses together, thereby giving itself legitimacy. It may even pay lip-service to such socialist methods as central planning, and when this happens we should remember the old saying, "Planning at the top is planning for the top."

Indeed, if a finger need to be pointed at all, it should be pointed at this native élite – the 400 or so families comprising the Filipino oligarchy – for they have plundered the country. As Salvador de Madariaga said, "A country need not be the colony of a foreign power; it can easily be the colony of its own leaders."

Culture of Philippine society

What is the culture of this society which we want to develop? How do the little people think? How do they live? How can we help them to help themselves?

Let me describe briefly the life in the village where I came from. The first truth about my village, of course, is its poverty. Even in Manila, malnutrition is evident in emaciated bodies, dirty skins, glazed eyes.

The other fact is ethnicity. In my village, we were all Ilokanos who prided ourselves in our thrift and industry. We looked with condescension at the Pangasinans in the other towns, for we regarded them as lazy and incapable of putting order in their homes.

Beyond the village, the society continues to be tribal. In recent times, Ilokanos and Leyteños were the favoured ethnic groups because President Marcos was Ilokano and his wife is from Leyte. At other times, when the President was Pampango, Boholano, or Cebuano, it was also the people from these regions who dominated our power structure. Cory Aquino is from Tarlac. I need not say more.

In describing my boyhood, I will be describing the lives of millions of Filipinos to this day, for after a few decades of dramatic changes elsewhere, not much has really changed in our rural areas, except perhaps the status symbols.

When I was young, for instance, a man carrying a fountain pen was supposed to be educated, so there were those who were not happy with one pen – they carried three! The college diploma was prominently displayed in the living room, for this meant there was an educated member in the household but, most of all, they had the money to send their child through college. The sewing machine was a status symbol, but in middle-class homes it was the refrigerator which was displayed in the living room. A couple of decades ago, it was the transistor radio; now it is the motorcycle and the television set.

Our life revolved around the rice crop, the tedium of planting and harvesting. Although there was no chapel in the village, we were religious and we trooped to town, particularly during the Holy Week when the evening processions were marked with awesome piety. In fact, this kind of religiosity, belief in the miraculous powers of religious images, may be witnessed every Friday in Manila, in Quiapo church, where hundreds of devotees flock to fulfil vows or ask the Black Nazarene for favours.

We also believed in malevolent spirits which inhabited big trees with fireflies or the mounds in the fields. When someone fell ill, it was not the doctor who was immediately called but the *herbolario*, the herb doctor, who plastered the afflicted parts of the body with nameless leaves and recited an *oración* or prayer. Offerings of gelatinous rice cakes, embedded with hard-boiled eggs, betel nut, and leaf cigars were then laid at the foot of the tree and the assistance of the spirits was invoked.

If someone was born, if someone got married, fell ill, or died, the landlord who lived in town was approached for money – to be repaid with 100 per cent interest the next harvest time. Today, the rural banks are supposed to supplant the usurious money lender, but all the rural banks in the country combined have less capital than the poorest commercial bank in Manila.

Our meals were always spartan. We raised chickens and hogs to sell. Magsaysay and his programme of providing artesian wells in all villages was the butt of jokes in Manila, but in many villages today there is still no potable water and, of course, no electricity.

We had a *barrio* school though, and a farmer would sell his last water buffalo to send his son to school so that he would be spared the drudgery of the farm.

Every so often, I visit the village where I was born. As a writer, I need to hear again and again the sounds of my own language, to nurture my roots. I see my childhood friends, now old and defeated, and the village itself as poor as it has always been. In fact, it has now become a rural slum.

And I know that the freedom I enjoy is alien to them although, every so often, they elect town mayors, congressmen, even the president of my country. What does democracy mean to them if it cannot assure them three meals a day and a system of justice that would punish those who oppress them?

On the other hand, there is Manila with its modern hospitals, its splendid residences, its millionaires who are at home in Paris and New York. Still, they are not free from the ethnic demands of society, or family. Many believe in faith healers and no less than the late President Marcos was supposed to possess a charm that gave him luck and longevity. Seven was his magic number and the most significant dates in his career were related to this number.

Given these cultural characteristics, it is easy to read the Filipino. The bonding element in the power structure is determined by ethnicity, relationships – never ideology. To understand how a political leader reacts, one must know where he comes from, his relatives, his schoolmates. Everything is personal and it is this same personalism that dictates political behaviour. And to trace corruption of public servants is easy. Look at their houses – the ultimate status symbol. Can they afford those mansions with their salaries? But then, as has often happened, they can always claim having won several first prizes in the sweepstakes.

Filipinos desiring modernity have often looked towards Japan and its Meijis for guidance; they often wish that they could get from the West only its technology, not its culture. But we know culture cannot be imported in isolation, nor can the native culture be ignored.

American initiatives in the Philippine countryside came in distinct waves in the post-war period; they were inspired and assisted by aid programmes, the Foundations, and were welcomed by Filipino leaders who felt they could ride the wave and at the same time benefit from American largesse.

At the height of the Huk uprising in the early 1950s, the community development programme was launched. President Magsaysay even set up the office of Presidential Assistant for Community Development. Together with this office, a cooperative movement funded by the Government was also set up. In less than three years, the cooperatives were all in shambles, victims of corruption or inefficiency. They did not grow because they were forced upon the rural people from above. As creations of government, they were easy prey. Stealing from the Government, in spite of the exhortations against corruption, is not perceived by many Filipinos as so grave a crime as stealing from individual Filipinos.

All over the country, millions of pesos were spent in what were called reading centres for the rural people. They were built of wood and concrete, depending on the enthusiasm of the village. Reading materials from the United States Information Service and the Government were stocked in these centres.

In another year, they had all fallen apart, ravaged by the weather and unattended. Why did this happen? Rural Filipinos don't really read. They listen to the radio, and if they read at all, it is the vernacular magazines, the comics. And most of all, they don't congregate in libraries – they gather at the village store. While education is valued, he who reads is considered lazy.

Then there was the Green Revolution. The emphasis was on food production, on new species of rice, particularly fast growing varieties. To be sure, the rice programme was an unqualified success. Technology was absorbed by the peasantry. Briefly, the Philippines became a rice exporter.

But studies also showed the high cost of fertilizers, the vast expenditures for infrastructures that the programme demanded. In the final reckoning, it was the big landlords who benefited most and the tenant farmer was back to square one.

On a strictly cultural plane, the native culture sometimes works against innovation. In the early 1950s, for instance, an enterprising industrialist set up a dairy farm in the province of Bulacan with acclimatized cattle from India and the United States. He thought he would be able to sell fresh milk in bottles like soft drinks and, thus, simplify the marketing problem.

But we Filipinos have never really been milk drinkers. In the village, milk is for the sick and for babies, or making candles. If the older people wanted to put in place the young who talk out of turn, they would say "your mouth still smells of milk."

The project collapsed in three years.

In the 1950s the population of Manila could no longer be confined to the city limits. Through private initiative, decongestion was started by the Zobel family, who owned the whole of a suburb called Makati. As everyone can see today, the problem of Makati is that it was patterned after the urban movement in the United States in the 1950s.

By the time the Americans realized their mistake, it was too late for the Makati developers to change theirs.

Thus, the business area of Makati today is dead at night, just like Wall Street or Manhattan in the East Fifties. There are no spaces between the buildings. And since Makati was planned by the upper class, there is no housing for clerks or secretaries. There are no restaurants for drivers and employees at the lower echelon. But more than anything, Makati and its élite residential area, Forbes Park, stand as *the* anomalous symbol of disparity between the many who are poor and the few who are rich.

Today, aid emphasis is on birth control. I need not detail the criticism on this programme but I see its necessity in the same way that China imposes a rigid birth control programme. Six decades ago, China, with 400 million people, had famine almost every year. But today, with a billion people, China has no famine. It is not so much the number of people, therefore, that causes poverty, but the way the leaders waste the resources which from the beginning have not been equitably distributed.

I question the emphasis on birth control based on fear of instability that enormous populations would bring to the global order. Instability, after all, will destroy the status quo upon which the imperial order feeds. And here we come to the most fundamental contradiction in the traditional view of development.

Revolutions in poor countries are feared, for they result in instability. But the instability I want for my country is the harbinger of change and, therefore, of justice. To put it another way, it seems to me that the imperial order wants the peace and stability of the cemetery for us who are poor.

Filipino revolution in the mind

Lenin asked, "What is to be done?"

I would rather that we ask, "What is to be undone?"

The first is for us to champion Filipino originality at the risk of being chauvinists. To do this, first and foremost, we must "kill" our Western father, cast aside everything Western from our minds and start with what we have – the mud of our villages, the poverty of our slums. We should build from there, no matter how arduous the effort, no matter how niggardly our materials.

I say all these knowing that the real revolution takes place first in the mind.

The banishment of our internal contradictions, in fact, the building of our culture and our nation, is not the task of foreigners; it is wholly and solely a Filipino responsibility. There can be no question about foreign goodwill which exists in the highest echelons of power, but it is necessary to cut off the links of an irresponsible and rapacious Filipino élite to its Western counterparts, not so much because these ties perpetuate the colonial relationship but because these ties condition us into accepting wholly and uncritically the Western model.

If we are to be free, we should pay the cost of that freedom.

But do we really want to be free?

Like the first educated Filipinos of the 1880s who wanted seats in the Spanish Cortes and equality with the Spaniards, Filipinos today do not seek freedom from the West, particularly the United States. The long lines of Filipinos applying for immigrant visas at the American Embassy everyday belie this assumption as well. In fact, if the 51st State of the Union movement was not quelled and submitted to a referendum, the majority of the Filipinos would probably opt for American sovereignty.

What has happened, I fear, is that most of us – because we wanted to be equals with our former rulers – have acquired not their virtues but their vices. The work ethic, the high standards of efficiency, the democratic ideal – these are just slogans never to be lived.

Who then will create the myths, the soul, the spirit with which a new nation will be shaped?

It is here, of course, where the Filipino artists, the Filipino writers – as creators of myth – are saddled with the horrendous job of recasting the national character. And this job becomes more difficult, for they must start with no classical tradition to fall back on in the manner that other Asian artists have. Perhaps it is just as well, for, like Americans, the cathedrals that we will build will be uniquely our own.

Philippine history in brief

Our history – the last 400 years of it – abounds with examples of how the foreign intruder used his communication skills to subjugate the country, then exploit it. In fairness to the Spanish friars who braved the unknown seas and a hostile land, they learned the native languages so they could preach to the natives in their own tongue. In the process, however, they destroyed their native scripts and, perhaps, all chances for an indigenous culture to grow and flower.

"I will learn your language so I can damn you" – so goes the old saying. It took some time – more than 300 years – before this was possible. Though the University of Santo Tomas was founded in 1611, it was not till the middle of the nineteenth century that the Indios – as we Filipinos were then called – were accepted in it.

The first educated Filipinos were half-breeds, usually children of the wealthy, and some of whom joined the priesthood. By 1880, the first major group was in schools in Europe, and there they started propagandizing for reforms. The *Ilustrados*, as they were called, set up a fortnightly called *La Solidaridad* wherein they wrote with intelligence and artistry.

It is now argued that the Spaniards could not bring to the Philippines a system they did not possess. It was the Americans who brought the public schools, and they comprise America's brightest colonial legacy.

The first American soldiers who defeated General Emilio Aguinaldo's ragtag army in 1901 became English teachers, conducting classes under the trees. Then, on 21 August 1901, the SS *Thomas* – a cattle ship – landed 540 teachers, almost all of them volunteers. Within six months, 27 of them died of tropical diseases. With their families, they were dispersed throughout the archipelago, in the malarial jungles of Mindanao, and among the head-hunting tribes in the mountains of northern Luzon; to these, they brought the shining symbols of the American ethos – the log cabin, the cherry tree. There is no village in the Philippines which does not have a schoolhouse, and our literacy is more than 80 per cent.

I will now recall some memories of this public school system without which I would most probably be a barefoot peasant in some benighted Ilokano barrio.

I went to grade school in the 1930s with American textbooks. I memorized the Gettysburg address and many Filipinos of my generation came to believe that in a democracy it is possible for anyone born in a log cabin – or in a nipa hut – to be President.

To be sure, we took a lot of inappropriate models. In literature, for instance, we read Longfellow, O. Henry. It was only much later that we got to appreciate Emerson, Whitman, Hemingway, Faulkner – all those writers who gave American literature its sinews.

But until today, many of our textbooks are still direct imports from the United States. To blame colonialism for this is to flog a dead horse. Since 1935, when we became a commonwealth, our educational system was completely in Filipino hands, and it was possible even then to redirect our education curriculum. Indeed, there is much to be said about a truly Filipino education as propounded by our leading anthropologist, F. Landa Jocano, who believes that our failure to appreciate our history – a prerequisite for development – stems from a maladjustment in the educational system.

First, the language. If the Americans had not come in 1896, we would probably be speaking Japanese today. I have to write in a language which is not mine and in the process, I console myself that language is just an instrument. But I know it brings with it a whole new culture, for now, whether I like it or not, I have joined the mainstream of English letters. Chaucer, Shakespeare, Steinbeck – they have become part of my tradition – a tradition I refuse to accept, for what I cling to is what I know, what I am, the village I have left, and its implacable poverty.

I feel that the Filipino artist is burdened with challenges sometimes too heavy and too complex for him to bear. He must give meaning, a direction to his work, so that it will not just be adornment; art will then be utilitarian, in the sense that it can incite, teach, and motivate. The artist would need not just an original sensibility but excellence and honesty. The excellence he must acquire himself, perhaps, by learning from the West; the honesty he would practise with courage to show clearly what is, as it really is.

In saying this, I bring to mind Rizal's two novels in Spanish. Here is art and honesty now embedded in our subconscious, showing the way from that dark night that we went through. For what Rizal, the artist, had done was to go straight to the heart as no textbook ever will.

With these in mind, I would like to see the educational system utilize our creative genius that will then lift our youth from the dungheap of colonial dependency. I would like to see this done by emphasizing what we have. To be more specific, in our humanities courses, we have to recast our views on aesthetics, and understand and synthesize our preoccupation with space as something different from those of other peoples. We fill up everything, whether it is the park in Manila with its well-manicured lawns and gewgaws, or the jeepney which lords it over Manila's streets. I would like our artists to draw from their own experience and not make facile copies of the latest fads in Soho or Paris. They could refine our folk crafts and provide our modern art with an indelible Filipino character.

I would ask our builders to stop thinking of mega-structures, such as one sees in the ancient world or in New York, and concentrate on native motifs, bearing in mind that we are a tropical country.

But, above all, I would like to see our intellectuals contribute to an educational system that would liberate our people from their own perception that they are "little," an education that would imbue our people with the capacity to stand up to the "big" people, and wrest from them the democracy which had been their sole preserve. Democracy would then mean what are taken for granted in the West – three meals, education, safe drinking water, and, most important, a system of justice that they can trust.

Democracy would then mean that labour leaders will come from the shop floor, that farm leaders will have dirt under their fingernails, and that such leaders would be in Congress.

I recognize the contributions of radical movements like the New Peoples' Army and the Moro National Liberation Front to the political upliftment of the "little people." Even if these movements fail, in the words of Salud Algabre, who led the peasant Sakdal uprising in 1935, "No revolution ever fails – each is a step forward."

Conclusion

I have tried to present, perhaps superficially, Filipino society and the reasons for its continuing poverty. Filipino development hinges primarily on the capacity of Filipinos to "kill" their Western father and to do it alone, never to eschew violence as an alternative, for it is the intellectual revolutionary after all who is the real modernizer. I do not propose a hermetically sealed culture, although, on second thought, it may not be such a bad idea after all.

If true development starts in the mind, then the country's myth makers – the artists, the writers, and the humanists – without the classical traditions of their neighbours to draw from – are burdened with an awesome duty.

The single, most important perception that needs to be altered or acquired is our attitude towards development itself. Development always implies economic and, therefore, material development, the unlimited acquisition of goods. It means taking on the American model and all its wasteful consequences. Already, our landscape is studded with such folly.

I suggest, therefore, that qualitative approach to development be taken, its humanist aspects emphasized.

I say this knowing that in the Philippines, the little people did not object to the imposition of martial law in September 1972, for freedom did not mean much to them, associated as it was with anarchy and exploitation. They just wanted peace and order so that they could pursue their miserable lives without being molested.

The other is that though we set up the first republic in Asia in 1898 and had a lot of American assistance in nurturing our fledgling democracy, that democracy was easily discredited – its institutions were destroyed by one man and they may not be revived again. Unless....

And, finally, I ask that development be equated with justice. With this in mind, it becomes easier to plan for alternative futures, for then we would not be thinking too much of resources and GNPs as we would of those institutions that would promote justice.

8

Culture, development, and democracy: Role of intellectuals in Africa

Alexander Kwapong

I am most grateful to the United Nations University, and especially my good friend and former colleague, Roland Fuchs, for the kind invitation to join in this international conference which the University has organized here at Yogyakarta to honour the memory of the late Soedjatmoko, the second Rector of the UNU. As I look back to my association with our beloved Koko, from our first meeting in Aspen, Colorado, in 1972 as members of the Aspen Institute for Humanistic Studies' Board of Trustees to the seven years I spent with him in Tokyo from 1980 to 1987 as one of his close colleagues during his rectorship, I cannot conceive of a better tribute to his memory than this conference. Nothing could pay more appropriate homage to his life's work or to the ideals which he so passionately espoused than for such a group of international scholars to be brought together to discuss the subject that was so dear to his heart and which consumed him so passionately throughout his whole lifetime: culture, development, and democracy. It was Koko's total commitment to the primacy of the human intellect as an agent in attaining development on the basis of culture and democracy that made him, uniquely and *par excellence*, the intellectual. He was not only an Indonesian and an Asian intellectual; he was, at the same time, *Homo universalis*, totally devoid of any trace of bigotry, whether racial, ethnic, cultural, or religious. A devout Muslim, Koko wore his religion lightly and with humanity. I recall, in particular, his lack of rancour or bitterness towards the Dutch, the erstwhile colonial overlords of his native land (whose language he spoke so fluently), or against the Japanese who violently interrupted his university medical education and so decisively shaped his later political and intellectual career.

In some respects, Koko was indeed an intellectual to a fault, more concerned with theoria than praxis. When it came to translating the intellectual mandate of the UNU into practical institutional and programmatic reality, or how to move from the grand ideas to specific practical implementation, one had one's differences with him. Inevitably, as colleagues, we did have our moments of disagreements, some of them quite heated, but they were never personal. The challenge of working together in the enterprise of creating the UNU blossomed into genuine friendship and grew into an exercise in building human cooperation and interracial cooperation, subject, of course, to the constraints of the UN system. That is the Koko whom we honour here together. History will, I believe, accord him a high place in the assessment of his contribution to the bold concept of the UNU, which was no less than to "help identify and find solutions to the pressing global problems of human survival, development, and welfare that are the concerns of the United Nations and its agencies."

I would like to think that I bring to the discussion of the subject of this conference an African background which is the product of an African birth, upbringing, and education in Ghana, a formal university specialization in classical studies in Cambridge, England, and professional involvement in higher education and international development. While I cannot claim that the views I will express are typically African, I can fairly say, however, that many share them and that there is very lively interest in sub-Saharan Africa today and especially among thoughtful Africans, both young and old, in the issues of democracy, culture, and development and the roles which intellectuals should play both in the academic world and in their various societies. Certainly, speaking for myself, my special interest in the interaction between culture and development was strongly stimulated by the 12½ years I spent in Japan during the foundation and formative period of the UNU. These years coincided with Japan's remarkable recovery from the ashes of Hiroshima and its rise to the status of economic superpower and "The Japan that can now say no" in Shitaro Ishihara's provocative phrase.

The current African economic and social crisis has given rise to many reactions, both among Africans and non-Africans. Several international observers have tended to write off Africa and see no prospects for its future recovery. Typical of the gloom and doom predictions are observers like Marvin Cetron and Owen Davies who have this to say:

> This giant troublesome continent has had a difficult past, and there is regrettably little that is good to be said about its future. Slight economic improvement combined with a rapidly growing population spells ruin for Africa.... Desertification, drought, and famine remain constant threats. The next 10 years will be bleak ones for the dark continent.... For the rest of the world, throughout the foreseeable future, Africa will remain a source of oil; scarce non-renewable resources; and worry. To its own inhabitants, Africa offers little more than survival, and, in many cases, not even that. It will benefit little, and late, from the burst of prosperity and seems ready to overtake the developed world.[1]

But as the Roman historian, Pliny, said, "*ex Africa, semper, aliquid novi.*" Africa has certainly come up with something new. 1991 has indeed been a dramatic year for sub-Saharan Africa, no less than it has been for Eastern Europe and the Soviet Union. The release of Nelson Mandela in South Africa and Namibian independence have been followed by tremendous political changes in the continent such as the collapse of the Mengistu regime in Ethiopia, and of Nguesso in Congo, the end of the Angolan conflict, the stirrings everywhere as military governments and authoritarian regimes are challenged by the rising tide of multi-party democracies, the most dramatic being the peaceful end through the ballot box of Kaunda's long reign in Zambia. All these developments have given rise to justifiable optimism among African people that their countries have now entered upon "a second liberation struggle."

After the first liberation struggle of the 1960s against alien rule, we are now witnessing what Ali Mazrui has called "the new crusade for African democracy":

> If the first liberation was for political independence, this second struggle is for wider human rights. If the first endeavour is for collective self-determination, this second liberation is for individual fulfilment. Africa fought hard for decolonization; Africa will fight equally hard for democratization in this second challenge.[2]

Ali Mazrui is one of my favourite African intellectuals, but he is not alone. There are several others and a growing number of scholars, writers, university professors, journalists, lawyers, human right activists, and ordinary citizens, all of whom are demonstrating their conviction that democratic governance is the key to the recovery of their countries from the present economic and social malaise.

Arguments over the precise prescriptions of the structural adjustment economic reforms adopted by some 30 African governments, particularly over economic conditionalities and their social impact on vulnerable groups like children, women, and the poor, are now giving way to an increasing concern for good governance and the basic elements of democracy: accountability of governments and the critical right to dissent; a free press; open debate; meritocracy in the civil service and an independent judiciary; institutional pluralism and popular participation. African intellectuals are spearheading the demands for an end to wasteful spending, an end to widespread corruption, and for more political freedom. The tired justification put forward by authoritarian one-party governments that more political freedom will intensify tribalism no longer carries conviction.

The African crisis is now viewed as a more complex, general crisis of development which requires a comprehensive, sustained, and systematic response, with a long-term focus on all fronts – economic, social, and political. The alleviation of poverty should be an overall, central objective for which high economic growth in food and agricultural production, and in all other sectors, is an essential condition. But higher economic growth must be human-centred and must go hand in hand with the pursuit of equity and the satisfaction of the "basic needs" of adequate food and nutrition, health, education, and shelter for all people, regardless of partisan political, ethnic, linguistic, religious, and other such considerations. Such development must also be sustainable. As the World Commission on the Environment and Development (Brundtland Commission) has demonstrated, poverty and environmental degradation are intimately linked, both domestically and globally. The failure in Africa of previous development efforts has eroded the natural resource base and threatens to compromise the ability of future generations to meet their development needs.

A key requirement for the success of economic and social reform is that they should not only be relevant to specific country situations, but that "they must be designed, implemented, and owned by the African countries themselves." And for this, African countries must possess the technical, analytical, management, and institutional capacities. This requirement has clearly not been met, judging from the failures of the last decade of African development efforts. A very strong consensus has therefore emerged, both among African intellectuals and governments and the international donor community, that a central challenge to African development efforts to which they must accord the topmost priority is the building of African human and institutional capacity. Africans need to build their capacities through institutional reforms at all levels of government, the private sector, and non-governmental organizations, and they must adopt measures in all three sectors to empower women to play their full role in economic and social development. African countries must invest more in human capital and institutions and make the best possible use of the human capital and institutions that they have.

Compared with the developing nations of Asia and Latin America, which show a gradual build-up in investment in their own human capital and institutions, African development approaches have lacked the central ingredient of capacity building of their indigenous skills, knowledge, and institutions. "Donor assistance strategists," as E.V.K. Jaycox, Vice-President of the World Bank, has correctly pointed out, "supported capacity building in Asia and Latin America through substantial and long-term investment in human resource development and institutional building. Africa, on the other hand, has been treated differently and has suffered from 'crisis management' and 'crisis response' by donors."[3] This is clearly one of the visible effects of the colonial overhang which bedevils African development and has contributed to the continuing dependency syndrome. In Africa, this is perhaps one of the most challenging tasks confronting African development practitioners and intellectuals.

Central to this objective of strengthening the intellectual capacity and knowledge base in Africa is the overhaul and revitalization of all segments of African education – primary, secondary, and tertiary – which after the promising growth of the initial post-independence years, has suffered a serious decline in quality because of the lack of financial and physical resources and facilities such as classrooms, laboratories, basic inputs like books, journals, and other learning materials. There is above all, at all levels, a serious shortage of teachers, researchers, and managers. A largely illiterate people cannot achieve meaningful, long-term, sustainable human development.

It is particularly urgent to arrest the critical decline in the quality of African research and advanced training institutions such as universities, agricultural, health, engineering and scientific and technical institutions, and other tertiary centres and thereby enhance African capacity to generate and apply new knowledge and manage change. There is the paradox of increasing numbers of unemployed and underemployed graduates being turned out by African universities side by side with the shortage of skilled and technical manpower with the relevant skills and technical expertise in agriculture, health, nutrition, commerce, industry, engineering, management, and policy analysis, etc. A major challenge is to enhance the quality and output of scientific research and training in the region.

Another urgent challenge is to arrest the external brain drain of such skilled and trained people from the continent to the developed countries. In recent years, this drain has become a haemorrhage. Whatever its complex political, financial, and social causes, there is little doubt that the continuing emigration of doctors and other technically skilled professionals constitutes a particularly costly resource loss in skills and human capital in African countries. All the gains from the reform efforts to build capacity will come to nought unless African governments, policy makers, and professional organizations take practical steps to give to the brain drain phenomenon the highest priority in their reform programmes. They need to attract back from abroad, through incentive schemes and other mechanisms, their skilled African professionals and experts now living and working overseas; and even more importantly, they must make every effort to retain and add to those who have been trained and are currently working in various institutions in Africa. An interesting initiative in this regard to help build capacity is the African Capacity Building Foundation, recently established by the African Development Bank, the United Nations Development Programme and the World Bank with its headquarters in Harare, Zimbabwe, which is designed to build capacity in policy analysis and development management.

Thus the agenda for capacity building is comprehensive and long-term. But with the acute shortage of financial resources, to build capacity at the national level alone will not be enough. Priority should be given to creating selected regional centres or "nodes" for research and training with a "critical mass" of experts and researchers and the necessary financial resources and physical facilities to serve as centres of excellence. Such centres can form appropriate cooperative networks for scientific research and training.

I would now put this challenge of capacity building in Africa within the emerging global or international context. As the world moves towards the twenty-first century, it is clear that outside of the emerging regional economic power blocs that we see in North America, Europe after 1992, and the Pacific Rim countries, comprising Japan and the NICs, the African continent risks becoming marginalized unless it is able to share in the profound changes being brought about by the two global revolutions in information and biology which are fuelled by advances in micro-electronics, material sciences, and biotechnology. Can the African countries position themselves through state-of-the-art skills and capability at the cutting edge of these information and biological revolutions and thereby share in their benefits, or are they to be bypassed or involuntarily "delinked" from the rest of the world? Building capacity in scientific research and development can transform African agriculture, health, and industry and ensure that, in all these areas, the African countries can maintain competitiveness and high quality.

This brings me to the issue of modernization, to science and technology, and their relationship with culture. Unquestionably, Africa is lowest in the scale in the growing technological gap between the developing and the developed nations. Basic science and its thorough mastery is an essential first step to any meaningful technology acquisition, transfer, and creation. Technology is a product of a very specific human activity within certain socio-economic relations and *cultural* and value systems. The so-called transfer of technology is no more than the transfer of products of that technology with all the values and lifestyles in them. The mere transfer of technology does not lead to technology transfer unless one has the capacity to understand fully the knowledge and the skills behind these techniques. Therefore, building national and regional research systems and improving one's educational capability should be the major prerequisite. So the cultural dimension must be constantly borne in mind and indeed integrated into research and development programmes. The task is therefore to harness recent advances in the new frontiers of science so as to upgrade traditional skills and occupations. As the distinguished Indian scientist, Dr. M.S. Swaminathan, has well observed:

> In the past, industrialization was synonymous with urbanization, centralization, automation, and pollution. Today, it is possible to promote in rural areas sophisticated agro-industrial complexes based on decentralized infrastructure and production techniques that will help to marry the techniques of science with the *culture* and skills of the people. Science and technology are important components of the wall dividing poverty and prosperity. Today, there are unusual opportunities for all developing countries, especially those bypassed by the great benefits of science and technology, to improve the quality of life of their rural and urban poor through the integration of traditional and emerging technologies.[4]

As the experience of Japan and the Asian NICs has clearly shown, the real challenge for Africa is to ensure that the advances of science and technology are combined with relevance to the African cultural endowment and the social reality of mass rural and urban poverty throughout the continent. The cultural dimension is the basic framework within which sustainable long-term development must be built.

Twelve-and-a-half years of experience of the Japanese economic miracle from the vantage point of the UNU in Tokyo brought home to me this essential truth of the close connection between a nation's cultural endowment and authenticity and its ability to master science and technology and development. Language, the arts, poetry, music, religion, and shared values are all important ingredients which cannot be separated from the economic factors that make for successful development.

"Economists," as P. Worsley observed, "have long used the term 'social' in a residual sense to denote relations other than those entailed in production and the market. In doing so, they necessarily conflate vast and varied domains of social life, religion, sport, sexual mores, art; as if these constituted some kind of outer space through which the spaceship of the economy floats.... It is necessary to avoid not only the assumption that the 'cultural' is a *separate* sphere but that it is causally *secondary* (merely 'super-structural'). It is in fact the realm of those crucial institutions in which the ideas we live by are produced and through which they are communicated – and penetrate even the economy."[5]

But all this has to be seen within the historical dimension. The great problem about African development has been the neglect of the historical dimension. When the continent was arbitrarily divided up by the imperial powers in Berlin in 1884, they paid scant regard to the ethnic and cultural realities that they found among the African people on the continent, and effectively used the imperial principle of divide and rule to reduce the continent to their subjection. A serious consequence of colonial rule has been to exacerbate African ethnic divisions and disunity; but an even graver consequence was the cultural alienation of many African peoples. This has been a serious impediment to any meaningful modernization.

It is not for nothing that in the first liberation of the 1960s, nationalist leaders like Kwame Nkrumah strove to achieve pan-African unity and in fact named the organization they created the Organization of African Unity (OAU). Ethnic diversity, endemic in most nation states, as recent events in other parts of the world have shown, was fanned into "tribalism" and the Organization of African Unity, which was founded on the principle of non-interference in the internal affairs of member States, has in fact been fighting the battle for African unity with one hand tied, as it were, behind its back. The division into the various language zones of the former colonial powers – anglophone, francophone, lusiphone, etc. – has been a serious impediment to the attainment of genuine unity and hence effective cooperation for development. African scholars, poets, intellectuals, artists, whether in their universities or research centres, have to meet the serious challenge posed by the ethnic and tribal Balkanization. Good progress has been made in a number of research centres and institutes of African studies which have been established in several African countries to undertake teaching and research in African history, languages, art, music, the dance, religion, and moral values. The long-term success of such efforts will be evident when the educational systems of the various countries begin to reflect the work of such institutions, leading to better integration of development programmes and policies. Without such integration, African development efforts will be rootless and will not be sustainable.

There is understandably very growing interest in Africa in learning from the lessons of the success stories of the Asian Tigers and the second generation NICs which are seeking to emulate their success. *The Economist*, in November 1991, devoted to a survey of Asia's emerging economies, has listed the following lessons: "(a) the priority of state action should be economic development, defined by growth in output productivity and, above all, international competitiveness; (b) a strong commitment to the market and private property; (c) markets do not have to be completely free but need guidance of the State through acting with an élite bureaucracy; (d) equal distribution of income and relatively low taxes serve as essential incentives; and, most important, (e) investing in education pays handsome dividends: the Tigers' single biggest source of competitive advantage is their well-educated workers."[6]

Mr. Lee Kuan Yew has asked the following question: "If countries have access to more or less the same technology and the same resources and they all operate essentially free market systems, competing on a level playing-field, what makes some more successful than others?" His answer is "the intangibles": "the coherence of a society, its commitment to common ideals, goals, and values. A belief in hard work, thrift, filial piety, national pride."[7] These are largely derived from the Confucian ethic.

In the African historical experience, in which the slave trade, colonial rule, and post-colonial exploitation have played an indelible role, such values and, above all, the political space and cultural homogeneity have not been easy to come by. African governments, scholars, and intellectuals should assiduously seek to cultivate these if their development efforts are to succeed. There is no question in my mind that an indispensable condition for such successful development is "a benign and enabling environment," in which traditional and modern values are harmoniously blended. An essential element of this environment is the right to good governance and the respect for human freedom and dignity. That is the principal challenge for African intellectuals.

Notes

1. *Crystal Globe* (New York: St. Martin's Press, 1991), pp. 185, 196.
2. *West Africa magazine*, 2–8 September 1991, p. 1450.
3. *Capacity Building and Human Resource Development in Africa* (Dalhousie University, 1989), pp. 113–114.
4. E.U. von Weizsacker, M.S. Swaminathan, and Aklilu Lemma, eds., *New Frontiers in Technology Application: Integration of Emerging and Traditional Technologies* (Dublin: United Nations, Tycooly International Publishing, 1983), p. xiv.
5. P. Worsley, *The Three Worlds: Culture and World Development* (Chicago: University of Chicago Press, 1984), pp. 50–60, 246–252, 337–340.
6. "A Survey: Asia's Emerging Economies." *The Economist*, 16–21 November 1991, London, pp. 5–6.
7. Ibid.

9

The culture of resistance in Latin America: New thinking about old issues

Rodolfo Stavenhagen

As the world prepares to celebrate the 500th anniversary of the misnamed Discovery of America in 1992, the indigenous peoples of the American continent reflect openly about five years of genocide and resistance.[1] Their numerous organizations and sympathizers are ready to confront the official ceremonies sponsored by governments and academic institutions with counter-commemorations and alternative demonstrations. While some people may dismiss this controversy as a bit of folkloric entertainment, the debate itself about the nature of the "Encounter of Two Worlds," as it is now called, points to the persistence of the as yet unresolved and still acute "national question" in the Americas, 500 years later. It also underlines the fact that a historical event such as the landfall of Columbus in the Caribbean in October 1492 still generates considerable debate at present and expresses deep ideological rifts among Latin America's intellectuals. At issue is not the voyage of Columbus as such, but the nature of the conquest and colonization of America and its influence upon contemporary society; as well as the perception and interpretation of this, even in today's intellectual currents.

Whereas the historical roots of today's problems are indeed to be found in the colonial history of the continent, the social and economic structures which gave rise to today's "national question" emerged during the nineteenth century, after political independence had been achieved. To many observers, at that time the Latin American countries were not yet national states at all, but rather a series of loosely knit regional units, based on a partially self-sufficient agrarian economy.

Once independence had been obtained by force of arms (Bolívar, O'Higgins, Hidalgo, etc.) the rulers of the new states were faced with the daunting task of building new nations. It was no small matter to forge viable polities out of the fragmented remains of the Spanish empire, that might serve the interests of the new ruling groups, particularly in view of the highly stratified and hierarchical nature of the social system inherited from the colonial period and the ethnic and racial diversity of the population. Well known are the words of Simón Bolívar, the "Liberator of America," who realized the difficulties of creating unified nations out of such mixed populations, and warned in 1819:

> We must keep in mind that our people are neither European nor North American: rather, they are a mixture of African and the Americans who originated in Europe.... It is impossible to determine with any degree of accuracy where we belong in the human family. The greater portion of the native Indians have been annihilated; Spaniards have mixed with Americans and Africans, and Africans with Indians and Spaniards. While we have all been born of the same mother, our fathers, different in origin and in blood, are foreigners, and all differ visibly as to the color of their skin: a dissimilarity which places upon us an obligation of the greatest importance.[2]

Bolívar was not alone in expressing qualms about his ethnic identity and his place in "the human family" (he himself was of mixed origin, though a prominent member of the dominant creole class). Others doubted that civilized nations could emerge at all from such diverse racial and ethnic backgrounds. Domingo Faustino Sarmiento, Argentine writer and statesman, asked later in the century:

> Are we Europeans? So many copper-colored faces deny it! Are we indigenous? Perhaps the answer is given by the condescending smiles of our blonde ladies. Mixed? Nobody wants to be it, and there are thousands who would want to be called neither Americans nor Argentinians. Are we a nation? A nation without the accumulation of mixed materials, without the adjustment of foundations?[3]

So it became necessary to create and invent nations, to construct national identities, which was the task that the intellectuals set for themselves in the nineteenth century. By some accounts this task has not yet been completed, for the search for national identity is still a principal concern of Latin American intellectuals to this day.[4]

No wonder, then, that the Latin American élites adopted nationalist ideology as a guiding orientation in their search for legitimation. This meant that once the new republican political units had been established, the true nations would have to be constituted as an act of state and government. In Latin America, as in so many other post-colonial societies, it is the State and its intellectual and political élites who create the nation, and not the sociological nation which struggles to create its own state (as happened – and, indeed, is again happening – in Europe).[5]

A persistent rift existed along class lines, between the small ruling groups, owners of the land and the mines, and the subordinate Indian peasantry. In fact, in most countries the Indians made up the majority of the population and occupied the lowest rungs of the social and economic ladder. The Latin American countries have at times been described as "dual societies," and the highly polarized social and economic structures persisted in most countries up to the twentieth century.

Class cleavage was also a cultural cleavage. The subordinate Indian populations had been incorporated by the Spaniards as servile labour into the colonial economy, and a rigid system of stratification and segregation kept them effectively outside the political process. After independence, slavery and serfdom were abolished and legal equality of all citizens was proclaimed. In fact, the subordination and exploitation of the Indians continued, mainly through the operation of the landholding system.[6]

The concept of the nation state and of national culture was developed by the upper classes, the white descendants of the European settlers, the landholding aristocracy, the urban bourgeois elements. The model of the modern nation which evolved together with the expanding capitalist economy was that of the Western liberal democracies on the French, British, and American patterns. In fact, Latin American political constitutions were almost exact copies of the American constitution and Napoleonic legal systems were introduced. The Latin American élites considered themselves as part and parcel of Western civilization; by religion, language, and cultural ethos.[7]

The fact that in most countries by the beginning of the twentieth century the majority of the population still spoke one of many hundreds of Indian languages and lived in closed, semi-isolated village or tribal communities according to their ancestral customs, did not basically alter the national self-perception of the dominant classes.

Though lip-service was given to the indigenous roots of modern Latin American societies, the cultural and political leaders of the independent republics were reluctant to recognize the native Indian peoples as part of the new nations in the making. Indeed, the Indians were explicitly rejected and excluded. As long as they were geographically isolated and numerically insignificant, this approach did not threaten the self-image of the élites, who first affirmed their new-found national identities against the former colonial power, Spain, and later against the upcoming continental hegemonic power, the "Anglo-Saxon" United States (Sarmiento, Rodó, etc.).[8]

As elsewhere in the world, it was the ruling class and the intelligentsia who imagined and invented the modern Latin American nations, trying to shape them in their own image. The indigenous cultures were excluded from the "national projects" that emerged in the nineteenth century; they have remained in the background since then, shadowy figures which, like Greek choruses, step into the historical limelight on certain occasions (revolutions, rebellions, uprisings, etc.) only to recede again into a forgotten world.

Sarmiento and so many others were convinced that as long as there were indigenous peoples around, the Latin American countries would be unable to join the civilized nations of the world. Just as the political constitutions were drawn from the Constitution of the United States, so the legal institutions, the educational system, and varieties of cultural policies were taken from European models to serve the *criollo* upper classes. While the indigenous peoples were recognized as distinct and separate cultures, neither their languages nor their social, religious, and political institutions were incorporated into the dominant mode of governance. Indian cultures were at best ignored, and at worst exterminated.

The Indians were considered an obstacle to national integration and therefore a threat to the rightful place which the national élites considered to be theirs among the civilized nations of the world. The principal intellectual leaders of the nineteenth century were openly contemptuous of the Indian cultures and considered them to be inferior to the dominant culture of the times.[9]

The prevailing ideology (based on liberalism and positivism) considered that the Indian or indigenous element had no place in the new national cultures which were being built. The State and the ruling classes used a number of mechanisms to try to do away with this "blemish" which they considered imperilled their chances to become truly modern nations. In a number of countries, state violence and military expeditions "cleared the land" for the cattle ranchers and the new entrepreneurs of the agricultural frontier so that many Indian peoples were physically exterminated.[10]

A good deal of racism was involved in this process. According to the racist ideology in vogue during the latter part of the nineteenth and the first half of the twentieth century, which was eagerly accepted by many members of the Latin American cultural élite, the indigenous people were to be considered racially inferior to the whites of European stock and thus incapable of acceding to the higher levels of civilized life. This same appraisal was often extended to the growing numbers of mestizos, the biologically mixed population who were to become the majority ethnic element in most Latin American countries by the twentieth century. But as regards the Indians, the racist ideology suggested that the only possible way out for the Latin American countries was to proceed towards an improvement of the "biological stock" of the population, through massive European immigration.[11]

It has sometimes been stated that racism was absent from Latin American history and that the mixing of the races began early in colonial history. While the latter is of course true, the former is not.[12] A strong undercurrent of racist thinking characterized the cultural evolution of the nineteenth and twentieth centuries and contributed to a cultural profile, effectively wielded by the ruling classes, from which the subordinate Indian peoples (with their languages, customs and traditions, world-view, and social organization, as well as artistic achievements) were practically excluded.[13]

The major ethnic fact of the twentieth century, in the countries where the Indians had not been completely exterminated, was the rapid growth of the mestizo, i.e., the biologically mixed population. The "pure" whites were rapidly diminishing in numbers, as was the relative proportion in the total population of the "pure" Indians. The mestizo population also occupied the middle rungs of the social and economic stratification system and has been increasingly identified in recent years with the growing Latin American "middle classes."

During the early colonial period, the mestizo population had only a slightly higher status than the Indians, usually rejected by both the Spanish upper strata and the indigenous communities. Marginal to both cultures, the mestizos lacked a coherent identity of their own, a problem which has preoccupied intellectuals, psychologists, and sociologists to this day. The racial theories of the nineteenth century, which Latin America's élites willingly imported from Europe and the United States, considered not only the Indians but also the mixed-breed mestizos as inferior human groups. What kind of a modern nation could be built upon so flimsy a human material? No wonder so many intellectuals despaired of their nations and their continent. While the Indians were rejected outright as passive, dependent, fatalistic, docile, stupid, incapable of higher civilization, lacking in emotions and sensitivity, impervious to pain and suffering, unable even to improve their miserable conditions of living, and therefore generally seen as a major obstacle to the progress of the Latin American countries, the mestizos were said to embody the worst elements of both their ancestors: they were hot-headed, violent, unreliable, dishonest, shiftless, opportunistic, passionate, power-hungry, lazy, and generally considered less than ideal to rule and run their countries.

But times changed. The mestizos did in fact come to occupy the occupational slots and the economic and social space which neither the reduced criollo upper groups nor the Indian peasantries were able to control. With the capitalist expansion of the economy and the growth of cities, trade, services, and industry, the mestizo soon became identified with the national mainstream, the driving force of economic and social, as well as eventually political, progress. The earlier doubts about the mestizo's biological and pyschological capabilities vanished, except among some foreign observers who still conveyed the old stereotypes well into the twentieth century.

By now, the mestizos had developed their own distinct culture; they became the bearers of truly nationalist sentiments. Moreover, the mestizos became identified with the burgeoning urban middle classes, and thus with progress, change, and modernization. An ideological reversal had occurred. Mestizo intellectuals themselves sang the virtues *mestizaje* as not only a biological process, but rather as a cultural and political condition leading to economic development and political democracy. *Por mi raza hablará el espíritu* ("The spirit will speak for my race"), proclaims the slogan of the National University of Mexico, coined by José Vasconcelos, Minister of Education in one of Mexico's post-revolutionary governments and standard-bearer of the mestizos as a new "cosmic race" in Latin America.[14]

Shunned and despised at first, by the present century the mestizos were considered to have incorporated the best features of the two original races (the white and the Indian) which had intervened in their make-up. They became the bearers of the new concept of nationality which evolved together with the strengthening of the nation state. The rise of the mestizo, now extolled in literature, social science, and political discourse, coincided with the growing political presence of middle-class parties and social movements which by the mid-twentieth century had practically displaced the more traditional oligarchic parties from the centre of the stage.

While Europe was regressing to the myth of racial purity and superiority, and white supremacy was still legally enshrined in the United States, the idealization of the mixed-blood mestizo in the Latin America of the 1920s and 1930s could be considered as something of a heterodox if not a revolutionary position. The identification of the mestizo population with national culture, the middle classes, and economic progress soon became the ideological underpinning of various kinds of government policies designed to strengthen the unitary nation state and the incorporation of the "non-national" elements, namely, the Indian peoples.

To the extent that the "racial" (or rather, racist) solution to the problem of ethnic and cultural diversity (as considered by the ruling élites) has fallen out of favour, emphasis has increasingly come to be placed upon cultural issues. Indigenous peoples are no longer considered to be racially inferior to whites and mestizos, but Indian cultures are thought to be backward, traditional, and not conducive to progress and modernity. Furthermore, the existence of a diversity of Indian cultures, distinct from the dominant, Western, urban culture of the wielders of political and economic power, has been considered as undermining efforts towards national unity and development. Thus, the "solution" found by governments and social scientists in the twentieth century has been to further what has variously been called acculturation, assimilation, incorporation, or integration. For this purpose, the State set up specialized institutions and followed specific policies in the educational, cultural, economic and social fields designed to "integrate" the Indian populations into the so-called national mainstream.

By the 1940s a set of government policies had been devised, known by the name of *indigenismo*, in order to carry out the "national integration" of the indigenous communities, i.e., to effect the social and cultural changes necessary for their assimilation into the mestizo national model. By then, indigenous cultures had already changed considerably, and many observers considered that they were no longer viable and would soon disappear of their own accord. Thus, government policy would only hasten their demise and help along a "natural" and inevitable process.

The supposed inferiority of the indigenous peoples was now no longer phrased in biological terms, but rather in the fashionable language of the times: culture and levels of socio-economic development. Indigenous cultures were deemed to be underdeveloped, archaic, backward, traditional, simple rather than complex, communalistic rather than individualistic, parochial rather than universalistic, and so on. Theories of the social sciences were invoked to explain the differences between the Indian communities and the national societies, and they provided the parameters for public policy. The writings of Durkheim, Spencer and Tönnies, Weber and Parsons, Boas and Redfield were gleaned for insights which would then justify *indigenista* policies.[15]

In modern Latin America, the concept of national culture has been predicated upon the idea that Indian cultures do not exist. When, as in most countries, their existence cannot be simply wished away, it is officially stated that they have nothing or little to do with "national" culture and that, at any rate, they have nothing or very little to contribute to national culture (their greatness, if any, lies in the historical past). Indigenous cultures, if they are recognized as such at all, are considered only as diminished remnants of their former splendour and are thought to be naturally disappearing; therefore, the best which an enlightened government can do is to hasten their demise. In this fashion, so the argument goes, is not only national culture and unity strengthened but the indigenous peoples themselves will greatly benefit in terms of material and spiritual development, modernization, and progress.

Modernization, national integration, and development became the political catchwords of the twentieth century and states fashioned different kinds of policies accordingly: investments, infrastructure, industrialization, urbanization, education. While in some instances national revolutionary or populist regimes attempted to transform the traditional hierarchical social structures of inequality and injustice through reformist measures such as land redistribution, or to strengthen the domestic market through import substitution policies, in most cases economic development strategies have strengthened, albeit modernized, inequalities and accentuated regional and social disparities. In the heyday of "economic development," during the two or three decades after the Second World War, it was held that economic growth policies would contribute to closing the gap between the "modern" and the "traditional" sectors; the "dual society" would tend to disappear, the "backward" regions and populations would catch up with the modern, urban centres. While things have changed considerably in both the modern and the traditional sectors over the last two or three decades, in fact a new kind of polarization has developed. Economic development policies, which have benefited the new urban and rural upper classes, the new bourgeoisies, the new and fast-growing middle sectors, have hardly brought solace to millions of poor peasants and urban shanty town dwellers.

Before the late 1950s and 1960s, Latin America's political parties and movements had not dealt with the Indian question to any great extent, a position which reflected the marginality of these issues in the body politic and the fact that politics itself was still the domain of a relatively small "political class." However, the two principal ideological currents of the times had rather clear ideas about how to deal with *el problema indígena*.

Neo-liberal thinkers considered that the problem of the Indian populations was simply one of underdevelopment, technological backwardness, traditionalism, and marginality. Within the generally accepted framework of modernization politics and economic and social development conceived as a unilinear process or a series of necessary stages, economists, anthropologists, and politicians decided that the so-called Indian problem would disappear by way of community development, regional planning, education, technological innovations, and paternalistically guided acculturation. The responsibility for carrying out these policies lay in the hands of the State, which had a tutelary role to play. Through such policies, Indian subsistence peasants would become modern farmers, traditional values which were considered to be inimical to progress would have to be changed through modern education; the virtues of individualism and entrepreneurship would have to be learned; the bonds of the local community would have to broken so that the outside world could penetrate and impart its bounties. For many observers of the time – the heyday of developmentalism – the indigenous *problématique* was merely an economic problem, to be solved by technological change, investments, cash crops, wage labour, profit maximization, and, in general, the monetarization of the local subsistence economy.

Development policies targeted at the Indian populations had two principal justifications. On the one hand, it was thought that only by means of such policies would the conditions of life of the Indians improve. On the other hand, it was felt that as long as the indigenous peoples lived in poverty and backwardness, isolated from the centres of modernization and growth, the country as a whole would remain backward and underdeveloped. Not only that, but such countries would be particularly vulnerable to foreign interference and interests, especially the economic imperialism coming from the North. As long as the Latin American nations were internally fragmented and polarized (the concept of the "dual society" was often invoked), they would be weak and unable to assert their sovereignty and independence in the world. Except in museums, handicrafts, and folklore, and as tourist attractions, Indians have been denied a cultural collective existence in Latin America. Whereas in some countries Indians do represent relatively small and regionally isolated minorities, in others they make up fully half, if not more, of the total population.[16] In all of Latin America, there are over 400 different Indian ethnic groups, each with its own language and distinctive culture and way of life. They range from small bands of isolated jungle dwellers whose physical survival is constantly threatened by the advancing frontier of the national society, to the several million-strong Indian peasant societies of the Andean highlands. While estimates vary and census returns are unreliable, it is safe to state that Indian populations today might well represent around 35 million people on the subcontinent (about 10 per cent of the total population of Latin America), and their numbers are growing.

During the last two decades, social scientists, political activists, and, more recently, indigenous leaders themselves, have debated at length about the relations between the State, the nation, the class structure, and the indigenous peoples. Their controversies illustrate more than a bit of cultural history; they also constitute an example of how intellectual perceptions not only interpret but can indeed shape the course of events. Three principal approaches, with their internal variations, may be identified.

First, an earlier approach, developed by anthropologists and generally accepted by governments as indicated above, considered that in the process of "modernization" the backward, traditional cultures would disappear and through "acculturation" become integrated or assimilated into the "national" or mainstream society. A vigorous school of "applied anthropology," linked to *indigenismo*, fostered the theory and praxis of this approach.[17]

A second approach, within the analytical framework of Marxism, which became hegemonic in the 1960s and 1970s, reduced the Indian populations to the category of exploited social classes. Indeed, they were recognized as probably being the most exploited and backward fraction of the working class, and totally lacking in class consciousness precisely because of their community-centred, traditionalistic world outlook. Moreover, their cultural distinctiveness (language, dress, religious organization, family, and community structures) which set them apart from the mestizo population, allowed the bourgeoisie and the landholding oligarchies to super-exploit them by depressing wages, maintaining different kinds of forced and servile labour (peonage) and thus preventing them from joining forces with the revolutionary proletariat in the class struggle. Indeed, it was held that the maintenance of indigenous cultural specificity was actually in the interests of the bourgeoisie (or at least its more backward fractions) within the framework of underdeveloped and dependent capitalism for which Latin America became notorious in the 1960s.[18] Indigenous cultures were treated simply as insignificant remnants of a pre-capitalist stage of development or as artificial constructs fostered by an oppressive ruling class to better exploit indigenous labour. Indian and non-Indian peasants were held to share the same class interests and, in activist terms, the indigenous peasantry should be mobilized in the class struggle.

The Marxist controversy regarding the indigenous peoples (sometimes framed as "the national question" in reference to the debates among Marxists in central and eastern Europe before the First World War), continued well into the 1980s.[19] While much of the debate took place at first in the academic environment, it progressively filtered into leftist political movements and the revolutionary guerrilla activities which emerged in many parts of the continent as a consequence of the Cuban revolution. Che Guevara's attempt to spark a revolutionary uprising in Bolivia in the 1960s probably failed, among other reasons, because Guevara was unaware of, or insensitive to, the "national question" in that country, or rather because revolutionary theory at that point did not find such issues relevant.

A number of revolutionary guerrilla groups in Guatemala from the 1960s onward were easily isolated and eliminated by repressive, US-backed military regimes because they had not been able to deal adequately (that is, in theoretical and political terms) with the fact that the majority of Guatemala's population is Indian.[20] One of the reasons why revolutionary activity has continued, despite brutal repression bordering on genocide, is that the revolutionary organizations have now revised the "class" approach of traditional Marxist analysis and have framed their struggle in terms of a "national question," challenging not only class rule but also the dominant view of the nation state. With this they have been able to get a foothold among the indigenous peoples.[21]

More widely known, because of the media attention it received, was the conflict between the Miskito Indians and the Sandinista government in Nicaragua during the 1980s. This conflict arose because the Sandinistas, basing their policies on class analysis, felt that the Indians of the Atlantic coast had a natural interest in joining forces with them. It came as a surprise to the Sandinistas that the Indian organizations had a different agenda, and they quickly attributed counter-revolutionary intentions to the latter. This unnecessary, if inevitable, confrontation had disastrous consequences in terms of lives and resources lost, and weakened the political position of the Sandinista government both at home and abroad. (The Reagan administration was of course quick to take up the Miskito cause as a major human rights issue in its undeclared war against Nicaragua.) By the time the Sandinistas recognized their mistakes in the mid-1980s, the damage had been done.[22]

Though originating in different intellectual traditions and based on different analyses and interpretations of social and economic dynamics, the neo-liberal and the orthodox Marxist approaches to the indigenous *problématique* in Latin America had one thing in common: they shared the view that the indigenous peoples as such constituted an obstacle to development and progress. Both approaches set out to devise policies to overcome such obstacles; in one case it became "acculturation" and "modernization"; in the other, the "class struggle." In both scenarios, indigenous cultures would have to disappear eventually, and probably the sooner the better. They also shared the fact that indigenous peoples had not participated in the formulation of either scenario. Both these approaches consider the indigenous cultures as expendable and destined to disappear; in practical terms they resulted in policies which in fact hastened the ethnocide of the indigenous peoples. Moreover, they were developed by non-Indian social scientists and were later criticized by the emerging Indian intellectuals.

The third approach bases its analysis on the relation between the dominant nation state, controlled by the white and mestizo ruling class, and the subordinate indigenous peasantry. The concept most aptly used to describe this situation has been "internal colonialism," now linked to the alternatives of "ethnodevelopment," "Indian liberation," and "self-determination." While not denying the exploitative class relations which have determined the Indians' subordinate position in the wider society, it emphasized Indian identity and the specificity of indigenous ethnicity as explanatory categories as well as dynamic mobilizing forces in social struggles and the dialectics of change.[23]

While at one extreme of the theoretical debate Indians are seen mainly as exploited peasants, at the other extreme some scholars see a profound civilizational divide between Indians and non-Indians, regardless of class dynamics, and question the legitimacy of the nation state itself.[24]

From the sixteenth century to the 1960s indigenous peoples had been the object but never the subject of their own history, except for brief flashes such as the uprising of Tupac Amaru in Peru or the caste war in Mexico, and countless smaller and localized revolts and rebellions, always suppressed, never successful, and which have not found their way into official historiography. As scholars now acknowledge, Indian opposition to domination took the form of passive resistance, of turning inwards and building protective shells around community life and cultural identity. This is what enabled so many indigenous cultures to survive into the twentieth century, though countless others did indeed in time disappear.

As the indigenous peoples became the victims of renewed assaults upon their lands, resources, and cultures in the latter half of the present century, they began to adopt new forms of resistance and defence. Beginning in the 1970s (though there were scattered initiatives before that), various sorts of political organizations of indigenous peoples emerged which expressed claims about Indian rights that had only been stated occasionally and unsystematically before. National and regional congresses were held. Some of these were local associations, others became regional; national coalitions and federations followed; finally international organizations were set up. As in other forms of social and political mobilization, factionalism, divisions, and rivalries appeared. Grass-roots organizations sprang up in different areas; local groups merged to structure organizations along ethnic-group lines (for example, the Shuar federation in eastern Ecuador); professional interest groups were also formed (e.g., indigenous plantation workers, bilingual schoolteachers, Indian lawyers, etc.). Some (not very successful) attempts were made to set up indigenous political parties (for example, *Katarismo* in Bolivia; an Indian political party in Guatemala); in other parts indigenous "sectors" of existing parties appeared (the PRI in Mexico organized a National

Council of Indigenous Peoples). A number of organizations, particularly at the national and international levels, were structured from the top down. While in the 1960s, probably not more than a smattering of indigenous organizations existed, by the beginning of the 1990s dozens of such groups have been identified as established and representative associations in every country, and hundreds probably continent-wide. No exact count is available.

In all of these efforts, a newly emerging indigenous intelligentsia has played a fundamental role, aided by Indian advocates from the social sciences, the churches, and a number of political formations. In earlier years, the intelligentsia would have been syphoned off and assimilated into the dominant society. While this is still an ongoing process, indigenous professional people, intellectuals, and political activists are increasingly adopting consciously their ethnic identity and provide leadership to their communities.[25] The new leadership is also displacing the more traditional kind of community authority which has played such a fundamental role in the period of passive resistance and retrenchment when, as anthropologists would have it, Indian peoples lived in "closed, corporate communities." As Indian communities are also becoming internally differentiated according to socio-economic criteria, so the new indigenous leaders often reflect different interests in the community itself. Whether this leadership represents the interests of the indigenous ethnic groups at large, or only those of an emerging "indigenous bourgeoisie" is being widely debated currently.

Indian peoples' organizations are a relatively recent phenomenon in Latin America, perhaps not more than 20 years old. Their number and political importance has grown significantly in the last two decades, and they may be seen as forming part of the "new social movements" which are so characteristic of the contemporary world. Through the activities of such organizations the indigenous peoples have acquired a new awareness of their past and present situation and have become political actors in their own right. There is not one single model of such ethnic organizations, but rather different types of associations that reflect different kinds of circumstances. Thus we may find indigenous sections of wider trade union organizations (as, for example, the guaymí in the banana workers union in Panama). Or all of the members of an Indian ethnic group in one organization, which is the case of the Shuar Federation in eastern Ecuador (actually, one of the earliest Indian organizations in Latin America) and the National Mapuche Federation in Chile. There are also multi-ethnic regional organizations, such as the *Consejo Regional Indígena del Cauca* (CRIC) in Colombia or the *Consejo Regional de Pueblos Indios* (CORPI) in Central America, as well as multi-ethnic national-level organizations such as the *União de Nações Indígenas* (UNI) in Brazil, which includes over 100 different groups, and the *Unión de Indígenas de El Salvador* (UNIS).[26]

The activities of these organizations also vary considerably. Three main kinds of orientations may be distinguished. There are those which are basically economically motivated, struggling for trade union benefits, land rights, or similar issues, and which include ethnic and communal grievances and petitions in their negotiations with the State. Then there are the strictly ethnic movements, which develop integral communal projects and demands. Yet another type of organization is principally political, usually made up of a small group of motivated intellectuals and activists, who develop and promote the ethnic ideology of "Indianity" in its various guises.

Many of the indigenous organizations received early support from outside sympathizers, who were at times instrumental in their emergence. Christian missionaries were particularly active in the 1960s and 1970s in setting up some of these organizations.[27] Yet as time has passed, local and autochthonous leadership has taken over and external advisers have become secondary. Occasionally, governments have fostered and tried to control such organizations, basically in order to pre-empt possible oppositional activity.[28] More commonly, however, governments have tried to disarticulate these movements and in more than one case have they suffered severe repression at the hands of the military. Colombia, Chile and Guatemala during the 1970s and 1980s are cases in point.

The emergence of the Indian ethnic organizations has underlined the principal issues that the indigenous peoples are facing. These can be summarized as follows:[29]

(1) *Definition, membership, and legal status.* It may seem surprising that the question of definition of and membership in indigenous groups is an issue of some concern both to the Indians themselves and to the states in whose territories they live. Yet the question arises, because the definition of indigenous peoples is directly linked to the nature of the relationship between the group and the State, and the issue of membership is frequently linked to the enjoyment of certain rights and privileges or, conversely, to the imposition of disabilities and the limitation of political and civil rights. Therefore this question has become a claim put forward by

the indigenous organizations, and is also being dealt with by international organizations.

National governments may define indigenous groups for administrative purposes or to provide legal status; such definitions may serve to grant or withhold rights and privileges. Indigenous organizations complain that definitions in which they have not been directly involved are generally used not in their best interests, but rather in the interests of the states. When no definitions exist, and the fiction of a homogeneous mass of equal citizens is maintained, then frequently indigenous populations are also short-changed.

The question of definition has to do with the relative importance accorded to collective and individual human rights. When an indigenous or tribal people possesses a clearly identified territory and constitutes a recognizable administrative and/or social unit, then the question of definition and membership should not pose a particularly difficult problem, except if governments refuse to recognize a group as such, which is often the case. A more complex situation arises in the case of indigenous peoples who emigrate from their original communities to become part of the modern, urban industrial, and service economy. Over the last decades, millions of members of highland Indian communities have moved to the cities to join the ranks of the services and so-called informal sector.

In fact, Indian ethnicity is no longer a purely rural phenomenon, and this poses a challenge for the issue of definition. Indigenous identification and membership may be important for some people in the urban environment, even when they are distant from their original communities, and it poses special problems relating to the uses of law and language and the provision of educational services.

(2) *Land, territory, and resources.* Land is the principal claim of indigenous peoples at the present time, and not only in Latin America. Ever since European expansion into the region, the land issue has been in the forefront of the conflicts with national governments. The Europeans considered that the "newly discovered" territories lacked inhabitants and/or owners and appropriated for themselves vast expanses of land, on the flimsy theories of "right of discovery," the concept of *terra nullius*, or the idea of waste or idle lands. Indigenous prior occupancy and property rights were largely ignored and hardly ever recognized or respected. On the American continent, indigenous peoples who formerly roamed freely on their earth, were pushed into reservations or on to barren lands, and frequently had to find refuge on mountain fastnesses and impenetrable jungles. But

capitalist expansion kept pursuing them, and, particularly in recent decades, the onslaught on indigenous lands has again taken on dramatic proportions.

Indians have always had a special relationship with land. It has been, and to a great extent still is, the source of their basic sustenance. The majority are to a large extent agriculturalists, hunters, or gatherers. Their culture and way of life is linked to the land; they have been called "geocentric" peoples. But the land is not only an economic factor of production; it is the basis of cultural and social identity; the home of the ancestors, the site of religious and mythical links to the past and to the supernatural. This is something special which government planners and economic developers have consistently refused to understand, when they simply push indigenous peoples off their land, or when they glibly offer "monetary compensation" or relocation in exchange of land expropriations. The World Council of Indigenous Peoples has stated this special relationship eloquently:

> The Earth is the foundation of Indigenous Peoples. It is the seat of spirituality, the foundation from which our cultures and languages flourish. The Earth is our historian, the keeper of events, and the bones of our forefathers. Earth provides us food, medicine, shelter, and clothing. It is the source of our independence; it is our Mother. We do not dominate Her: we must harmonize with Her. Next to shooting Indigenous Peoples, the surest way to kill us is to separate us from our part of the Earth.[30]

For most indigenous peoples, land thus has a double role. On the one hand, it is frequently the basis for the economic sustenance of the group, tribe, or community. On the other hand, for many indigenous peoples a given territory is considered their homeland, it is the physical, historical, and often mythical space with which the group identifies and without which its very survival is at stake.

Indigenous peoples are aware of the fact that unless they are able to retain control over their land and territories, their survival as identifiable, distinct societies and cultures is seriously endangered. Traditionally, the greatest threat to their ancestral habitats came from the national governments; nowadays the multinational corporations also play an increasingly important role. More and more governments have been impelled to recognize the legitimacy of indigenous land claims, and protective legislations have been adopted by a number of states. Much damage has been done to indigenous peoples through economic development projects, particularly hydroelectric dams and other regional development schemes. The isolated, marginal areas they often occupy constitute the last great and until recently unexploited reserves of natural resources. Neither state planners nor multinational corporations nor international development agencies have hesitated to implement strategies to "incorporate" these areas into the national and international economy. In the process, the Indians have suffered genocide and ethnocide. Usually the grandiose development schemes that governments are so fond of are not designed to benefit the local population, but rather the urban and rural élites. Indeed, when indigenous populations exist, the idea is that they must be removed to make way for "progress."

(3) *Language, education, and culture.* In many Latin American countries, in the absence of other valid criteria, the only test for the existence and quantification of indigenous peoples is their language. A language is basically a means of communication, but it is much more than that. Languages are an integral part of cultures; through its language, a given group expresses its own culture, its own societal identity; languages are related to thought processes and to the way the members of a certain linguistic group perceive nature, the universe, and society. In the tropical jungles, the languages of local tribes are capable of designating and naming the myriad objects and forms of the jungle environment, which no other language is capable of doing. In other contexts also, languages express cultural patterns and social relations and in turn help shape these patterns and relations. Moreover, languages are the vehicles for literary and poetic expression; they are the instruments whereby oral history, myths, and beliefs are shared by a community and transmitted from generation to generation. Just as an Indian without land is a dead Indian, as the World Council of Indigenous Peoples states, so also an ethnic community without a language is a dying community. On the other hand, language has always been an instrument of conquest and empire. Nebrija, a Castillian grammarian and adviser to Queen Isabel the Catholic in the fifteenth century, published his Spanish grammar the same year Columbus reached America, and advised his queen to use the language as an instrument for the good government of the empire. Both the Spanish Crown and the Church took the advice to heart, for Spanish did become one of the universal languages of the modern world. But many Indian languages survived, and some are still used widely today. In Paraguay, most of the population speaks Guarani, but the indigenous peoples in that country are victims of ethnocide and genocide.[31] Quechua actually became a lingua franca in the Andes after the Spanish conquest.

As a result of discrimination-forced linguistic acculturation, many indigenous peoples have internalized the negative attitudes of the dominant society against their languages and cultures. Particularly when they leave their communities, they tend to deny their identity and feel ashamed of being "aboriginal" or "native" or "Indian" or "primitive." Self-hatred and internalized racism is a common occurrence, which has been instilled by the dominant society.[32]

In recent years, indigenous peoples have begun to resist the "natural" or forced disappearance of their languages and cultures, and slowly a growing awareness has arisen among social scientists, humanists, educators, and politicians, that the maintenance of indigenous languages within the concept of cultural pluralism is not necessarily undesirable.[33]

The struggle for language rights has become a major issue among indigenous organizations at the present time. At the regional level, the periodic inter-American indigenist congresses, a meeting of governments belonging to the Organization of American States, has reaffirmed for several years the linguistic rights of the indigenous populations of the American continent, even though a number of member states do not appear to pay much attention to these resolutions domestically. UNESCO has also affirmed the importance of the use of vernacular languages as an integral part of the cultural policies of states, and particularly as regards education for minority groups.

In Latin America, in some recent national constitutions and general laws, indigenous languages have finally been recognized as part of the "national culture."[34] Not only are Indian languages threatened. Discrimination and persecution of indigenous cultures span a wide variety of aspects, including:

- religion (prohibition to practise indigenous religion, forced conversion, taking of children from families and putting them into Christian schools. In this respect international missionary institutions such as the Summer Institute of Linguistics which works among hundreds of indigenous and tribal peoples in the world, have been particularly destructive of native cultures);[35]
- the use of traditional dress or names. The use of traditional costumes was prohibited for many years in numerous mestizo cities and is still today a stigma that Indians wish to overcome, now that international tourism has appropriated "ethnic" clothing world-wide;[36]
- the violation of sacred and burial sites (Indians claim that numerous objects and artifacts in museums and private collections around the world have been vandalized, pillaged, and stolen from

sites and monuments which still have cultural and symbolic meaning at the present time. Sacred sites are constantly being destroyed by land developers, government projects, military activity, grave-diggers, or treasure hunters);

- the exploitation of the artistic expressions (visual arts, dances, ceremonies, music, etc.) for tourism, with complete disregard for authenticity and preservation, thus contributing to what many observers have termed the prostitution and degeneration of indigenous cultures.[37]

(4) *Indigenous law and social organization.* One of the factors which has enabled indigenous and tribal peoples to survive in the face of the persistent assaults against them by the dominant society, is their internal coherence, their social organization, as well as the maintenance of their own traditions, laws, and customs, including local political authority. The distinct personality of indigenous peoples is not only a question of language or other cultural expressions, but the result of the permanent social reproduction of the group through the functioning of its own social, political, and frequently religious institutions. Of course, there are exceptions, and in general terms indigenous peoples who lose their social institutions will also, in the long run, tend to lose their ethnic identity. There may also be cases in which, despite internal divisions and strife, or the breakdown of traditional institutions, a given group is able to conserve its identity.

Many governments consider that the existence of such institutions distinct from the constitutional or legal mechanisms developed by the State, constitute a form of separatism, a threat to national unity. Most national legal systems do not recognize indigenous law and political institutions. On the contrary, they may argue that if equality before the law, as established in all international human rights instruments, is to be a reality, then no particular ethnic group should have a right to its own separate legal and political institutions. Many observers, however, have pointed out that equality before the law is a pious fiction when indigenous peoples are concerned, and that one of the best instruments that these people have to defend their human rights is precisely the validity of their own institutions.

Indigenous peoples have demanded that their own customary legal and political institutions be recognized by the State and respected in practice. There are two arguments to sustain this demand. One is that only by doing so will individual human rights actually be protected. The other is the collective right of a people to survival as a group. Indigenous organizations are increasingly making statements to this effect at their meetings and congresses. In 1985, the Inter-Americanist Indigenist Congress, a periodic intergovernmental event, took up this demand in one of its resolutions. National governments are beginning to consider this possibility seriously, and some legislative changes have accordingly already been made. The problem lies not so much in formal legal mechanisms, but rather in their implementation.

Contrary to common belief, and widely disregarded by anthropologists for a long time, indigenous customary law or alternative legal systems as they are sometimes called, are quite active in Latin America. They operate basically at the community level. They refer to land and resource use and rights, the maintenance of internal social order, the management and resolution of conflict, the definition, control, and prevention of delinquency and antisocial behaviour, the rules of marriage and inheritance, etc. Contradictions and controversies may arise between customary legal practices and the official legal system, and the sometimes uncritical application of the latter in total ignorance and disregard for the indigenous social structure is just one more form of domination and discrimination.[38]

(5) *Self-government, autonomy, and self-determination.* The question of legal systems and customary law is directly related to tribal and community government, and to the political status of the indigenous peoples within the contemporary nation state. From time immemorial, the indigenous peoples have been jealous of their sovereignty and independence, though they have been incorporated against their will into administrative systems not of their own choosing. They were reduced to "minority" status, whose lives and fortunes were determined and controlled by special ministries or departments, or by religious institutions. They lacked political rights and were excluded from political participation and representation. Many of them never knew what states they actually "belonged" to, till recent times.

Indigenous organizations are now claiming the right to self-government and autonomy. Some countries have granted this. Panama's constitution of 1972 recognizes the tribal territory of some indigenous groups, and others in that country are negotiating for similar treatment. In Nicaragua, the constitution of 1986 establishes a measure of autonomy for the communities of the Atlantic Coast and recognizes their right to establish their own forms of social organization and to administer their local affairs according to their own traditions. A further Statute of Autonomy of the Regions of the Atlantic Coast spells out the social, economic, political, and cultural rights of the local communities.[39]

Self-determination has recently become a major political claim of indigenous peoples, especially in international bodies. They base their demands on the human right of self-determination of peoples as spelled out in Article 1 of the two International Covenants on Human Rights.[40] They claim that being the original "First Nations" of the territories which they inhabit, and having been subordinated generally against their choosing to the suzerainty of other states and governments, usually in the form of invasion, conquest, and colonialism, they have the right to self-determination just as so many other peoples who have shaken off colonialism. Moreover, they demand the right to be considered "peoples," and not mere "populations" as has been the custom in international organizations. Likewise, they reject being considered as "ethnic minorities" and thus refuse to be dealt with according to Article 27 of the ICCPR. These demands have been taken up by the specialized bodies of the United Nations which are currently dealing with the rights of indigenous peoples. Thus, both Convention 169 of the International Labour Organization and a Draft Universal Declaration on Indigenous Rights being prepared in the United Nations, use the term people instead of the former word populations.[41] In the Inter-American Commission on Human Rights of the Organization of American States, preliminary steps are being taken which may lead eventually to a new regional human rights instrument for the indigenous peoples of the continent.

At a time when in several parts of the world non-state peoples are questioning the legitimacy of existing state structures and boundaries, the struggles of the indigenous people of Latin America for self-determination raises the national question to more than a rhetorical issue. Beyond the problems of "human rights" and "development" which dominated political discourse for so long, the 500th anniversary will be an occasion for forging a new historical compact between the indigenous peoples and the wider national societies of which they are a part.

Notes

1. In October 1991, the second continental conference of indigenous peoples took place in Guatemala City, attended by hundreds of representatives from all over the Americas, under the banner of "Five Hundred Years of Resistance."
2. Simón Bolívar, *Discurso de Angostura*, *Latinoamérica* 30, *Cuadernos de Cultura Latinoamericana* (Mexico: UNAM, 1978). English version in Vicente Lecuna, *Selected Writings of Bolívar*, 2 vols. Harold A. Beirck, ed. (New York: Colonial Press, 1951), vol. 1, p. 181.
3. Domingo Faustino Sarmiento, *Conflicto y armonía de las razas en América* (Buenos Aires:

Editorial Intermundo, 1946), p. 27. Quoted in Leopoldo Zea, *Discurso desde de la marginación y la barbarie* (Mexico: Fundo de Cultura Económica, 1990), p. 102. Translation by the author. Sarmiento became President of Argentina in the late 1880s; he is usually considered one of the "intellectual fathers" of the Argentine nation.

4. Pablo Gonzalez Casanova, ed., *Cultura y creación intelectual en América Latina* (Mexico: Siglo XXI, 1979); Hugo Zemelman, ed., *Cultura y política en América Latina* (Mexico: Siglo XXI, 1990); Leopoldo Zea, *The Latin American Mind* (Norman: University of Oklahoma Press, 1963).
5. Anthony D. Smith, *National Identity* (Harmondsworth: Penguin, 1991).
6. On Latin America's landholding system, see Solon Barraclough and Arthur Domike, "Agrarian Structure in Seven Latin American Countries," Rodolfo Stavenhagen, ed., *Agrarian Problems and Peasant Movements in Latin America* (New York: Anchor Books).
7. In fact, they still do. In July 1991, there was an Ibero-American "summit" meeting in Mexico which brought together the presidents of the Spanish- and Portuguese-speaking states of Latin America ... with the King of Spain and the President of Portugal. The English-speaking countries and Haiti, which is usually considered as part of Latin America, were not invited.
8. Leopoldo Zea, *Discurso desde la marginación y la barbarie* (Mexico: Fondo de Cultura Económica, 1990). José Enrique Rodó, Uruguayan philosopher, wrote at the turn of the century about Latin America's "Nordomania," the attempt to copy everything from the North.
9. Rodolfo Stavenhagen, *The Ethnic Question: Conflicts, Development, and Human Rights* (Tokyo: United Nations University Press, 1990), chap. 4.
10. This happened principally in Uruguay, Argentina, Chile, and Brazil, countries which later received great numbers of immigrants. In the Caribbean islands, the indigenous population had been exterminated by the middle of the sixteenth century.
11. A number of countries such as Argentina, Uruguay, Chile, Brazil, Venezuela, Costa Rica, and to a lesser extent some others, embarked upon a systematic policy of attracting European immigrants, who were to provide technology, capital, know-how, and entrepreneurship to the backward countries and who would eventually contribute to a racial "whitening" of the population and, thus, to improvement and progress (the concept of "development" had not yet been coined) of these nations.
12. See Magnus Mörner, *Race Mixture in the History of Latin America* (Boston: Little Brown, 1967), and Richard Graham, ed., *The Idea of Race in Latin America, 1870–1940* (Austin: University of Texas Press, 1990).
13. The same must be said about the negation and exclusion of persons of African descent from the self-perception of the national ruling élites. There are, as yet, few studies on racial prejudice and discrimination in Latin America. For a recent contribution see Winthrop R. Wright, *Café con Leche, Race, Class, and National Image in Venezuela* (Austin: University of Texas Press, 1990).
14. José Casconcelos, *La raza cósmica, misión de la raza iberoamericana* (Paris: Agencia Mundial de Librería, 1925). October 12 (Columbus Day in North America) is celebrated as *día de la raza* in Mexico. Chicanos in the south-western United States identify themselves as la raza.
15. For an assessment of *indigenismo* in Mexico, see Alan Knight, "Racism, Revolution and *Indigenismo*: Mexico, 1910–1940." In: Richard Graham, ed., *The Idea of Race in Latin America, 1870–1940* (Austin: University of Texas Press, 1990).
16. In Bolivia and Guatemala, the indigenous population amounts to more than 50 per cent.
17. The role of social anthropologists in formulating *indigenista* policies and providing theoretical support for them must be stressed. In Mexico, Alfonso Caso, Julio de la Fuente, Gonzalo Aguirre Beltrán are the best known, and their writings influenced generations of "applied anthropologists" in Mexico and other Latin American countries.
18. Fernando Henrique Cardoso and Enzo Paletto, *Dependence and Development in Latin America* (Berkeley: University of California Press, 1979).

19. Hector Díaz Polanco Hector, *La cuestion étnico-nacional* (Mexico: Editorial Línea, 1985).
20. Cf. *inter alia*, Martinez Peláez, Severo, *La patria del criollo* (Guatemala: Editorial Universitaria, 1971), Flores Alvarado, Humberto, *La proletarización del campesino de Guatemala* (Quetzaltenango: Rumbos Nuevos, 1971). For a critique, see Necker, L, "*A propos de quelques thèses sur l'Indianité*," *De l'empreinte à l'emprise* (Geneva: IUDED, 1982).
21. Arturo Arias, "Changing Indian Identity: Guatemala's Violent Transition to Modernity," Carol A. Smith, ed., *Guatemalan Indians and the State, 1540–1988* (Austin: The University of Texas Press, 1990). See also Susanne Jonas, *The Battle for Guatemala* (Boulder: Westview Press, 1991), chap. 7.
22. Carlos Vilas, *State, Class and Ethnicity in Nicaragua* (Boulder: Lynne Reinner Publishers, 1989).
23. For an earlier treatment of "internal colonialism" see Rodolfo Stavenhagen, "*Clases, colonialism y aculturación*," *América Latina* (Rio de Janeiro: 1964). Also Guillermo Bonfil, "*El concepto de indio en América: una categoría de la situación colonial*," *Anales de Antropología* (Mexico: UNAM, 1971), IV, 3; Guzmán Böckler, Carlos and Jean-Louis Herbert, *Guatemala: una interpretación histórico-social* (Mexico: Siglo XXI, 1970); Carol A. Smith, ed., *Guatemalan Indians and the State, 1540 to 1988* (Austin: University of Texas Press, 1990).
24. See, for example, Guillermo Bonfil, *México profundo* (Mexico: Secretaría de Educación Pública, 1987), as well as the writings of some Indian intellectuals such as Ramiro Reynaga in Bolivia, and political manifestos of a number of indigenous organizations.
25. Guillermo Bonfil, *Utopía y Revolución: el pensamiento político contemporáneo de los indios en América Latina* (Mexico: Nueva Imagen, 1981).
26. It is well to remember that in the early 1930s the Salvadorean government massacred over 30,000 Indians. The repression continued over many years so that the official position was that there were no longer any Indians in El Salvador. During the last decade of the civil war, the indigenous peoples, of whom there are over half a million, and who are the most notorious victims of military violence, have begun to organize themselves politically.
27. Catholic missionaries created the first Shuar organizations in Ecuador; the Moravian church organized the Miskitos in Nicaragua.
28. The association of indigenous bilingual teachers (ANPIBAC) and the local indigenous peoples' councils (*Consejos de Pueblos Indigenas*) in Mexico, co-opted by the official party and the Government; Somoza's use of the early Miskito organization on the Atlantic Coast; Torrijos' attempt to co-opt the Kuna confederation in Panama, etc.
29. Rodolfo Stavenhagen, *The Ethnic Question: Conflicts, Development, and Human Rights* (Tokyo: United Nations University Press, 1990), chap. 8.
30. World Council of Indigenous Peoples, "Rights of indigenous peoples to the earth" submission by the WCIP to the UN Working Group on Indigenous Populations, Geneva, 30 July 1985. Quoted in Julian Burger, *Report from the Frontier* (London: Zed Books, 1987), p. 14.
31. Cf. Mark Münzel, *The Aché Indians: Genocide in Paraguay* (Copenhagen: International Work Group for Indigenous Affairs), IWGIA Report No. 11, and by the same author, *The Aché: Genocide Continues in Paraguay* (Copenhagen: International Work Group for Indigenous Affairs), IWGIA Report No. 17.
32. At a public meeting in Mexico some years ago, which I attended, an elderly indigenous man apologized to the audience, in broken Spanish, for being an Indian. Among the Guaymi in Panama, says one observer, "internalized racism results in passivity, helplessness, and deference to the dominant ethnic group." See Philippe I. Bourgois, *Ethnicity at Work. Divided Labour on a Central American Banana Plantation* (Baltimore: The Johns Hopkins University Press, 1989), p. 143.
33. In Peru the Velasco regime officialized quechua and aymara in the early 1970s, but a later government revoked this measure. See Stefano Varese, "*Derechos étnicos en Péru*." In: Rodolfo Stavenhagen, *Derecho indígena y derechos humanos en América Latina* (Mexico: El Colegio de México y Instituto Interamericano de Derechos Humanos, 1988).

34. Argentina, Brazil, Guatemala, Nicaragua, Peru among others. Cf. Rodolfo Stavenhagen, op. cit.
35. David Stoll, *Fishers of Men or Founders of Empire?* (London: Zed Press, 1982); Soren Hvalkof and Peter Aaby, *Is God an American?* (Copenhagen: International Work Group for Indigenous Affairs and Survival International, 1981).
36. When I worked as a young applied anthropologist in south-eastern Mexico in the early 1950s, the local schoolteacher insisted that indigenous schoolchildren be known only by saints' names and not by the ones their parents gave them in the local language. As late as October 1988, a Brazilian judge refused to deal with Indian litigants who wore their ethnic attire; the Indians in turn refused to deal with the judge unless so dressed.
37. The "Declaration of Quito," adopted by a continent-wide meeting of indigenous organizations in July 1990, states that they "affirm our decision to defend our culture, education, and religion as fundamental to our identity as peoples, reclaiming and maintaining our own forms of spiritual life and communal existence; in an intimate relationship with our Mother Earth."
38. See Rodolfo Stavenhagen and Diego Iturralde, eds., *Entre la ley y la costumbre. El derecho consuetudinario indígena en América Latina* (Mexico: Instituto Interamericano de Derechos Humanos y Instituto Indigenista Interamericano, 1990).
39. For Panama, see James Howe, *The Kuna Gathering: Contemporary Village Politics in Panama* (Austin: University of Texas Press, 1986); for Nicaragua, CIDCA, *Ethnic Groups and the Nation State. The Case of the Atlantic Coast in Nicaragua* (University of Stockholm, 1987); Rupesinghe, Kumar, ed., *Ethnic Conflict and Human Rights* (Oslo: The United Nations University and the University of Oslo Press, 1987).
40. Article 1 of the International Covenant on Economic, Social, and Cultural Rights and of the International Covenant on Civil and Political Rights are identical: "All peoples have the right to self-determination. By virtue of that right they freely determine their political status and freely pursue their economic, social, and cultural development."
41. The ILO approved Convention 169, a revision of Convention 107 (1957) on indigenous and tribal peoples. The earlier convention had been criticized for being assimilationist and paternalistic. A handful of indigenous representatives took part in the discussions leading up to the adoption of Convention 169 by the ILO General Conference in 1988. It has to be ratified by a sufficient number of states in order to replace Convention 107, which still remains on the books. Since 1985, the UN Sub-Commission on the Prevention of Discrimination and Protection of Minorities has been preparing a draft Declaration of the Rights of Indigenous Peoples, which is expected to be approved by the General Assembly of the United Nations. In the yearly public sessions of the Working Group on Indigenous Peoples, in Geneva, numerous indigenous organizations from around the world participate actively.

10

The dynamics of reshaping the social order: Old actors, new actors

Elise Boulding

Introduction

Culture is the all-embracing context in which development takes place, and cannot be separated from it. Culture is inherently participatory, in that it only exists in process and practice. It is constantly being shaped by its members, from the youngest to the oldest. When the civic dimension of a culture is strongly developed, so that its members have the capacity to discern the public good, and the participatory skills for creating the conditions that maintain that public good for all the citizenry, regardless of social categories, then that culture can be called democratic. The role of intellectuals is to articulate the public good, and to guard it.

A "developed" society, then, is a participatory society with a strong civic culture. It is a "learning society," both adventurous and peaceable; ready to try new things, but not at the expense of the needs of its members. It is a society alive with diversity, and by necessity possessing to a high degree the skills of conflict resolution and negotiation; a society of shared abundance in which the arts and humanities thrive alongside science and technology, in a carefully sustained and vigilantly nurtured natural environment.

What I have described is a utopia (*ou topos*, or a not-place). As we look around us we see on every continent rising tides of violence, widening gulfs between rich and poor, deteriorating ecosystems. Yet the "developed" society I have just described would be recognized by those who consider themselves citizens of the modern world, as what we are supposed to be moving toward. Whether delusion or aspiration, it is a concept known to us.

Not only is it a recognizable concept today, it has ancient roots. With appropriate modifications, this is the age-old image of the good society. It is Plato's *Republic*. In more mythic language it is the image of the Elysian Fields, of the Plains of Asgaard, of Mount Zion, of the garden paradise in the desert of Arabian legend.[1]

In more recent history, the world-wide axial age known in the West as the Renaissance brought the good society up to date by exploring new potentials, new dimensions of *Homo* and *Mulier sapiens*.[2] The Enlightenment in Eurasia then gave rise to the social sciences, articulating the details of a human social order, and to a revolutionary phase in the physical sciences enabling the harnessing of nature's resources for human use on an unprecedented scale. Everything good was possible, although Ibn Khaldun (1332–1406) warned us that every flowering of civilization bears the seeds of its own decay (Ibn Khaldun 1958).

So what went wrong? Why did Herbert Spencer's (1874) thesis of the industrial age as an age of human peaceableness give way to the reality of developments in science and technology that have led to a fear of extinction of the human race, through nuclear war and/or environmental destruction?

In order to understand the complex role intellectuals have played in bringing the world to its present precarious state, and to understand the alternative intellectual currents that have remained strong and viable as potentials for the future, I propose to discuss the Now in the context of what I call the 200-year present. Because change processes move both more rapidly and more slowly than we think, only by looking at the present in this expanded time frame can we grasp what is actually going on. The 200-year time unit is also the longest time span we can encompass organically through our own life experience:

> The 200-year present moment begins 100 years ago today, on the day of birth of those in our society who are centenarians, celebrating their hundredth birthday today. The other boundary of this present moment is the hundredth birthday of babies born today. It is a continuously moving moment, always reaching out one hundred years in either direction from the day we are in. We are linked with both boundaries of this moment by the

people among us whose life began or will end at one of those boundaries, $3\frac{1}{2}$ generations each way in time (Boulding 1978).

Acknowledging the events occurring in the international system in the 1890s as part of our present makes the structure of those events psychologically more accessible to us; it makes the 1990s less confusing, and the 2090s less mysterious. Our crisis did not simply erupt out of nowhere, and our responses will not be random.

In what follows I will focus on the role of an internationally oriented intellectual community whose major contribution to the unfolding of the 200-year present has been in the formation of transnational networks that have fostered the dynamics of development throughout the period. The intellectuals of this global community are a very special breed, not to be confused with intellectuals who retreat to the deserts of the mind and do not necessarily connect with the human condition. They are the thinkers who have broken free, as the poet pleads:

> The intellectual has a roof of zinc,
> Sheltering his spirit from the rain of grace,
> The quiet, vast, night rain, that in this place
> Sputters and patters with metallic clink!
> Strange that the source and substance of all drink
> Should sound so dry – that roof should so efface
> All hints of vastness, in this tiny space,
> This airless, lamplit chamber without chink.
>
> O Friend break out, out, out into the night
> And marvel with the silence, how the ground
> Receives the living drops with such small sound;
> And better, still thyself, and so incite
> The inward ear to catch the sudden winging,
> The universe, crammed full with angels, singing.
>
> (Kenneth Boulding 1975).

1891

We will take the 200-year present as falling between 1891 and 2091. At the beginning of this elongated present moment we are in the heyday of Western-style internationalism, a time of exuberant claiming of the world beyond the borders of the "core" European states. Having steadily encroached on native territories by right of conquest for several centuries, European statesmen by 1891 have placed most of Africa formally under colonial rule. In Asia, colonial rule is in midstream, having started about a century earlier. In Latin America, colonial rule has already been over for 50 years, and now a neocolonial relationship exists with the United States. The colonial rulers of the two-thirds world soon include Belgium, France, Germany, Italy, Japan, the Netherlands, Portugal, Spain, Turkey, and the United Kingdom. If there is a rhetoric in public parlance about the brotherhood of man, few see any inconsistency between this talk and the ruthless policies of colonial occupation in Africa and parts of Asia. Mankind is not a concept that includes people of other skin colours (or women).

The rhetoric, however, is there. A series of world fairs, beginning with the great London Exposition of 1851, by providing occasions for contact and exchange of ideas among people who had hitherto worked in more limited spheres, has fired the enthusiasm of scientists, educators, and advocates of social reform. The United States, as a sign of its coming of age, will be hosting the Chicago World Exposition in 1893. Inspired by Tsar Nicholas's call for an intergovernmental peace conference at The Hague to begin the process of replacing war by arbitration, peace organizations have begun to gather the million signatures in support of the conference purposes that will be presented when the conference is convened in 1898 – the first large-scale peace demonstration at an international meeting of diplomats.

While statesmen are inching along towards the establishment of the first International Court of Arbitration and the international bodies that will follow from it, a new phenomenon is coming to birth: the transnationalization of the civil society. The scientists, educators, and reformers who have been meeting at the world's fairs have started to form associations based on their common interests. It is now in fashion in these circles to call oneself a "world citizen" (ter Meulen 1917). These transnational networks linking individuals across national boundaries independently of national citizenship on the basis of perceived common interests and common tasks are to become known as INGOs, international non-governmental organizations. Every INGO represents a new global identity and a new social role for those who belong, whether as a member of a social movement, a profession, a common religion, or other social identities such as parenthood, political ideology, occupation, or special creative talents (see table 1).

Table 1 **Categories of non-governmental organizations as listed in the Yearbook of International Organizations***

Religion, ethics	Economics, finance
Social sciences, humanistic studies	Commerce, industry
International relations	Agriculture
Politics, law, administration	Transport, travel
Social welfare	Science
Health, medicine	Education, youth
Arts, literature, radio, cinema, TV	Sport, recreation
Nation NGOs with UN consultative status	EEC/EFTA NGOs
Professions, employers	Short entries
Trade unions	Dead organizations

*Yearbook of International Organizations, 1972.

The precursors of later concepts of social and economic development can be found in these early INGOs, more than half a century before states will take such concepts seriously. Intellectual leadership for the new concepts of "brotherhood of man" and "world citizenship" is provided by teachers and other professionals in a cluster of new, rapidly forming peace organizations, strongly focused on the study of international law and arbitration procedures. The Third Universal Peace Congress in Rome in July, 1891, establishes the International Peace Bureau which will carry out an effective programme in research, education, and international coordination of peace development work right up to its centenary in 1991, the midpoint of our 200-year present (Santi 1991).

The vision of a world rule of law emerging from these activities points the way to a new kind of education that will be necessary to train future generations to negotiate rather than fight in future conflicts. Peace education as a social philosophy, a political agenda, and school curriculum becomes visible with the first published peace education bibliography in 1888 (Carroll et al. 1983). By 1894, a proposal will be made to establish an international university where history and problem-solving will be taught from an international perspective. Such a university will actually be established briefly in 1920, by the Union of International Associations in Brussels (Boulding 1987).

Another type of intellectual leadership is coming from women's organizations. Leaping ahead of their brothers in the international Christian missionary movement, women carry a social and human development agenda to the continents of Asia, Africa, and Latin America, establishing schools, hospitals, vocational training, and welfare services for women and children. The World Young Woman's Christian Association (WYWCA) and the World Women's Christian Temperance Union (WWCTU), along with their more secular sisters in the International Council of Nurses and the International Council of Women, represent a generation of fearless feminists at work in the villages and cities of the two-thirds world by the 1890s. Frances Willard, a founder of the WWCTU, reflects the philosophy and spirit of these women:

> We are a world republic of women – without distinction of race or colour – who recognize no sectarianism in religion, no sectionalism in politics, no sex in citizenship. Each of us is as much a part of the world's union as any other woman; it is our great, growing beautiful home (Gordon 1924:69).

The women's sisterhood approach stands in sharp contrast to that of the colonial administrators who take land right out from under whole populations of settled villages "in the name of the crown," then tax resettled "natives" for the right to build new houses. Highly evolved indigenous systems of governance and laws, land tenure, and agricultural practices are brushed aside without being noticed. "New ideas must be implanted to replace the old" is the colonialist motto. There is no dearth of anthropologists to study the curious tribal ways – only a powerful cultural insulation that prevents an understanding of what is observed.

Back home in Europe this is an era of utopian experiments and the intense idealism of the socialist international movement, seeking justice for workers and peace for all. It just happens that tribal peoples are not conceived as also being workers, and in need of justice. *Their* utopian experiments go unnoticed. The old internationalism, for all its idealism, has simply swallowed whole, in total unawareness, the rich on-the-ground diversity of colonized peoples.

1991

As we move forward toward the midpoint of the 200-year present, i.e. today, we see the fruits of the West's failure to use its centuries of exploring other continents to learn from the peoples encountered there. The Old Club of 50 states and vast colonial territories has now been replaced by a heterogeneous collection of 170 states. Looking back to the beginning of our extended present, we see how the early efforts by states to invent order-creating structures at the interstate level, via first the International Court of Arbitration, then the League of Nations, and then finally the United Nations, have led to this new political map. The cultural and economic context for this new map, however, is still very weak. The United Nations serves as an uneasy buffer between the old and the new. The senior cohorts that fill the European and North American diplomatic corps and government halls have been socialized into a world in which the Africans who are now their colleagues were till only recently thought of as "primitives." The tail end of the 45-year-long process of establishing new political sovereignties and patching up colonial economies to function in international markets has left the old rich industrial nations of the North and the new poor non-industrial nations of the South – in Africa, Asia, and "old but poor" Latin America – mutually distrustful of each other.

The evolutionary optimism of earlier decades lead the industrially successful members of the Old Club to first try a benevolent "open door" to development: a *suitable* development for the two-thirds world will come about if only the less developed nations adopt the necessary economic, social, and political measures (including controlling the labour force) that will make their countries look attractive to foreign investment (Wolpin 1977). The enclave development characteristic of the old colonized society is reinforced by the new investment policies, and the subsistence sector, which includes the bulk of the population, is left largely untouched. The overall poverty of two-thirds world societies (apart from their urban élites, who are doing well) becomes increasingly visible through the modern accounting measures introduced by the North. The North's advice to develop capital-intensive heavy industry in the modern enclave ensures the rise of the GNP growth rate at the expense of more labour-intensive light industries that might employ the masses of unemployed young. When agricultural development does get on the agenda, it is with the aid of capital-intensive equipment requiring large acreages. Subsistence farmers are pushed on to marginal lands with rapidly deteriorating soils.

The vague concept of overall human betterment implied in the 1890s thinking about economy and polity are now reduced to an economistic focus on GNP growth. Certainly Adam Smith cannot be blamed for this reductionism. His entire theory of societal development as spelled out in The Theory of Moral Sentiments (Smith 1759) rested on the concept of *sympathy*, of being able to recognize how another feels and respond to that recognition. That concept is hard to find in contemporary economic thinking about development in the West. Persistent failures of Western economic development models in the South lead to the formulation of an International Development Strategy and the Development Decade programmes – and continuing lack of success.

Finally, the Group of 77 (eventually 118 states) try to take matters into their own hands by devising their own strategy for full development in every desired dimension, economic, social, and cultural. Temporary clout from the oil crises of the 1970s facilitate adoption in 1974 of the Programme of Action on the Establishment of a New International Economic Order by the UN General Assembly. In principle, this programme commits the industrial North to the principle of indexation – the linking of prices of exports of developing countries to the prices of imports from developed countries, so that when the latter increase, the former will also increase. In addition, developed countries are asked to provide debt moratoriums and increased financial and technical assistance under more flexible conditions, and also to provide for developing countries a larger share in the world industrial production.

The fact is, however, that the one-third world has rejected – first in practice and then in plain speech – the New International Economic Order. Euro-North American concepts of equity are not seen by the North as applying to North-South relations. The North-South divide remains. Decline of solidarity among the countries of the two-thirds world and growing debt problems further contribute to the fading into obscurity of the unborn new order.

The UN system has been unable to cope with the stresses of growing inequality between North and South; ECOSOC, for example, has never been permitted to function as it was designed to; nor have the independent agencies, the World Bank, and the International Monetary Fund, been able to do better (Urquidi 1991). The goals of the North have shrunk from a rhetorical commitment to an equitable international economic order to the bare alleviation of extreme poverty in the two-thirds world. Poverty alleviation as a policy deliberately ignores "the basics of development through which inequality and poverty are supposed to have originated and should be resolved" (Urquidi p. 9).

The new economic strategy is to focus on growth, not on development of human beings in the context of their cultures and their environments. Why? There were warnings as far back as the early 1950s that there could be no long-term economic development without taking account of resources within existing cultures, that the motto of "new ideas must be implanted to replace the old" could not work (Meynaud 1963).

The failure of the Old Club to heed these warnings has affected the countries of the North as much as the countries of the South. Somehow in the process of industrialization people have come to be seduced by the illusory effortlessness of technological solutions to social problems. By the same token, labour-saving devices that made it possible to accomplish tasks effortlessly came to be sought for their own sake, labour and effort themselves being devalued. The word *development* has come to mean economic development instead of human and social development. This misconstrual of development has led to a misapplication of technologies for human and environmental exploitation, resulting in both economic and social stagnation and the ready resort to force when conflicts arise. The most misapplied technologies of all relate to massive world-wide military build-ups that have created an autonomous military forcing system threatening the survival of the planet.[3]

The challenge now is to reconceptualize development in terms of human and social development, and to shift policy goals to address that kind of development. Such a process is indeed slowly and painfully under way. What does human and social development mean? The maturing of individual human persons in family, school, and community settings. It means designing economically productive activity that makes possible an integrated intellectual, emotional, and spiritual development of men and women workers over a lifetime. It means valuing a diversity of social roles in the public and private spheres for men and women from childhood on.

A focus on human and social development requires a redefinition of productivity in terms of quality of work life for society as a whole, with production technologies geared to the creation of satisfying employment for everyone in moderately labour-intensive situations; the development of measures to identify the quality of work life. It requires a high value set on diversity: cultural diversity, multilingualism, diversity in agriculture, in natural ecosystems, diversity in production systems, transportation systems, and diversity in size and patterning of human settlements. All this to be accompanied by a recognition of the limits of diversity, and the development of skills in dealing with the conflicts generated by it. Needless to say, this involves a very different kind of social and economic bookkeeping than is practised in any country today.

The long road to 2091

Reconceptualization is an arduous task, the more because it requires conscious effort to depart from what is comfortable and familiar. It doesn't just happen of itself because the time is ripe. History is littered with the stories of failed societies that did not respond to the challenge of reconceptualization, as Toynbee has noted at length (Toynbee 1954). We can take hope from the fact that the process is going on, the challenge is being met, only not in ways that we might expect. Let us examine some of the actors in that process. These are the resources for reconceptualization of our time. The intellectual leadership for this reconceptualization comes from within the UN system, from articulate members of the "10,000 societies," and from INGOs.

The UN system

It is easy to point to failures of the United Nations in relation to the development story, yet much significant intellectual leadership for reconceptualization has come from the United Nations. From its founding it has attracted an outstanding group of world citizens who have been willing to serve that world as international civil servants in the United Nations, and to create the structures of a sustainable world society long before the word "sustainable" came into use. The early Secretaries-General of the United Nations, and practical visionaries such as Wilfred Jenks (1967) of the International Labour Organization, were such citizens. But the organization itself has grown like Topsy, so each division, agency, or institute has tended to operate in isolation from every other, in spite of heroic efforts by the Secretary-General's office to encourage coordination. Reports of exciting developments out in the field on the part of the UNDP or other agencies come back to the United Nations in New York rather than to fellow UN workers in other agencies in the same region actually working on similar tasks, and so the multiplier effects of creativity and collaboration are often lost.

UNESCO has over the decades tried to be faithful to its name (Educational, Science, and Culture Organization) and has produced important work on the interrelationship of education, science, culture, economic development, environmental conservation, human rights, and peace. Its roster of publications, conferences, and local projects provide a litany of wisdom ignored. The failure of too many international studies scholars in the United States to cite UNESCO publications or to assign them for student reading is a loss for everyone concerned. The failure of the governments of the United States and the United Kingdom to support UNESCO itself; the failure of development professionals from the North to draw on UNESCO's development literature, and finally the failure adequately to acknowledge and participate in the World Decade for Cultural Development are current examples of a persistent blindness on the part of large sections of academia. All 15 of the specialized agencies of the United Nations, as well as UN departments, divisions and regional commissions, and its research and training bodies, including UNRISD, UNITAR, the UNU, INSTRAW (the UN Institute for Research on the Advancement of Women), the Centre for Social Development and Humanitarian Affairs, and the Centre for Human Rights, have all made significant contributions over the past three decades to a multidimensional, multicultural understanding of development and the importance of local participation in the development process.

ACUNS (Academic Council of the United Nations System), a new INGO dedicated to teaching and research on the UN system and dialogue among members of the academy, the scientific community, governments, and the United Nations to increase the latter's effectiveness, are trying to call attention to the 900 information systems operated by the United Nations and the vital information these systems carry.[4] Yet governments, with a few notable exceptions such as the Nordic countries and Canada, ignore these findings in their aid programmes. Governments of the South ignore them too, being too heavily tied to the traditional aid programmes of the North and too heavily in debt to feel free to strike out with different programmes realistically based on actual needs, strengths, and resources. There is nothing more depressing than the general ignorance of the remarkable work accomplished daily by the United Nations, an ignorance not only on the part of governments but on the part of leaders of thought in the countries of the one-third world.

The UNU, as the key UN contact point for world academe, is in a position to provide the intellectual leadership for this reconceptualization through its programmes at university centres around the world. In fact, it has done so, notably under the charismatic rectorship of Soedjatmoko, whose life and work we are honouring at this conference. He was able to build on the work of his predecessor, James Hester, who introduced the theme of human and social development as a major focus of UNU research and training. Under various labels, this theme has continued to be central to UNU work. WIDER, its research and training centre in Helsinki (World Institute for Development Economics Research), is particularly important in this regard, and special programmes like the Household, Gender and Age project uncover the hidden aspects of human development in the household, where policy makers rarely look.

The genius of the UNU lies in its linking of the micro and macro, and its networking approach to relations with scholars around the world. Addressing the "global *problématique*" (as the UNU mission is sometimes referred to) calls for interdisciplinary thinkers with world system perspectives. Kenneth Boulding's seminars on "The World as a Total System" (K. Boulding 1985) at the UNU in 1984, at the invitation of Rector Soedjatmoko, may be taken as representative of the continual expansion of intellectual horizons generated by this institution, one of the later-born offspring of the UN system. However, the UNU is itself handicapped by the relative weakness and fragmentation into disciplinary specialities of world academe. The old *universitas* is no more, and yet the memory of it lingers. A second flowering of the *universitas* may be aided by the present surge in creative energy now taking place within the scientific and professional communities of INGOs, as will be discussed shortly.

It must not be forgotten that the United Nations is made up of its member States, plus the auxiliary problem-solving capabilities of the 2,000 IGOs (intergovernmental organizations) that facilitate regional and global cooperation in such matters as common markets, joint control of waterways, and other transboundary issues. Effective IGOs depend on strong leadership to overcome rigidities generated by narrow conceptions of national interest and national sovereignty. Such leadership can also help states deal with problems of internal minorities, a subject we will now turn to.

The 10,000 societies

The modern state, thought to be the great achievement of twentieth-century development, is a beleaguered institution. In the closing decades of the twentieth century there has been an increasing unease in the relationship between the "10,000 societies"[5] – ethnically, linguistically, or religion-based identity groups spread over the 170 nation states of the contemporary world – and the states which they inhabit. Supposedly extinct ethnicities are reappearing at a rapid rate.

Strong ethnic identities are today frequently seen as a source of social disintegration, violence, and terror, a retrogression to a less evolved social condition. Yet over most of human history, as well as in the present, different ethnic, cultural, linguistic, and religious groups have coexisted peacefully on common or adjacent terrains. The current revival of communal identities in all states, from the most to the least "developed," and even the creation of new mythical identities with no clear historical foundation suggests that these identity groups may have an important function to serve in sustaining the social order. The resurgence may in fact be a response to the failure of the modern state to meet the needs of its diverse populations – not only the need for the equitable distribution of resources and opportunities, but the need for meaning and a sense of self-worth.

Identity groups may contribute in important ways to the solution of some of the structural problems of the nation state: (1) the problem of scale, with the centre unable to manage its peripheries effectively; (2) the problem of adequate knowledge of local terrains, where many of the resources for problem-solving are located; and (3) the problem of relevant skills for the issues at hand. Identity groups are to varying degrees storehouses of folk wisdom and technical problem-solving skills that increase the chances of survival for their members within the polities where they are disadvantaged. These skills include conflict resolution skills for use within the identity group and with outsiders, and knowledge of how to use environmental resources, rural or urban. The ethnic wisdom/skill complex may undergo distortion and even degeneration in interaction with an indifferent or hostile state. If this is true, a viable political future for the twenty-first century may depend on new constitutive orders substantially modified from the present nation-state system, political orders that permit much wider participation of identity groups in shaping the polities of which they are a part. The intense and continuing efforts to evolve new constitutional formats in countries with strong identity groups like Canada, Switzerland, Belgium, Spain, the republics of what had been the Soviet Union, and other Eastern European countries, as well as in many countries of the South including Nigeria, Sudan, Malaysia, and India may be harbingers of a new, more democratic, and more peaceful constitutive order of the twenty-first century (Boulding 1991).

One particular arena in which ethnic knowledge is of critical importance is in reference to traditional agricultural practices. These practices are based on a knowledge of social, environmental, and climatic conditions that may have been acquired over centuries, and are patterned by forms of social organization that are only now being studied by agricultural development experts after decades of disastrous agricultural advice imported from the North and grounded in ignorance of local conditions (Boulding 1989).

One thing ethnic groups offer is *participation*. While ethnic groups in struggle with the larger society of which they are a part sometimes suffer the domination of internally oppressive ethnic élites, and traditional village councils too often exclude women's voices, many societies have traditional participation patterns that are being or can be revitalized, made more inclusive, and generally adapted to contemporary conditions in a creative problem-solving way.

The World Decade for Cultural Development (1988–1997) provides a remarkable opportunity for identifying these resources of knowledge and skill woven into nurturant community life at the local level, on different continents. Directed precisely at the inevitable fourth Development Decade, its goals are to introduce cultural factors and a focus on human beings into all development projects; to transform tourism from exploitative trespassing to opportunities for cultural learning, and to create a new awareness of the multiculturalism of the planet (UNESCO 1990). The Decade still has six years to go. It is urgent that a greater priority be given to Decade activities at the governmental level in member States of the United Nations, together with a well-thought-out linkage to national development policies. This will only come about through INGO activities, to which we now turn.

INGOs

The 170 or so INGOs of 1900 have now grown to 18,000. The growth of these people's networks over the first half of our 200-year present is perhaps the single greatest change that has taken place in the international system.[6] While INGOs remained primarily Eurocentric until the 1960s – a luxury of those who could afford to travel – today there are many INGOs indigenous to the two-thirds world, and the intercontinental INGOs have much stronger two-thirds world representation.

Because most INGOs, in contrast to states and multinational corporations, are small, relatively non-hierarchical grass-roots associations and strongly oriented to human welfare across the boundaries of states, class, race, religion, and gender, they are uniquely situated to further what has been called development with a human face. Although relatively few INGOs have development as their primary concern, many have in recent years included on their agenda a focus on the betterment of the conditions of life for their fellows in the two-thirds world. This is particularly true for the 1980s as INGOs have become more aware, due to their growing membership constituency in the South, of the poverty gap between North and South. The projects they undertake are rarely purely economic in character.

As an example of the increasing tendency of INGOs to concern themselves with human and social development, the OECD listed 2,500 INGOs as having development programmes in 1980. By 1990 the number had nearly doubled, to over 4,000 (Dichter 1991). The very smallness and ubiquity of the projects are their greatest strength, since this means they are more likely to be locally rooted, participatory, and building on the cultural strengths of the communities where projects take place. "Trickle up" rather than "trickle down" is the motto of many INGOs, and one INGO actually goes by the name of Trickle Up. This is not to say that Western-based INGOs have not made their share of serious mistakes. Fortunately, the recipients of these mistakes are now speaking up (Tandon 1991), letting the one-third world know how much it has to learn.

Because of their very nature, INGO projects are resistant to pressures for large-scale replication, and are thus more likely to accept the uniqueness of each situation in which they work. This cultural sensitivity, when INGOs are at their best, is working to moderate the economistic and often culturally insensitive programmes of such bodies as the World Bank. A recent report on cooperation between the World Bank and INGOs (World Bank 1991) indicates that the number of INGOs in collaborative activities with the Bank have come close to doubling in the past decade. Further evidence in this direction comes from a study of development projects in Asia and the Pacific, indicating a process of devolution from central control of projects to local government, and a transfer of functions from public to NGO bodies (Siedentopf 1991). A parallel process of Asian INGOs forming networks to coordinate their activities more effectively can be found in Japan. One hundred and sixteen Japanese non-governmental associations have recently formed JANIC, a mutual support network to facilitate extension of work in Japan on the environment, peace, human rights, and related social issues to other countries of the South, in a new partnership with national and international NGOs and governments of the two-thirds world (TRANET 1991).

Another arena closely related to development in which INGOs are having an increasing policy impact is in peace, security, and defence studies. A new generation of peace research and peace education INGOs first came to life in the undergrounds of war-torn Europe and Asia during the Second World War and have been growing rapidly (with significant help from UNESCO) in national, regional, and international associations committed to understanding the conditions of peace and the causes of war and other forms of violence. In the research field the strategies of non-offensive defence, zones of peace, tension reduction, and confidence-building projects and scenarios have contributed to changing conceptions of national defence and to ending the cold war. This same research is also broadening the concept of security beyond military security to include the dimensions of environmental and human rights security and the security of livelihood, or economic security. This means that development in both social and economic terms is now seen as central to societal security by peace researchers (Oswald 1992; Boulding 1992), a position also strongly supported by the Palme (1983) and Brundtland (1987) Reports on common security.

In the education field, peace research has given rise to peace studies programmes in universities around the world. The Peace Education Commission of the International Peace Research Association, Global Education Associates, the Talloires Group of university presidents,[7] and other bodies, represent strong and growing networks connecting hundreds of teaching programmes from continent to continent. The vision first articulated at the beginning of our 200-year present of preparing a new generation to manage conflicts without resort to war is now being realized. The same linking of development issues with peace, environment, and human rights issues that is happening in peace research is also happening in peace studies, so in effect the current student generation is being prepared for a new kind of human and social development work. The peace education networks are now being extended to high schools and elementary schools, as educators become aware of the importance of peace learning at an early age. The problem-solving skills that come from these programmes are increasingly being seen as essential to effective participatory economic and social development.

How strong is the civil society of the 1990s? Its strength is to a considerable extent the strength of its peoples' associations, and the global civil society rests heavily on some important characteristics of INGOs: (1) the very fact that every INGO is a transnational network means that there are regional and global communication and cooperation systems available to individuals and groups independently of the state in which they reside, systems that can and do penetrate the barriers of even the most authoritarian state. (2) the physical and social science know-how of the twentieth century, and its aesthetic and humanitarian capabilities, are located in the INGOs, not in governments. For example, governments and the United Nations alike depend on INGOs for information on what is happening to the geosphere/biosphere/sociosphere.[8] They depend on INGOs for problem-solving skills. While military power is in the hands of governments, military power has few problem-solving capabilities. (3) INGOs are becoming increasingly aware of their growing international role, and have developed strategies for making the most of their interfaces with government and the United Nations. One of these is to form special-interest clusters, or networks of networks. There are consultative bodies bringing together all INGOs interested in development. Similarly there are consultative bodies for INGOs in the fields of environment, peace, human rights, and women's issues. (4) INGOs, unlike governments, which operate under pressure on short policy deadlines, have a broader historical sense of social process and social goals. In a sense they actually live in the 200-year present we have been exploring. Their sense of the possible will play a key role in bringing about a more humane and peaceable future.

The United Nations itself has played an important role in the growth in number and effectiveness of INGOs, through its procedures for giving them consultative status with the appropriate UN bodies, and through the machinery associated with its holding of world conferences on major world problems. The first of these was the Stockholm Conference on the Environment; this was where INGOs first developed their technique of holding parallel peoples' gatherings at the same location as the intergovernmental conference, bringing their unique transnational combination of scientific expertise and humanitarian concern to the issue at hand. These parallel conferences not only greatly speeded up the networking among INGOs with common concerns, they became the breeding ground for new INGOs as it became evident that governments were not dealing adequately with the problems the UN conferences were posing.

Table 2 **Focus of activity of 30 recently founded women's INGOs**

Development	7
Development, Equality	6
Development, Research	4
Development, Media	3
Development, Health	1
Development, Environment	1
Equality, Human Rights	5
Peace	3
	30

Source: E. Boulding, "Women's Movements and Social Transformation in the Twentieth Century," in *The Changing Structure of World Politics*, ed., Yoshikazu Sakamoto, Iwanami Shoten Publishers, Tokyo, 1990.

A good example of the rapid development of a new set of INGOs in response to unaddressed development needs, and the creation of interfaces between INGOs, governments and the United Nations, can be found in women's INGOs. Between 1973 and 1986, women's INGOs grew from 47 to 189, a fourfold increase, in a shift from an earlier Eurocentrism to a much broader representation of different continental perspectives. The shift was also from the more traditional hierarchical organizational formats of an earlier era to more loosely structured decentralized organizations (Boulding 1990). At the same time, women's INGOs expanded their professional competence, with large increases in INGOs representing women in the professions. Of particular interest is how many of the newer women's NGOs have a direct focus on various aspects of development, as can be seen from table 2.

The link between development and women's roles had been accepted as a theoretical proposition by governments at the beginning of the Second Development Decade, but spelling that out in practice was everywhere resisted. The draft Plan of Action prepared for the 1974 UN World Population Year Conference contained no mention of women at all. The same was true of the 1974 Rome World Food Conference and the 1979 Conference on Science and Technology. In each case, women's networks were activated and the final conference documents incorporated statements about the role of women. The strategy did not always succeed, however, because women could not always mobilize their networks in time. That is why 1975, International Women's Year, represents a major step forward. Women's Year created a context for focused activity on the part of women to produce models, scenarios, and strategies that would take account of women's centrality in the development process. The Women's World Plan of Action (United Nations 1975) spells this out in detail. As a result, a great deal happened in the first Women's Decade, 1975–1985. The conference that is currently planned to mark the end of the second Women's Decade in 1995 will show a comparable, if less dramatic, growth in women's networks. The most important contribution of women's INGOs has been to show concretely how centrally involved women are in development-related activities, from child-rearing and home-based craft work to food production, processing and distribution to health maintenance and community services – and to reveal the absurdity of development programmes that ignore them. Women's INGOs are highly articulate about a future in which women and men work together as equal partners, not only in decision-making, but in child-rearing – the nurturing of the next generation.

Interfaces

We have looked at the 10,000 societies, the 170 states and their intergovernmental organizations, the United Nations and the 18,000 INGOs. It is in the interfacing between these different sets of actors that the dynamics of getting through the second half of our 200-year present lies. There is not space here to spell out all these interfaces, but every one of these entities interacts with every other. The 10,000 societies negotiate endlessly with the governments of the territories they inhabit. (For example, native Americans are engaged in an almost continuous process of negotiating with the US government concerning its violations of treaties signed with various tribes in the previous century.) The World Council of Indigenous Peoples and several other bodies representing tribal peoples and unrecognized ethnic groups have formed INGOs and achieved consultative status at the United Nations, giving them an opportunity to place their case before the UN General Assembly on one hand, and providing legitimation and status for placing their case before national governments on the other. The United Nations functions to provide a platform and public voice to groups with special competence in a wide variety of global issues, enabling INGOs to speak to world assemblies, to governments, and to local communities. Each of these entities – the

10,000 societies, the 170 states with their 2,000 IGOs, the United Nations and the 18,000 INGOs – need each other as their members address the difficult task of disentangling the contemporary world from violence and destruction and getting on with human and social development.

The Middle East can be taken as a sad example of ignored interfaces. The massive multilateral military build-up in the Gulf and the ensuing war to drive Hussein out of Kuwait has left widespread environmental destruction, thousands of refugees, and economic hardship for surrounding states, including already hard-pressed African states. If the past three decades of calls from concerned and knowledgeable observers for a total arms embargo on arms to the Middle East had been heeded, military action could have been replaced by diplomacy long ago. Even while arming, the states of the region have in recent decades participated in extensive intergovernmental networks which could have been used to deal with the boundary conflicts that led to the war. Such networks, however, need physical and psychological space in which to work. That space was too heavily pressured during the recent crisis, so diplomacy did not have a proper chance to show what it could do.

Table 3 shows how the countries of the Middle East are situated with regard to IGO, INGO, and UN networks, taken as indicators of diplomatic capability, in relation to their military expenditures as a per cent of GNP (1986 data), taken as indicators of military capability. It will be noted that Iran, Iraq, Israel, and Saudi Arabia have spent the most on arms, but these countries also (together with Egypt, Jordan, Libya, and Lebanon) are each part of 40 or more IGO networks and have between 200 and 456 transnational NGOs represented in their countries.[9] Not only are most of them members of the Economic Commission for West Asia, but Iraq formerly housed the secretariat for that Commission in Baghdad. Every country has at least one UN centre except Qatar (no information on Kuwait), and they are all connected into UN information centres (14 in Egypt's case). The Arab League, which gets most attention in the public press, is only one of 40 or more IGO structures in which these countries are involved. Each structure represents problem-solving and conflict resolution resources. In short, there are substantial diplomatic capabilities available. The forcing system of military intervention has created great obstacles to the full use of these capabilities.

Still, rather than bemoan missed opportunities, one can marvel that the transition decade to the twenty-first century offers so many chan-

Table 3 **Military and diplomatic capability of 14 Middle East countries: Military expenditures; IGO, NGO and UN participation**

Countries	Military expenditure as % of GNP	UN region[a]	NGO	IGO	UN Regional Centres	UN Regional Information systems
Bahrein	5.0	ECWA	111	27	1	1
Egypt	8.9	ECWA	655	52	11	14
Iran	20.0	ESCAP	456	40	2	2
Iraq	32.0	ECWA	308	51	2	2
Israel	19.2	–[b]	1032	36	2	2
Jordan	13.8	ECWA	254	42	2	2
Kuwait	5.8	ECWA	233	39	–	–
Libya	12.0	ECA	201	48	1	1
Lebanon	–	ECWA	456	40	8	8
Qatar	5.0	ECWA	77	35	0	1
Saudi Arabia	22.7	ECWA	230	42	1	–
Syria	14.7	ECWA	268	43	2	2
United Arab Emirates	8.8	ECWA	103	36	1	1
Yemen Arab Republic	6.8	ECWA	64	30	1	1

Sources: Military expenditures from Sivard, *World Military and Social Expenditures 1989*; UN regional memberships from *Everyone's United Nations*, 1979; NGO and IGO figures from the *1983 Yearbook of International Organizations*, UN centres and information systems from *Directory of United Nations Information System*, Vols. 1 and 2, 1980.

a. The Economic Commission for West Asia was founded in 1973. Countries in this biocultural region already belonging to ESCAP or ECA remain outside ECWA.

b. As far as can be ascertained at this writing, Israel is not a member of any UN regional commission. This exclusion is contrary to the UN charter.

nels of communication and instruments for collaboration among the diverse human groupings of the international system. They need to be known, to know each other. The study of those channels and instruments should comprise the ABCs of the curriculum of every child in every elementary school classroom in the world. Only then can the instruments be as frequently and effectively used as our crisis situation calls for.

2091

It is important to allow our imaginations to wander in thinking about 2091 – to engage in what might be called social day dreaming. What do we want the world to be like at this other boundary of our 200-

year present? We can't work for a future we can't even imagine. In so far as intellectuals are being true to their calling to provide creative leadership, they are futurists, skilled in social day dreaming. A society's capacity to change, however, depends on the extent to which thoughtful citizenry also have positive ideas about the future. For the past decade I have conducted workshops on imaging a future world without weapons with participants of all ages, from a variety of backgrounds, from different parts of the world. The workshop approach is based on the thesis developed by Fred Polak (1955) that societies' images of the future act as a dynamic force to empower peoples' actions in the present in order to bring about the envisioned future. Because 100 years into the future seems far away to the average person, we only ask that people step 30 years – three decades – into the future. This will be a future in which they are likely to be alive and present, so they can relate to it in a very direct way. However, the three-decade horizon is really only a heuristic device. In fact participants are describing situations that are much more likely to require a century to come about. Let us look at the themes that appear in their imagined futures as possible clues for 2091.

What do people see when they step into the imagined future?

Some find a village or a farm, some find a city, but there are certain features of this world they all identify at once. Whatever people are doing, women and men are doing it together. Children and the elderly seem to be everywhere – there is no age segregation. Communities are also described as racially mixed. Learning seems to take place throughout the day, in many settings, for all ages. This is a "learning society."

It is a non-hierarchical world; there are no visible authority figures. It is also one in which locality is very important, and there is a lot of group decision-making. Connections with other localities are gradually discovered, but the first impression is of a strong sense of place. Community gardens and local growing of food are widely seen, with larger farms in the hinterlands. Technology is low profile but it does exist and everyone reports that it is shared. There are no technological haves and have-nots. Interestingly, production technologies are rarely paid attention to. The technologies described usually involve communication and transport. Computers turn out to be omnipresent, and are a major knowledge resource in the localist society. They are also a source of social connectedness. There is widespread reporting that people are operating out of a different sense of awareness than that of 30 years ago; this is felt in an increased sense of interpersonal security and a general inclination of peaceableness.

Other themes, not as universally reported, include: (1) "boundarylessness" – an awareness of a free flow of people and thoughts and activities, unimpeded by formal structures or by occupational and political barriers; (2) a "bright, clean, green" world, with feelings of closeness to the earth that have an almost tactile quality; (3) a world in which everyone belongs, in which there is much community celebration; (4) a great variety of types of households and familial groups, but everyone belongs somewhere.

After the fantasy imaging, people are instructed to analyse the institutional infrastructure that would make the world they visited in imagination possible in reality, and then to design appropriate institutions for such a world. They soon discover it is easier to fantasize than to design viable institutions! The analysis of the structures they design has been described elsewhere.[10] However, the fantasy themes are useful for our purposes here since they reflect an intuitive sense of the difference in future lifeways required to live in a peaceable world (Boulding 1992).

The localism that appears in so much of the imagery from these workshops suggests that in 2091 the world may be seen as a gentler, freer place, in which states are less important, people live in harmony with each other and their environment, and technology serves to nurture human potentials and creative community life. This sounds like the fully developed participatory civic culture of the peaceable, adventurous, learning society described at the beginning of this paper.

Imagination is not prediction. But it is profoundly important to know that these are the longings of some significant sector of human beings in the twentieth century, and that these longings have deep roots in the human imagination as we look back into history. It is also important to know that the positive interplay of human creativity, with emergent social structures and technological capabilities that has been described here as taking place in the first half of the 200-year present in parallel with more destructive phenomena, has the possibility of bringing that destructiveness under control. That interplay might indeed produce in the second half of the extended present an adventurously peaceable social order with open-ended possibilities for later centuries.

Notes

1. Mythic images of the good society can be found in: T. Bulfinch, *Bulfinch Mythology* (New York: Thomas Y. Crowell, 1947); J. Macpherson, *The Four Ages of Man* (New York: St. Martin's Press, 1962); P.A. Munch, *Norse Mythology: Legends of Gods and Heroes*, trans. by S. Bernhardt, rev. by M. Olsen (New York: American Scandinavian Foundation, 1926); H. Stang, "Westernness and Islam." In: *Trends in Western Civilization Program No. 7*, Peace Research Institute Oslo (Oslo: University of Oslo, 1975); W.M. Watt, *What is Islam?* (New York: Praeger, 1968); C.Y. Chang (trans.), *Tao: A New Way of Thinking* (New York: Harper Colophon, 1975); and also in the Old (Hebrew Bible) and the New Testaments: Micah 4:3, Revelations 22:1–2.

2. The late chancellor Mujeeb of Jamia Millia University in New Delhi provides a fine overview of this axial age from a global perspective in his *World History, Our Heritage*, 1960.
3. See the *International Social Science Journal* issue on Reconciling the Sociosphere and the Biosphere: Global Change, Industrial Metabolism, Sustainable Development, Vulnerability, No. 121, August 1989, for an in-depth analysis of the system-wide effects of strong forcing functions on the ecosphere.
4. The Academic Council of the United Nations System (ACUNS), currently located at Dartmouth College, Hanover, New Hampshire, publishes research papers on the United Nations and provides bibliographic assistance for finding UN documents, as well as providing teaching materials on the United Nations.
5. The "10,000 societies" is a term loosely used by some anthropologists. According to Nietschman, quoted in Ted Gurr and James Scarritt, "Minorities Rights At Risk: A Global Survey," *Human Rights Quarterly* 11, 1989:375–404: there are "5000 distinct communities in the contemporary world (that) might claim they are national peoples on grounds that they share common ancestry, institutions, beliefs, language, and territory." In a 1979 study, I identified 6,276 significant ethnic groups in 159 countries, Elise Boulding, "Ethnic Separatism and World Development." In: Louis Kriesberg, ed., *Research in Social Movements, Conflicts and Change*, vol. 2 (Connecticut: JAL Press, 1979), 259–281. How many groups you find obviously depends on how you count them.
6. For more details on how INGOs function, see Elise Boulding, *Building a Global Civic Culture* (Syracuse: Syracuse University Press, 1990).
7. The Peace Education Secretariat is at the University of Malmo School of Education, Malmo, Sweden, with Ake Bjerstedt serving as Executive Secretary; Global Education Associates, under the direction of Patricia and Gerald Mische, is located at 475 Riverside Dr., New York City; the Talloires group has an office coordinated by Peter Wallensteen at the University of Uppsala, Sweden.
8. The UNU has played an important role in coordinating the activities of the International Council of Scientific Unions and the International Social Science Council in this arena. Note the following: Human Dimensions of Global Change Programme, Tokyo International Symposium on the Human Dimensions of Global Change, 11–22 September 1988 (Toronto: HDGS Secretariat, 1988); also International Geosphere-Biosphere Programme, Report No. 4: A Plan for Action (Stockholm: IGBP Secretariat, 1988).
9. This "case study" will be found in Elise Boulding, "States, Boundaries and Environmental Security," *Interdisciplinary Peace Research*.
10. For a fuller explanation of the workshops and their outcomes, see Elise Boulding, "Image and Action in Peace Building," *Journal of Social Issues*, 44(2) 1988, 17–37.

References

Boulding, Elise. 1978. "The Dynamics of Imaging Futures." *World Future Society Bulletin*, September–October: 1–8.

———. 1987. "Peace Education as Peace Development." *Transnational Associations*, 6:321–326.

———. 1988. "Image Before Action." *Journal of Social Issues*, 44(2):17–37.

———. 1989. "Cultural Perspectives on Development: The Relevance of Sociology and Anthropology." *Alternatives*, XIV:107–122.

———. 1990a. "Ethnicity and New Constitutive Orders: An Approach to Peace in the Twenty-First Century." In: Hisakazu Usui and Takeo Uchida, eds., *New Global Science: From Chaos to Order*. Tokyo: Yushindo Publishers (in Japanese).

———. 1990b. *Building a Global Civic Culture: Education for an Interdependent World.* Syracuse: Syracuse University Press.

———. 1990c. "Women's Movements and Social Transformation in the Twentieth Century." In: Yoshikazu Sakamoto, ed. *The Changing Structure of World Politics.* Tokyo: Iwanami Shoten Publishers (in Japanese).

———, ed. 1992a. *New Agendas for Peace Research: Conflict and Security Re-examined.* Boulder, CO: Lynne Rienner Publishers.

———. 1992b. States, Boundaries and Environmental Security. *Interdisciplinary Journal of Peace Research.*

———. 1992c. "The Concept of Peace Culture." In UNESCO Yearbook on Peace and Conflict Studies, *Democratization Processes and Their Implications for International Security.* Paris: UNESCO, in press.

Boulding, Kenneth. 1975. *Sonnets From the Interior Life.* Boulder, CO: Colorado University Press, p. 7.

———. 1985. *The World As A Total System.* Beverly Hills, CA: Sage Publications.

Brundtland Report, World Commission on Economic Development. 1987. *Our Common Future.* Oxford: Oxford University Press.

Carroll, Berenice, Clinton Fink and Jane Mohraz. 1983. *Peace and War: A Guide to Bibliographies.* Oxford ABC-CLIO Inc.

Dichter, Thomas. 1991. "NGOs and the Replication Trap." *Transnational Associations* 4:190–196.

Gordon, Elizabeth Putnam. (1924). *Women Torch Bearers: The Story of the Women's Christian Temperance Union.* Evanston IL: National Women's Christian Temperance Union Publishing House.

Jenks, Wilfred. 1967. *The World Beyond the Charter in Historical Perspective.* London: Rustin House.

Khaldun, Ibn. 1958. *The Muqaddimah: An Introduction to History*, vols. I–III, trans. by Franz Rosenthal. New York: Pantheon Books.

Masini, Eleanora and Stratigos, Susan. 1991. *Women, Households and Change.* Tokyo: United Nations University Press.

Meynaud, Jean, ed. 1963. *Social Change and Economic Development* (papers from a 1954 conference sponsored by the International Social Science Council). Paris: UNESCO.

Mujeeb, M. 1960. *World History, Our Heritage.* Bombay: Asia Publishing House.

Oswald, Ursula. 1992. "Ecodevelopment: What Security for the Third World?" In: Elise Boulding, ed. *New Agendas for Peace Research: Conflict and Security Reexamined.* Boulder, CO: Lynne Rienner Publishers.

Palme Report, Independent Commission for Disarmament and Security Issues. 1983. *Common Security: A Blueprint for Survival.* New York: Simon and Schuster.

Polak, Fred. 1955. *Image of the Future* (*De Toekomst is Verleden Tyd*, Utrecht: de Haan). English trans. & abr. by Elise Boulding. 1972. San Francisco: Jossey Bass/Elsevier.

Santi, Rainer. 1991. *One Hundred Years of Peace Making.* Geneva: International Peace Bureau.

Siedentopf, Heindrich. 1991. "Decentralization for Rural Development: Government Approaches and People's Initiatives in Asia and the Pacific." *Transnational Associations* 4:223–225.

Sivard, Ruth. 1989. *World Military and Social Expenditures*. Leesburg, VA: UMSE Publications.

Smith, Adam. 1853. *The Theory of Moral Sentiments*. First published in 1759; the 1853 edition reprinted by Augustus Kelley, New York, in 1966.

Spencer, Herbert. 1874. *The Study of Society*. New York: D. Appleton & Co.

Tandon, Yash. 1991. "Foreign NGOs: Uses and Abuses." *IFDA Dossier* April/June: 67–78.

ter Meulen, Jacob. 1917. *Das Gedanke der Internationalen Organization in seiner Entwicklung, 1300–1800*. The Hague: Martinus Nijhoff.

Toynbee, Arnold. 1954. *A Study of History* (2nd edition). New York: Oxford University Press.

Union of International Associations. 1973. *Yearbook of International Organizations*. Brussels: Union of International Associations.

———. 1983. *Yearbook of International Organizations*. Brussels: Union of International Associations.

Transnational Network for Appropriate/Alternative Technology. 1991. Report from Asia and the Pacific. *TRANET* 73 (November): 4.

Urquidi, Victor. 1991. *Can the UN System Meet the Challenges of the World Economy?* Hanover, NH: Academic Council on the UN System (ACUNS), Dartmouth College.

United Nations. 1975. *World Plan of Action of the World Conference of the International Women's Year, Mexico City June 19–July 2*. New York: United Nations.

———. 1979. *Everyone's United Nations*. New York: United Nations.

———. 1980. *Directory of United Nations Information Systems*. Vols 1 & 2. New York: United Nations.

UNESCO. 1990. *Final Report of the Intergovernmental Committee of the World Decade for Cultural Development, Second Session, Feb. 5–9*. Paris: UNESCO.

Wolpin, Miles. 1977. "Military Dependence as Development in the Third World." *Bulletin of Peace Proposals* 2:137–141.

World Bank. 1991. "Cooperation Between the World Bank and NGOs, Progress Report of the International Economic Relations Division." *Transnational Associations* 4:197–215.

11

Global development and the movement of peoples

Wang Gungwu

The essay looks at spatial relationships between people who live far apart, those who stay at home, and those who have moved away from their home to foreign lands, and more specifically at the conditions under which people have emigrated over great distances. Historians have always been concerned with the study of people over time, but the way economic and social developments have been globalized during the past decades requires that greater attention be paid to the linkages between the spaces people occupy. Where the movement of peoples is particularly relevant for this essay is in its external rather than internal form, notably what people who move out of their countries do to the space they leave and to the space they move into. The more people there are who are able to link those discrete areas of space they are involved in, and the more different such areas are from one another, the more people give shape to global development.

Historians often acknowledge the importance of geography, but more commonly in terms of chunks of territory. They are, therefore, more concerned with those who controlled territory, with tribes, king-

This is a topic Soedjatmoko and I had discussed several times. The essay is one I wish he could have read and offered his comments. That would have helped me improve it. Regrettably, all I can do now is to send it as a draft to mutual friends to be a small token of my respect for him. If it can assist the Soedjatmoko commemoration in any way, I will be satisfied. An earlier draft of this essay had been presented to a seminar on global history.

doms, empires, and their leaders and rulers. People were identified by the territory, whether large or small, to which they belonged. Entities like communities, nation states, confederations, and alliances were studied mainly in terms of places occupied and fought over. In this way, historians have ranged from local, national, and regional history to international, and even an interdependent world, history. Each kind of history reflects a primary concern for the politics of physical space. Globalization in the modern world leads us to a more diffuse sense of space, and invites us to explore the more fragmented linkages between people in smaller groups, even as families and as individuals who live in different parts of the globe.

Global development today assumes the linking of large numbers of people over time and space. There are different ways of studying this development. We could place the stress on ideals, common faiths, and values crossing national boundaries and even continents and point at features which show the oneness of mankind. On the other hand, we could focus on the linking of physical space and examine how this has become significant because of the spread of people and technology. The more recent migrations of large numbers of people who had not been allowed to move freely in the past have contributed to the recognition that another way of looking at the use of physical space may now be more fruitful. Modern transportation and communication have enabled more people to move from one place to another, not just once but again and again, to settle or remigrate, and to do so quickly and frequently. And, what is more, different kinds of people have begun to move, and migration in small groups, as nuclear families and as individuals, has become legitimate and acceptable as a new norm. This in turn has contributed to a new emphasis on the autonomy of such groups and the rights of their constituent members as individual persons. Global development would seem to have brought forth a more abstract perception of physical space, changing the emphasis from territorial and historical space to finer distinctions, as well as relationships, between public and private space. The part played by migration in this change is an important one which deserves attention. Certainly migration trends and patterns contribute to our understanding of the way globalization is happening. These trends and patterns will be examined in three parts.

The essay focuses on those aspects of global development which are influenced by the movement of peoples. How such development occurred despite the obstacles placed in the path of migration and how it evolved institutional and other methods of dealing with these obstacles has been of special interest to me. A brief look at three major varieties of migration would bring out the main outlines of what the essay seeks to do. Firstly, large-group migrations of tribes, nations, or whole communities would naturally lead to conflict, and either to conquest of territory or defeat and slaughter, and possible enslavement of the losers. The borders that are erected would end migrations for a long time. Then there are enforced migrations of smaller groups because of famines, plagues, and other disasters. Some of these groups become colonists, refugees, or offer themselves, if not as slaves then as bonded or contract labour of one kind or another. The obstacles to movement would be more diffuse; for example, host communities which despise the newcomers, and in modern times some immigration officials and trade unions. Finally, the sojourners who eventually become migrants. They are individuals and families who had not intended to migrate but left their countries to trade, to seek skilled employment, to escape temporarily or look for adventure and fresh opportunites for betterment, sometimes called economic refugees, but who eventually settled down. Sojourning is experimental migration which, in the face of uncertainty, suspicion, and the possibility of other options, can be indefinitely extended until a decision is inevitable. It is now increasingly the strategy of middle-class and educated people who postpone the final decision as long as possible.

The way these varieties of migration evolved and ebbed and flowed through time is worthy of consideration in any study of global development. Modern sojourning, in particular, can contribute to a better understanding of this development. The first part of this essay will begin with the phenomenon of sojourning as part of the traditions of two contrasting regions in which migration was discouraged, if not impossible. Eventually, sojourning became one of the strategies for dealing with the enemies of migration. The two regions are East Asia and South-East Asia. The second part will deal with the growth in modern nation states of formal structures to control and assist migration. It will highlight the paradox of how restrictive institutions came to enhance the significance of the people movement they were created to control. Finally, the essay looks at new varieties of migration and the advent of informal linkages across all boundaries in recent decades and how they redefine the global nature of people movement.

Sojourning in East and South-East Asia

There are excellent studies of migration history world wide, notably those of the Jewish Diaspora and, more recently, the peopling of the Americas. They have enriched our understanding of how such people movements encountered resistance or created obstacles for themselves and for others, and provide invaluable material for any study of global history. Migration in East and South-East Asian history has been less dramatic but its importance in giving shape to the history of at least the latter region has been recognised. It is less obvious that migrations in Asia have contributed to the globalization of history, but the regions are two key pieces of the jigsaw which need to be put in place, if only to point out the differences between their migration histories and those elsewhere.

The historiography of migrations of the regions is interesting. Indigenous writings give emphasis to different features of migration: in East Asia, to its involuntary nature and in South-East Asia, to the contrast between bonding the indigenous workforce and tolerating outsiders. Modern historical writings sharpen the picture further. For East Asia, they did so by placing migration in the context of a static agrarian society reinforced by Confucianized bureaucratic structures. In this way, migration was seen as marginal to its history and seems to have had minimal influence on the region's development. The enemies of migration prevailed. For South-East Asia, in contrast, scholarship since the nineteenth century has stressed the significance of people movements from the earliest times. Such movements would include the precursors of the Malays arriving from south-west China; similar peoples spreading from south-east China and Taiwan to various island groups in the Pacific and others across the Indian Ocean to Madagascar; the Burmans and the Thais following later also from south-west China; the Vietnamese moving south at the expense of the Chams and the Khmers; and the coming of Indians, Arabs, Chinese, and Europeans in recent centuries. There appears an unending process of peopling and successive dominance and retreat which has livened the region's history. But that picture has been overdrawn. While the contrast with East Asia is clear, the impression of continuous mobility is greatly exaggerated.

It is equally misleading to emphasize the relative immobility of the East Asian peoples. Filling empty spaces and displacing indigenous peoples from the borderlands have been a major part of Chinese history from the earliest times. Indeed, tribal migrations played an important part in the formation of petty states both in China and Korea and ancient overseas migrations enriched and strengthened the early Japanese state. But with the smaller territories of Korea and Japan soon filled up, further migration both inwards and outwards was no longer encouraged. As in China, the increasingly Confucianized societies developed good reasons to persuade people to stay at home wherever they were, but China had many more reasons to allow the movement of people within the empire. For one thing, there was much more room and an evolving technology to make use of less fertile lands. For another, there were many periods of disorder, famine, barbarian invasions, breakdown of central administration, especially in northern China, when people were forced to leave home. Peopling the southern provinces remained a straightforward option until at least the Ming dynasty (1368–1644). And, furthermore, moving people to the long land borders with various tribal confederations, whether Tibetan, Mongol, Turk, or Manchu, led to many official transfers of whole peasant populations to hostile frontier lands often not suitable for intensive agriculture.

Such internal migrations are part of conventional history and add little to global history. One could speculate, of course, on whether the famous naval expeditions between 1405 and 1435 of Admiral Cheng Ho which reached the East African coasts might have influenced global developments, but they led nowhere and represented more of an aberration than a new trend. In any case, they had nothing directly to do with migration. Nevertheless, the abrupt withdrawal of the treasure-ships did have consequences on the nature of Chinese trade with South-East Asia. The expeditions had raised great expectations among the maritime peoples of Fujian and Guangdong provinces, who had been expanding their trade relations with their southern neighbours rapidly since the twelfth century. The lack of official support of any kind after 1435 drove the coastal traders to greater risk-taking and to a kind of extended sojourning, or long periods of so-called temporary absences from China that verged on migration.

Why the extended periods of sojourning did not lead to colonization or full-scale migration is relevant to migration history. The phenomenon of *qiao* (sojourner) or *qiaoju* (sojourning) was a product of Confucian rhetoric, of the exhortations to be filial and loyal to heads of family and the clan-based village so prevalent in southern China. This was a powerful value system that enjoined everyone never to move away from *his* ancestral home (women were carefully excluded from any form of sojourning in order to ensure that the men returned). Migration was simply not an option; only sojourning on official duty or as a trader was permissible. Any other kind of departure amounted to rejection of the family, and life as an exile from home was punishment indeed in China because no other place would normally receive such people except in bondage. Leaving home was feared and seeking settlement elsewhere unwelcome.

Chinese traders thus sojourned in Japan and South-East Asia. Most of them returned after a few years overseas, but many stayed on to marry locally and establish second homes abroad. For some, they had to all intents and purposes settled down with their local descendants. But with advances in transportation during the last two centuries, links with their ancestral homes became easier and regular visits home were possible. Then came the massive migrations of largely unskilled labour of the nineteenth century, not only to South-East Asia but also to the Americas and Australasia. As the Chinese saw it, until the middle of twentieth century, this was not migration, but mere sojourning. But calling the phenomenon sojourning did not prevent migration and settlement. By the twentieth century, Chinese women could also leave their homes to join their husbands abroad and the conditions for settlement were complete.

Yet the concept of sojourning remained, even though its meaning had been modified. It had become possible to say that sojourning was not necessarily temporary but could be for life and could stretch over generations. It also meant that a highly particularistic loyalty towards family and the clan-based village could be the basis of linked space over great distances, thus creating the conditions for the kind of autonomy of small groups (independent of states and governments) which later advances in communications technology would continue to strengthen and support. It is comparable to the kind of autonomous space that enabled Jewish communities in different parts of the world to survive for centuries even though the Chinese idea of sojourning did not express itself in terms of a single unified and structured religion. The Chinese version was predicated on actual relationships with ancestral homes which did not materialize for the Jews until the creation of Israel; on the other hand, the Chinese sojourners never experienced the intensity of emotional and spiritual power that characterized the relations between Israel and the Diaspora.

The bulk of the Chinese sojourners went to South-East Asia and their millions of descendants are still to be found there. What has changed for them, however, is the emergence of new nation states after the period of Western colonialism. In the context of local nationalism and the powerful pressures of nation-building, these Chinese have adopted the nationalities of their adopted homes. But there remains doubt among South-East Asian national governments that many of their local Chinese are still unrepentant sojourners, while many others who have become loyal nationals find the tradition of linked spatial relationships with ancestral homes still invaluable for them to engage in the long-distance trade with Chinese and other descendants of Chinese elsewhere in the world. One might add that the hundreds of thousands of Chinese who travelled even greater distances to other parts of Asia and other Continents like the Americas, Australasia, Europe, and Africa had extended their sojourning pattern of spatial relationships everywhere. Also, it is interesting that other East Asians with comparable Confucian familial backgrounds, the Koreans and the Japanese, practised a diluted form of sojourning but nevertheless achieved in their own way the kind of linked spatial relationships over great distances. Despite the differences among the three major kinds of East Asians, it is noteworthy that their behaviour patterns and cultural manifestations are often perceived by other ethnic groups as the same, and there is a tendency to group them all together. What is striking, however, is that they are all attuned to the modern communications technology that makes the linking of spatial relationships relatively easy and ensure that their autonomy as small groups is well protected, if not invulnerable.

The Chinese concept of sojourning was largely evolved in South-East Asia. The centuries of experience there taught the Chinese what was or was not possible in long-distance spatial relationships, but even more important was the nature of South-East Asian societies where the efficacy of these sojourning links was proven. Let us return to the somewhat overdrawn picture referred to earlier on which seemed to suggest that most peoples migrated into the region from somewhere else from the earliest times. In its extreme form, the cultures of the region, too, appeared to have originated from somewhere else, from India (Hinduism and Buddhism) or further west (Islam and Christianity) or from China (Confucianism and a sinicized Buddhism in Viet Nam), In addition, there was a period of Western colonial domination from the eighteenth century to the first half of the twentieth century during which modern political and economic institutions, as well as most of the Chinese sojourning communities in the port cities of the region, were established.

The picture of extensive migrations of peoples and cultures that made South-East Asia what it is today is overdrawn because indigenous attitudes towards migration have been neglected. Migration in South-East Asia was either peripheral to mainstream society (as with the mainland states based on the great river valleys of the Irrawady, the Salween, the Menam, the Mekong, and the Red River), or integral and vital (as with the coastal and trading ports and kingdoms of the Malay archipelago). With the former mainland states, migration communities were rarely significant. But with the archipelago polities for all the centuries before European dominance, overseas trade was an overriding concern. For them, migrant traders in their port cities brought wealth and power. They were therefore welcome for their role in linking these ports with great ports in other regions, be they Chinese, Indian, Arab, or Persian. The spatial links were essential to the trading relationships. The autonomy of the small groups was a necessary part of those links, and the fact that many of these migrant groups settled down as loyal subjects to the local rulers did not mean that they had to lose the autonomy that made them the wealth-creating communities they had become. In this context, migration was not associated with absorption or assimilation or integration, but with usefulness as economic actors across great distances overseas, especially as skilled labour or as commercial agents and advisers. Certainly superior transport (in this case, shipping) technology had an impact in ways which were not true for overland trade until the modern advent of railways and highways. Hence, before the nineteenth century, migrants or sojourners who were masters of shipping technology were invaluable, but even those who accompanied them as merchants and skilled hands would have been welcomed.

The contrast between East Asia and South-East Asia is clear. People movement was difficult in East Asia where there were strong local identities in closed societies, where there was a centralized bureaucratic state, and where foreign trade was not important. This was also true in the mainland South-East Asian states which resembled their northern neighbour China in many ways. But in the archipelago states of South-East Asia, such movements were commonplace before the creation of the nation states that replaced the colonial administrations since the end of the Second World War. Today the nation state as an obstacle to easy movement of peoples seems to have come to stay in South-East Asia, yet there are extenuating factors which are worth noting in the archipelago states that, together with Thailand, have come to form the Association of South-East Asian States (ASEAN). While they are all building central bureaucracies and emphasizing strong local identities, they have affirmed the great importance of foreign or international trade and investment and kept their societies relatively open to outside influences. Because of their history of valuing long-distance links that were vital to their trading economies and because of their tolerance of autonomous migrant groups in their midst over the centuries, they are more open to external opportunities and in that way have made their contribution to the globalization of development.

The modern nation state is an institution created in the modern West but it had evolved from powerful kingly states, some of them (like the British Isles, Scandinavia, the Netherlands, and Portugal) not unlike the trading port cities and kingdoms of South-East Asia. Because these nation states had been evolutionary and the older ones had not emerged overnight as in South-East Asia, they are relatively open. There had not been the need (with the exception of Nazi Germany) for painful and melodramatic efforts at nation-building. Thus it is not the nation state itself that is necessarily hostile to migration but the artificial boundaries of some of the South-East Asian states and the haste with which they were created which made them feel politically insecure and, as a consequence, actively opposed to migration. Yet useful migrant groups remain free today in the ASEAN states to participate fully in commercial and industrial enterprises and even play a global role in international finance and trade.

Migrations beyond the nation state

In the two regions outlined above, the traditional bureaucratic empires and the modern nation state are as much obstacles to people movements as to other features of global development. Against that, the notion of sojourning in the relatively open trading societies of island South-East Asia was never threatening and therefore acceptable. Migration patterns based on acts of sojourning are reinforced by safer and faster forms of transport and further encouraged and strengthened by modern communications technology essential for international trade. And there is little doubt that the great trading nations and their finance and marketing centres contribute much to our understanding of global development. They are the centres of wealth and growth that draw people towards them as sojourners or migrants.

It is in the context of globalization of commerce that conventional migration might be usefully reexamined. Again, the large-scale movements of people in the formative periods of ancient kingdoms, empires, cultures, and civilizations are well known. Prior to the formation of strong centralized states, there were only natural borders consisting mostly of mountains, deserts, swamps, and river valleys which sooner or later some powerful tribe or tribal confederation would cross in mass migrations. The stories of the Aryans who entered India, the Turks who spread to China, Europe, and West Asia, the Arabs who fought their way across North Africa into the Iberian peninsula and traded south into sub-Saharan Africa, and the expansion of the Teutonic tribes at the expense of the Celts and the Slavs, are also somewhat overdrawn, but they have all been central to conventional history and made such history exciting and comprehensible. But mass migrations of this kind normally led to settlement and the filling up of empty spaces and therefore to new state formations and defensive structures. These structures were set up against the challenges of further sizeable migrations. Thus the migrations that led to large-scale settlement would very naturally create their own instruments for self-protection and survival which then became themselves hostile to future migrations. In themselves, the story of such migrations add little to the idea of globalization. The vast spaces they linked together were soon divided from one another. For such mass migrations, linked space was temporary, quickly to be succeeded by political and military barriers against future links.

Nevertheless, despite the barriers, migrations by individuals, families, and small groups continued as long as they were non-threatening to the already settled. It was also expected that the migrants would eventually be absorbed into the native population. And, until modern times, this was inevitable, if only because the means of transport allowing the migrants to return to their original homes were limited and difficult. Perhaps the only exception to the norm of assimilation were the Jews, whose struggle to survive as a distinct people was a truly remarkable story which would later have its input into global history. Before we turn to that, it would be necessary to focus attention on the paradoxes of migration history in the two major North Atlantic regions: Europe and North America.

Europe as a region fragmented throughout its history may be compared to South-East Asia, but it has been culturally homogeneous in ways that South-East Asia has never been. Except for brief interludes when Muslim forces led by the Arabs and the Turks dominated the Mediterranean and south-eastern Europe (and an even briefer period when Mongol armies rode in from the East), the heritage has been Christian. With a common religion, small group migrations from one part of Europe to another has never been a problem and has rarely made the history books. Much of conventional history has been concerned with dynastic wars, defences against the power of Islam, and the political and constitutional evolution from monarchies to democracies; qualitative changes in the feudal and capitalist economies of the region; overseas expansion since the sixteenth century; and the scientific and technological revolution that is still with us. The dynamics of historical development that led to world-wide modernization is obviously part of global history, but in so far as that development also created a plethora of nation states, one manifestation of the enemies of migration, it has also produced for us a paradox that needs to be explained.

The roots of that paradox may be found in the unique separation of Church and State common to the western and central parts of the Christian world. That separation produced parallel legal concepts if not systems that protected subjects from their rulers and the individual citizen from the authorities and eventually minorities from majorities and even migrants from the natives. These changes were indeed slow to come about, whether under monarchic or republican nation states. And when they were too slow, those who felt disadvantaged, dispossessed, and oppressed, and those who knew they were discriminated against, voted with their feet and migrated to new lands, especially those opened up for settlement in North America. Of course, not all migration from Europe was of this kind. There were the soldiers and officials who set up administrative and legal structures, the adventurers who pioneered the wilderness, and the traders who linked the newly settled places with the centres of civilization in the old world. But, unlike the usual migrants in search of land and wealth, there were also those who wanted to be free and equal, more specifically, free to worship their own faith and equal before God and the law. These were far-reaching concerns which proved to be difficult to achieve even among the migrants who had left their homes to seek them. But the ideals that were transplanted to what became migrant-established new states found the soil congenial and new and higher standards of rights and duties were determined.

Thus old-world states and societies spawned a number of migrant states in the Americas and Australasia. Thankfully, after a few decades of uncertainty during the first half of this century, these new states have not reproduced all the narrow-minded nationalisms of the old world. On the contrary, they have translated most of the old-world arbitrary controls of migration into controlled channels of regular and continuous migration. Four factors have assisted these developments, and these developments have in turn influenced migration policies of the old nation states of Europe and, to a lesser extent, even some of the new nation states elsewhere in the world. The four are the Holocaust experience and its ramifications; the new categories of refugees; the communications revolution; and the evolving concept of universal human rights.

The story of the Jewish Diaspora has been referred to above. As an unfinished migration history, it stands alone. As a chain of anti-Semitic pogroms and a symbol of unrelenting religious persecution, it also surpasses the experience of all other migrant groups. How that extraordinary heritage of an unassimilated migrant minority led to the Holocaust perpetrated by Nazi Germany belongs to the history of the explosive power of nationalism and the new nation state. Had the Germans succeeded in establishing the Third Reich in Europe, its racial policies would have led to the end of migration as a historical phenomenon. The only exceptions would have been the returning migrants of the same nation and culture as, for example, the Sudetan and Volga Germans and the German settlers in the Americas; otherwise, the solution was the expansion of Germany to encompass all those of the same "race." The horror of the Holocaust challenged some earlier claims to civilization. After the war was over, it led to the creation of the state of Israel, the idea of a historic homeland which the migrating Jews could return to or identify with. That is still a mixed blessing representing both a new nation state and the ideals of the rights of minorities. But the overall effect of the Holocaust upon the world was positive. The persecution of small groups of minorities has become less tolerable to more people. The idea of ethnic, even sub-ethnic, rights, including the right to remain different and unassimilated, is still being resisted, but the rhetoric of multiculturalism and cross-cultural understanding is unlikely now to go away. The chances of this rhetoric being embodied in law and turned into practice through a common basic education are now better than ever, especially in the migrant states of North America and Australasia.

The second new factor concerns a sub-type of migratory peoples, the refugees who had never sought to migrate. Starting with the displaced peoples of the First World War and the efforts of international organizations like the League of Nations and, after the Second World War, the United Nations, the idea of refugees has been greatly refined. In particular, refugees have become more than involuntary migrants in search of better living conditions or those escaping war and chaos, dire poverty, death by disease, and starvation. As with the migrations to North America since the seventeenth century, the new categories which have been extended to every part of the world now include those seeking freedom and protection from political persecution. This recent development adds another dimension to the concept of linked global space. It enables people of like political faiths and goals to globalize their ideals and have these values physically linked through networks that are independent of nation states and their narrowly defined migration targets. It has given new meaning to small groups, families, and individuals scattered about the world and placed them within the realm of global history.

As for the communications revolution which made fine technical networks of spatial relationships possible, that also sprang from Europe and North America but now reach every corner of the globe. All they need are people to use and service them, and the migrant peoples are those best positioned to take full advantage of their power and range. The rapid rate of scientific discovery in the field of transport and communications and the speed at which these discoveries have been translated into practical application has been a source of wonderment for decades. Even more so has been the ability of every country, city, and territory in the world to acquire the skills to use these applications effectively. The technological links established between distant places now reinforce the spatial relationships that have been created by past and present migrations. If the links are, in addition, open and accessible, they further reinforce the idea of ethnic minority rights, as well as the multicultural conditions which several migrant states have consciously supported. And not least, such links and conditions could encourage the globalization of the sojourning found in East and South-East Asia. The new communications links would enable many migrants or migrant communities to live, behave, think, and feel as if they had never really left home. The impact on the older ideas like settlement and assimilation would be considerable and much rethinking about the phenomenon in the context of global history would need to be done.

The fourth factor can be connected to the three already outlined above. The concept of universal human rights has become less abstract because of the shock of the Holocaust, the plight of political refugees and the widespread access to speedy communications. Although human rights appear superficially comparable with other more traditional ideas about the family of man, brotherhood, compassionate humanity, and equality before God, and therefore generally appealing to the common man, the concept is different in nature and goes much further than the earlier ideas. Human rights have to be traced to the same tradition of Church-State separation which was there at the beginning of modernization in western Europe. Hence its strong connection with the law that protects one's rights and with the individual who wishes to guard his right to be true to his own conscience. Already it has found application in the right to migrate whether as free labour or as refugees, and no doubt it will be further refined to defend the rights of migrants to preserve their cultural values and their private relationships with their ancestral homes. There is still a large gap in understanding between peoples and also in the kinds of institutional structures that are needed to implement such rights. There are also political barriers, both national and international, which would inhibit the rapid promotion of the idea of human rights for decades to come, but the first step in attempting to globalize the right of individuals to his own private spatial relationship with whomever he likes in the world has been taken.

Many remarkable developments have followed the globalization of issues and problems in modern history. Among them we must include the fact that obstacles to migration have been challenged and the paradox that the attempts to control migration have led to greater protection of migrant and refugee rights. In turn, closer study of migration issues should explain certain key features of global development.

Migrants and informal linkages

The outline above of the way migrations illuminate our understanding of the phenomenon of globalization may easily lead to a new Whig or positivist interpretation of history. Let me hasten to check myself from offering such a view. Global history is no substitute for the conventional local and national histories that more accurately reflect the actual concerns of governments and societies, including their glories and successes and their mistakes and disasters. But there are developments which require different approaches before they can be understood. The universality of science and technology is one, the common appreciation of popular art, music, and literature as well as some aspects of *haute* culture shared around the world is another, the integration of multinational networks of trade and finance is yet another, and no less significant is the growing range of linked spatial relationships that people are now beginning to cultivate. The way sojourner-migrants have responded to the informal linkages now open to them is of particular interest. Whether or not these linkages will last, whether new enemies of migration might appear if only to restore the great barriers of the past, is yet uncertain. What is unmistakable is that, for now, migrants can be long-term sojourners more easily than ever in the past.

The contrast with earlier migrations is obvious. In ancient times, whole tribes would have migrated, often joining related tribes in larger armed confederations. If they succeeded, they took over the spaces they marched into and either put the defeated to the sword or enslaved them. Such powerful migrant groups were collectives; loyalty was not only expected, but was often also absolute. The idea that smaller groups or families or individuals should be free to migrate or remigrate out of the new territory or return home without the agreement of the tribal leaders or the kings was unthinkable. No such group or individual would dare or be so foolish to cross over the borders controlled by their own kin. Only in times of great disorder would it ever be necessary for any of them to move away on their own and that would be either involuntary or enforced. The results were often tragic. Unless there were new empty spaces to move into, or spaces occupied by groups who were even smaller and weaker than themselves, the small groups, families, or individuals from an alien tribe would only be met by hostility wherever they went.

The only safe scenario for small group migrations was when the group possessed some special skill or skills which their hosts needed and did not have. Historical records show that the arts of the smith, the potter, and the apothecary were often welcome. Artists, performers, and cooks could hope to survive. Religious men and nimble fortune-tellers sometimes did well. With salesmanship, entrepreneurship, courage, and a bit of luck, the sojourning merchants would prosper. And there was always room for the linguist, the ubiquitous interpreter. Most of them travelled in small groups, some alone and a few with their families, depending on the skills they had to offer. But, until modern times, they could not remain in touch with their homes except at great expense or inconvenience to themselves. Even the Chinese merchant sojourners were forced to stay away for long periods, and many established second or more families who would normally identify with the land of their mothers and grow up as natives rather than migrants. Thus, successful migrants had three choices: that of settling down and bringing up native families; that of returning home with their fortunes after years of sojourning; or, if there was enough time, that of arranging chain migrations for kinfolk to join them and organize new migrant communities abroad. For the most part, it was easiest to settle down and be assimilated to the host culture provided the hosts allowed them to do so.

The globalization of the modern world has changed that. At stage one, following the end of the institution of slavery, large-scale migration of cheap contract labour was needed in various parts of the European empires to feed the industrial revolution in Europe. In North America, the demand was smaller because the freed slaves and the descendants of slaves could still work. And where their capitalists needed fresh industrial labour, they turned to the impoverished parts of Europe itself. In Asia and the Caribbean, however, most of the coolie labourers were Chinese and East Indians. They were shipped overseas to plantations and mines, to build roads and railways and clear jungles and bush. They were not skilled enough to be highly regarded or well rewarded, but they were useful, thus fulfilling one of the principal conditions of migration. In so far as they were useful to the colonial territories, many stayed on after the end of their contracts and settled down as migrants. Unfortunately for them, they encountered the phenomenon of White superiority which had emerged from the period of imperial power during the nineteenth century and was to last until the end of the Second World War. This had been tolerable in Asia where the Whites were few in number. But, in the migrant states of North America and Australasia, the Asian migrants could not assimilate as equal citizens, nor were they allowed to enlarge their communities through chain migrations. Many chose to go home instead, while those who stayed were allowed to remain on the periphery of White society as sojourners, an ambiguous state to be in at the time, but the only condition under which they could survive.

Stage two, after the end of the Second World War, was an improvement for migration, but only marginally so. On the one hand, concepts of racial superiority were on their way out and greater compassion was found for the victims of war and deprivation, the millions of displaced people and political refugees (especially from Europe) for whom homes had to be found. At the same time, the modern empires came to an end and they were succeeded by scores of new nation states. Although these new states subscribed to a United Nations Charter which endorsed great principles dedicated to supporting the poor and the oppressed and to assisting migrant labour as well as to protecting persecuted refugees, the available institutions to implement these principles were still subject to the traditional controls of national bodies. Migration was not a priority and its enemies stayed in control. What was remarkable, however, was the change in political conditions which created large numbers of upper- and middle-class refugees all over the world, followed by a change in values that permitted the same classes also to become sojourner-migrants. Also unprecedented was the way the modern skilled and educated classes responded to the pull of centres of power and wealth and the new transnational opportunities in trade and industry. These new types of migrants were articulate, politically sensitive, and knew how to move in high native circles. They knew the law and their rights and their successful adaptation to local conditions strengthened their capacity to transform the environment for all migrants. Most of all, as befitting their origins, they were masters not only in the handling of official and bureaucratic connections but also in the art of informal linkages. They very quickly laid the foundations for even greater changes.

The most dramatic transformation came about in the migrant states of North America and Australasia. These states were strongly affected by the four factors outlined earlier as the Holocaust, the politicization of refugees, the communications revolution, and the issue of human rights. Within a couple of decades after the end of the Second World War, a radical revision of assimilationist ("melting pot") and migration policies had taken place. In their place were calls for racial equality, multiculturalism, and selective but non-discriminatory migration. And much sooner than anyone expected, migrant communities were formally legitimized, their contacts with ancestral homes were restored, even encouraged, and the rights of migrant individuals and nuclear families were for the first time carefully protected.

These developments are recent and still evolving. It is difficult to evaluate them before they have worked themselves out. What is clear is that they reflect the globalization of major issues and problems that touch on individuals, families, and small minority groups. Where migrants and their communities are concerned, surprising progress has been made in the enhancement of informal linkages over great distances: the right to communicate, the means of staying in close personal touch, the use of international investment, and financial connections to bind distant kinsmen together, all contributing towards the unfolding of global history. It is too early to say if these friendly conditions have been entrenched in the migrant states and if they could ever be fully accepted into the nation states, but it is a measure of global change when the enemies of migration could be so thoroughly thwarted.

Contributors

ELISE MARIE BOULDING is an American sociologist and international organization executive. She graduated from Iowa State University and University of Michigan. She is currently Project Director of Commission of Peace Building in the Middle East. She served as Research Associate at University of Michigan (1957–1960), Professor of Sociology at University of Colorado (1967–1978), Chairperson of the Department of Sociology at Dartmouth College (1978–1985). She was also Editor of International Peace Research Newsletter (1963–1968, 1983–1987), Secretary-General of International Peace Research Association (1988–1991), and member of the UNU Council (1980–1985). She is the author of *Underside of History: A View of Women Through Time* (1976 and 1992), *Women in the 20th Century World* (1977), *Building Global Civic Culture* (1988), and *One Small Plot of Heaven* (1989). She received several awards such as Women of Conscience Award (1980) and National Women's Award (1985 and 1990).

MINE EDER received her Ph.D. from the University of Virginia in 1993. She is an authority in International Relations Theory and International Policy Economy. She was head teaching assistant for three years in GFIR 101, Introduction to International Politics. Her dissertation committee recommended her dissertation for a distinction. She is presently a member of the faculty of the Department of Political Science at Lewis and Clark College in Portland, Oregon. She has also taught at Washington and Lee University and the University of Virginia.

FRANSISCO SIONIL JOSÉ. Filipino writer and journalist. Chairman of the Solidarity Foundation and publisher/editor of *Solidarity*. He received Ph.D. in Humanities from University of the Philippines. He has been professorial lecturer on Philippine Culture both at University of the East (1974) and De La Salle University (1984–

1985), and visiting research scholar at the Centre for South-East Asian Studies, Kyoto University, Japan (1988). He is the author of *The Pretenders* (1962), *Two Filipino Women* (1981), *Mass* (1982), *Viajero* (1993), and other novels and short stories. He received several awards such as Ramon Magsaysay Award for Journalism, Literature, and Creative Communication Arts (1980), Outstanding Fulbrighters Award for Literature (1988), and Cultural Centre of the Philippines Award for Literature (1989).

ALEXANDER KING was born in Scotland in 1909, studied at the University of London (D.Sc) and did research in physical chemistry at the University of Munich. Senior Lecturer in physical chemistry at the Imperial College of Science and Technology (1931–1941), Deputy Science Adviser to British Minister of Production (1942–1944); Head of British Scientific Mission, and Science Councillor at British Embassy, Washington, DC (1944–1946). Science adviser to Lord President, London (1946–1951). Co-Director European Productivity Agency of OEEC, Paris 1957–1960, Director-General for Scientific Affairs and Education, OECD (1960–1974); Chairman International Federation of Institutes of Advanced Study (1974–1984). In 1968, together with the Italian industrialist, Aurelio Peccei, he created the Club of Rome, becoming its President in 1984 and now President Emeritus. Dr King was awarded the Erasmus Prize in 1987.

ALEXANDER KWAPONG is a graduate of Cambridge University. He was Visiting Professor at Princeton University (1962), Former Pro-Vice-Chancellor and Head of Classics Department of Ghana University and Vice-Chancellor (1966–1975). He was Vice-Rector for Institutional Planning and Resource Development of the United Nations University (1976–1988). He is the author of *Higher Education and Development in Africa Today: A Reappraisal* (1979), *The Role of Knowledge* (1980), *Culture, Development and African Unity* (1988), *Some Reflections on International Education in the 90s in the Role of Service Learning in International Education* (1989), *Meeting the Challenge, The African Capacity Building Initiative* (ed. with B. Lesser) (1992). He is a Fellow of Ghana Academy of Arts and Sciences. He received Honour of Doctor of Literature from the University of Ghana and Honour of LL.D from Princeton University.

SABURO OKITA (1914–1993). An eminent Japanese economist and former Minister for Foreign Affairs. He graduated from the University of Tokyo (1937). He served as Chief of the Research Section at the Economic Stabilization Board (1947) and Director General of Planning Bureau (1957). He was the Minister for Foreign Affairs (1979–1980), President and Chancellor of the International University of Japan (1982–1993). He also joined meetings and committees organized by international organizations, such as the Pearson Commission of International Development (1969–1970), Group of Experts on Structure of UN (1975), and UN Committee of Development Planning (1965–1980). He is the author of *The Future of Japan's Economy* (1960), *Japan and the World Economy* (1975), *Approaching the 21st Century: Japan's Role* (1990), and numerous articles. He received several honours; Honorable LL.D. from University of Michigan (1977) and from University of the Philippines (1990). He received awards of Ramon Magsaysay Award for International Understanding (1971), Indira Gandhi Prize for Peace, Disarmament, and Development (1992).

FARHANG RAJAEE received his Ph.D. from the University of Virginia in 1983. He is presently Associate Professor and Head of Cultural and Social Issues and is regularly a Visiting Professor at Shahid Beheshti University. He is also a member of the Iranian Academy of Philosophy. He is the author of *Political Wisdom in Ancient East*, *Iran-Iraq War: The Politics of Aggression* (ed.), and *Power* (1991).

SULAK SIVARAKSA was coordinator for the UNU's Project on *Buddhist Perception for Desirable Societies in the Future*, a book of this title has now been edited and published by him in Bangkok. His own writing includes *Seeds of Peace: A Buddhist Vision for Renewing Society*. He is founder of the International Network of Engaged Buddhists and has been a visiting professor at University of Toronto, University of California, Berkeley, Cornell, Hawaii and Swarthmore in North America as well as at Ryukoku University in Japan.

SELO SOEMARDJAN received his Ph.D. in sociology in 1959 at Cornell University, USA. Since then he has been teaching at Universitas Indonesia in Jakarta. Starting with political sociology at the time of the revolutionary changes in his country he has dedicated the last two decades to the study and extensive research of villages and isolated tribes as they respond to the national development programmes in Indonesia. Professor Selo Soemardjan is also senior adviser to five consultative Vice-Presidents and Chairman of the Indonesia Social Science Foundation. He is the author of *A Socio-Economic Profile* (1988).

RODOLFO STAVENHAGEN is a graduate of the Mexican School of Anthropology and received his Ph.D. in sociology at the University of Paris in 1964. He is currently research professor at El Colegio de Mexico. He is former Assistant Director-General of UNESCO for social sciences, and currently Chairman of the Fund for the Development of Indigenous Peoples of the Americas, as well as of International Alert, a non-governmental organization devoted to the peaceful solution of conflicts. The United Nations University has published his *The Ethnic Question: Conflicts, Development and Human Rights* (1990).

KENNETH W. THOMPSON received diploma of Public Administration from the University of London. He serves as Chief Technical Adviser of ILO/UNDP Social Security Project in Thailand since 1991. He served at the Social Security Office at ILO/UNDP Social Security Project in Ghana (1971–1973), Regional Adviser on Social Security for Asia and the Pacific, ILO in Thailand (1973–1977), Project Coordinator of ILO/UNDP Social Security Project in Myanmar (1977–1979), Chief of the Regional Activity Branch at the International Social Security Association in Switzerland (1979–1985), and Regional Adviser on Social Security for Asia and Pacific at ILO in Thailand (1985–1991). He is the author of *Political Realism and Crisis of World Politics* (1960), *Understanding World Politics* (1975), *Cold War Theories* (1981), and *Fathers of International Thought: The Legacy of Political Theory* (1994).

WANG GUNGWU. Historian and university Vice-Chancellor. He studied at National Central University in Nanjing, and graduated from University of Malaya, and University of London. He was Lecturer at University of Malaya, Singapore (1959), and Kuala Lumpur (1959–1961), Dean of Arts (1962–1963), and Professor of History (1963–1968). He was a Rockefeller Fellow at University of London (1961–1962),

Professor of Far Eastern History at Australian National University (1968–1986), and Professor Emeritus since 1988. He is also Vice-Chancellor of The University of Hong Kong since 1986. He is the author of 12 books including *The Chineseness of China* (1991), *China and the Chinese Overseas* (1991), *Community and Nation: China, South-East Asia, and Australia* (1992). He has also written numerous articles on Chinese and South-East Asian history.